Governance and European Civil Society

This book provides a critical analysis of the European Union's approach to 'governance', focusing on the way in which civil society is incorporated within the EU decision-making process and arguing that it is not conducive to the democratisation of EU governance.

Using a governmentality approach, Acar Kutay demonstrates that civic actors are not incorporated into EU decision-making processes as they are; rather, they are formed, manipulated and guided by political programming. The author explains how this acts to prescribe and construct particular types of subjectivities, thereby limiting and constraining the types of participation that might emerge as part of European civil society and the process of political participation.

Governance and European Civil Society will be of interest to students and scholars of European Union politics, global governance, civil society and democracy, Central and East European studies and political and international theory.

Acar Kutay is an Affiliated Researcher Fellow at the Christian Michelsen Institute in Bergen, Norway.

Routledge advances in European politics

1. **Russian Messianism**
   Third Rome, revolution,
   Communism and after
   Peter J.S. Duncan

2. **European Integration and the Postmodern Condition**
   Governance, democracy, identity
   Peter van Ham

3. **Nationalism in Italian Politics**
   The stories of the Northern League, 1980–2000
   Damian Tambini

4. **International Intervention in the Balkans since 1995**
   Edited by Peter Siani-Davies

5. **Widening the European Union**
   The politics of institutional change and reform
   Edited by Bernard Steunenberg

6. **Institutional Challenges in the European Union**
   Edited by Madeleine Hosli, Adrian van Deemen and Mika Widgrén

7. **Europe Unbound**
   Enlarging and reshaping the boundaries of the European Union
   Edited by Jan Zielonka

8. **Ethnic Cleansing in the Balkans**
   Nationalism and the destruction of tradition
   Cathie Carmichael

9. **Democracy and Enlargement in Post-Communist Europe**
   The democratisation of the general public in fifteen Central and Eastern European countries, 1991–1998
   Christian W. Haerpfer

10. **Private Sector Involvement in the Euro**
    The power of ideas
    Stefan Collignon and Daniela Schwarzer

11. **Europe**
    A Nietzschean perspective
    Stefan Elbe

12. **European Union and E-Voting**
    Addressing the European Parliament's internet voting challenge
    Edited by Alexander H. Trechsel and Fernando Mendez

13. **European Union Council Presidencies**
    A comparative perspective
    Edited by Ole Elgström

14 **European Governance and Supranational Institutions**
Making states comply
Jonas Tallberg

15 **European Union, NATO and Russia**
Martin Smith and Graham Timmins

16 **Business, The State and Economic Policy**
The case of Italy
G. Grant Amyot

17 **Europeanization and Transnational States**
Comparing Nordic central governments
Bengt Jacobsson, Per Lægreid and Ove K. Pedersen

18 **European Union Enlargement**
A comparative history
Edited by Wolfram Kaiser and Jürgen Elvert

19 **Gibraltar**
British or Spanish?
Peter Gold

20 **Gendering Spanish Democracy**
Monica Threlfall, Christine Cousins and Celia Valiente

21 **European Union Negotiations**
Processes, networks and negotiations
Edited by Ole Elgström and Christer Jönsson

22 **Evaluating Euro-Mediterranean Relations**
Stephen C. Calleya

23 **The Changing Face of European Identity**
A seven-nation study of (supra)national attachments
Edited by Richard Robyn

24 **Governing Europe**
Discourse, governmentality and European integration
William Walters and Jens Henrik Haahr

25 **Territory and Terror**
Conflicting nationalisms in the Basque country
Jan Mansvelt Beck

26 **Multilateralism, German Foreign Policy and Central Europe**
Claus Hofhansel

27 **Popular Protest in East Germany**
Gareth Dale

28 **Germany's Foreign Policy Towards Poland and the Czech Republic**
Ostpolitik revisited
Karl Cordell and Stefan Wolff

29 **Kosovo**
The politics of identity and space
Denisa Kostovicova

30 **The Politics of European Union Enlargement**
Theoretical approaches
Edited by Frank Schimmelfennig and Ulrich Sedelmeier

31 **Europeanizing Social Democracy?**
The rise of the party of European socialists
Simon Lightfoot

32 **Conflict and Change in EU Budgetary Politics**
Johannes Lindner

33 **Gibraltar, Identity and Empire**
E.G. Archer

34 **Governance Stories**
Mark Bevir and R.A.W. Rhodes

35 **Britain and the Balkans**
1991 until the present
Carole Hodge

36 **The Eastern Enlargement of the European Union**
John O'Brennan

37 **Values and Principles in European Union Foreign Policy**
Edited by Sonia Lucarelli and Ian Manners

38 **European Union and the Making of a Wider Northern Europe**
Pami Aalto

39 **Democracy in the European Union**
Towards the emergence of a public sphere
Edited by Liana Giorgi, Ingmar Von Homeyer and Wayne Parsons

40 **European Union Peacebuilding and Policing**
Michael Merlingen with Rasa Ostrauskaite

41 **The Conservative Party and European Integration since 1945**
At the heart of Europe?
N.J. Crowson

42 **E-Government in Europe**
Re-booting the state
Edited by Paul G. Nixon and Vassiliki N. Koutrakou

43 **EU Foreign and Interior Policies**
Cross-pillar politics and the social construction of sovereignty
Stephan Stetter

44 **Policy Transfer in European Union Governance**
Regulating the utilities
Simon Bulmer, David Dolowitz, Peter Humphreys and Stephen Padgett

45 **The Europeanization of National Political Parties**
Power and organizational adaptation
Edited by Thomas Poguntke, Nicholas Aylott, Elisabeth Carter, Robert Ladrech and Kurt Richard Luther

46 **Citizenship in Nordic Welfare States**
Dynamics of choice, duties and participation in a changing Europe
Edited by Bjørn Hvinden and Håkan Johansson

47 **National Parliaments within the Enlarged European Union**
From victims of integration to competitive actors?
Edited by John O'Brennan and Tapio Raunio

48 **Britain, Ireland and Northern Ireland since 1980**
The totality of relationships
Eamonn O'Kane

49 **The EU and the European Security Strategy**
Forging a global Europe
Edited by Sven Biscop and Jan Joel Andersson

50 **European Security and Defence Policy**
An implementation perspective
Edited by Michael Merlingen and Rasa Ostrauskaitė

51 **Women and British Party Politics**
Descriptive, substantive and symbolic representation
Sarah Childs

52 **The Selection of Ministers in Europe**
Hiring and firing
Edited by Keith Dowding and Patrick Dumont

53 **Energy Security**
Europe's new foreign policy challenge
Richard Youngs

54 **Institutional Challenges in Post-Constitutional Europe**
Governing change
Edited by Catherine Moury and Luís de Sousa

55 **The Struggle for the European Constitution**
A past and future history
Michael O'Neill

56 **Transnational Labour Solidarity**
Mechanisms of commitment to cooperation within the European Trade Union Movement
Katarzyna Gajewska

57 **The Illusion of Accountability in the European Union**
Edited by Sverker Gustavsson, Christer Karlsson, and Thomas Persson

58 **The European Union and Global Social Change**
A critical geopolitical-economic analysis
József Böröcz

59 **Citizenship and Collective Identity in Europe**
Ireneusz Pawel Karolewski

60 **EU Enlargement and Socialization**
Turkey and Cyprus
Stefan Engert

61 **The Politics of EU Accession**
Turkish challenges and Central European experiences
Edited by Lucie Tunkrová and Pavel Šaradín

62 **The Political History of European Integration**
The hypocrisy of democracy-through-market
Hagen Schulz-Forberg and Bo Stråth

63 **The Spatialities of Europeanization**
Power, governance and territory in Europe
Alun Jones and Julian Clark

64 **European Union Sanctions and Foreign Policy**
When and why do they work?
Clara Portela

65 **The EU's Role in World Politics**
A retreat from liberal internationalism
Richard Youngs

66 **Social Democracy and European Integration**
The politics of preference formation
Edited by Dionyssis Dimitrakopoulos

67 **The EU Presence in International Organizations**
Edited by Spyros Blavoukos and Dimitris Bourantonis

68 **Sustainability in European Environmental Policy**
Challenge of governance and knowledge
Edited by Rob Atkinson, Georgios Terizakis and Karsten Zimmermann

69 **Fifty Years of EU–Turkey Relations**
A Sisyphean story
Edited by Armagan Emre Çakir

70 **Europeanization and Foreign Policy**
State diversity in Finland and Britain
Juha Jokela

71 **EU Foreign Policy and Post-Soviet Conflicts**
Stealth intervention
Nicu Popescu

72 **Switzerland in Europe**
Continuity and change in the Swiss political economy
Edited by Christine Trampusch and André Mach

73 **The Political Economy of Noncompliance**
Adjusting to the single European Market
Scott Nicholas Siegel

74 **National and European Foreign Policy**
Towards Europeanization
Edited by Reuben Wong and Christopher Hill

75 **The European Union Diplomatic Service**
Ideas, preferences and identities
Caterina Carta

76 **Poland within the European Union**
New awkward partner or new heart of Europe?
Aleks Szczerbiak

77 **A Political Theory of Identity in European Integration**
Memory and policies
Catherine Guisan

78 **EU Foreign Policy and the Europeanization of Neutral States**
Comparing Irish and Austrian foreign policy
Nicole Alecu de Flers

79 **Party System Change in Western Europe**
Gemma Loomes

80 **The Second Tier of Local Government in Europe**
Provinces, counties, départements and Landkreise in comparison
Hubert Heinelt and Xavier Bertrana Horta

81 **Learning from the EU Constitutional Treaty**
Democratic constitutionalism beyond the nation-state
Ben Crum

82 **Human Rights and Democracy in EU Foreign Policy**
The cases of Ukraine and Egypt
Rosa Balfour

83 **Europeanization, Integration and Identity**
A social constructivist fusion perspective on Norway
Gamze Tanil

84 **The Impact of European Integration on Political Parties**
Beyond the permissive consensus
Dimitri Almeida

85 **Civic Resources and the Future of the European Union**
Victoria Kaina and Ireneusz Pawel Karolewski

86 **The Europeanization of National Foreign Policies towards Latin America**
Lorena Ruano

87 **The EU and Multilateral Security Governance**
Sonia Lucarelli, Luk Van Langenhove and Jan Wouters

88 **Security Challenges in the Euro-Med Area in the 21st Century**
Mare nostrum
Stephen C. Calleya

89 **Society and Democracy in Europe**
Oscar W. Gabriel and Silke Keil

90 **European Union Public Health Policy**
Regional and global trends
Edited by Scott L. Greer and Paulette Kurzer

91 **The New Member States and the European Union**
Foreign policy and Europeanization
Edited by Michael Baun and Dan Marek

92 **The Politics of Ratification of EU Treaties**
Carlos Closa

93 **Europeanization and New Member States**
A comparative social network analysis
Flavia Jurje

94 **National Perspectives on Russia**
European foreign policy in the making
Maxine David, Jackie Gower and Hiski Haukkala

95 **Institutional Legacies of Communism**
Change and continuities in minority protection
Edited by Karl Cordell, Timofey Agarin and Alexander Osipov

96 **Sustainable Development and Governance in Europe**
The evolution of the discourse on sustainability
Edited by Pamela M. Barnes and Thomas C. Hoerber

97 **Social Networks and Public Support for the European Union**
Elizabeth Radziszewski

98 **The EU's Democracy Promotion and the Mediterranean Neighbours**
Orientation, ownership and dialogue in Jordan and Turkey
Ann-Kristin Jonasson

99 **New Democracies in Crisis?**
A comparative constitutional study of the Czech Republic, Hungary, Poland, Romania and Slovakia
Paul Blokker

100 **Party Attitudes Towards the EU in the Member States**
Parties for Europe, parties against Europe
Nicolò Conti

101 **The European Union and Occupied Palestinian Territories**
State-building without a state
Dimitris Bouris

102 **Portugal in the European Union**
Assessing twenty-five years of integration experience
Laura C. Ferreira-Pereira

103 **Governance and European Civil Society**
Governmentality, discourse and NGOs
Acar Kutay

Governance and European Civil Society
Governmentality, discourse and NGOs

Acar Kutay

LONDON AND NEW YORK

First published 2014 by Routledge

2 Park Square, Milton Park, Abingdon, Oxfordshire OX14 4RN
711 Third Avenue, New York, NY 10017

Routledge is an imprint of the Taylor & Francis Group, an informa business

First issued in paperback 2018

Copyright © 2014 Acar Kutay

The right of Acar Kutay to be identified as editor of this work has been asserted by him in accordance with the Copyright, Designs and Patents Act 1988.

All rights reserved. No part of this book may be reprinted or reproduced or utilised in any form or by any electronic, mechanical, or other means, now known or hereafter invented, including photocopying and recording, or in any information storage or retrieval system, without permission in writing from the publishers.

Notice:
Product or corporate names may be trademarks or registered trademarks, and are used only for identification and explanation without intent to infringe.

British Library Cataloguing in Publication Data
A catalogue record for this book is available from the British Library

Library of Congress Cataloging in Publication Data
A catalog for this book has been requested.

ISBN: 978-0-415-70737-4 (hbk)
ISBN: 978-1-138-37736-3 (pbk)

Typeset in Times New Roman
by Wearset Ltd, Boldon, Tyne and Wear

To my family

Contents

Acknowledgements xv

Introduction 1
Governmentality and political phenomena 3

1 **Theoretical perspective: governmentality and discursive formation of European civil society** 17
 Governmentality, governance and NGO phenomenon 21
 Governing the EU and EU governance as a new form of governmentality 29

2 **Civil society participation in governance: a global project?** 45
 Political economy of civil society participation: neoliberal rationalities and government of the social 46

3 **European governance and civil society** 59
 European commission and proposing political projects 59
 Evolution of civil society discourse in EU 64
 The changing roles and discursive shifts of European civil society in EU governance 66
 Further extension of the discourse: European civil society and technologies of EU communication 74
 The stage and norms of civil society participation in EU governance: civil dialogue and consultations 88
 Competing discourses on defining civil society in EU institutions 95

4 **A case study on the Social Platform: a performing agent of European civil society** 112
  EU politics, governance turn and Platform 119
  Social Platform and social Europe 125
  Management of the Social Platform and influences of managerial formations 137
  Platform and participation discourses 152

5 **Conducting a European civil society agency: embedding neoliberal governance through managerial subjects** 171

References 188
Index 200

Acknowledgements

This book draws upon the research I did for my PhD dissertation, which was submitted to Middle East Technical University (METU), Ankara, Turkey. I wish to express my gratitude to my PhD supervisor Kürşad Ertuğrul for his guidance, advice, criticism, encouragement and insight throughout the period of research. I also owe special gratitude to Hakan G. Sicakkan, who helped me throughout the research and writing process. His influence on the progress of this book has been considerable. I am inspired by his work and the EUROSPHERE research project coordinated by him.

I am also grateful to my PhD defence committee, comprising: Atila Eralp, Galip Yalman, Mustafa Bayırbağ and Dimitris Tsarouhas. It was a long and thorough PhD defence, because the committee members had critically engaged in the earlier draft of this book. But it proved helpful in advancing my research.

I would also like to thank my colleagues Marybel Perez, Bjarte Folkestad, Monika Mokre, Elisabeth Ivarsflaten and Åse Gilje Østensen, and three anonymous reviewers who commented on some parts of this work. This study was chiefly supported by the EUROSPHERE research project (CIT4-CT-2006–028504). It has also benefited from the Jean Monnet Centre of Excellence award for research, which is provided by the Centre for European Studies, METU. The UiB Global, University of Bergen, was also very kind in providing an excellent research environment.

I have used some materials in Chapter 1 and Chapter 4 from my previously published work. These parts are reprinted with the permission of EURICOM from *Javnost – The Public*.

Finally, I should express my gratefulness to my wife, Jovita, for support and our newborn baby, Alp, for letting me get some sleep during the very critical stages of writing.

Without the contribution of all the aforementioned names, this book would not have emerged. However, I am responsible for the content.

Acar Kutay
Bergen July 2013

Introduction

This book critiques the common understanding of the organised actors of European civil society or NGO networks, which finds them to be conducive to the democratisation of EU governance.[1] Contrary to the common understanding, which often takes for granted that NGOs are essential actors of an emerging European civil society (ECS) and act as agents of democracy, the book starts with a *problematique* of what an NGO network identity actually comprises, and how it might relate to governing the EU and Europe.

In accordance with this objective, it avoids any normative orientation that would suggest the incorporation of NGOs into the EU decision-making processes was good and desirable, or the opposite, bad and undesirable. A study of this kind would answer the question of whether NGOs are democratising or not and conclude that: 'yes' they are democratising, or 'no' they are not democratising; that they are democratising, but not sufficient; or, that they are gradually democratising. In contrast, in this book I argue that the EU, particularly the European Commission, defines and constitutes NGOs both as subjects and objects of European government.

This argument implies that the discourse on European civil society and activities of NGOs can be constituted by political programming. A political intervention that orients to define and constitute is, however, an intricate act. Theoretical and analytical reflection is needed to understand what it means for a political institution to engage in such an act and to make sense of the instruments and practices that a political institution employs in relation to an act to define and constitute. To cast light on this theoretical and analytical issue, the survey thus interrogates: the descent of the notion of NGOs and civil society within the institutional discourses of EU documents and global governance; the means of their engagement in governance settings; and the perception of the former two by an NGO network. Hence, when (or if) the EU describes and prescribes a certain form of civil society participation, (then) this restricts or limits possible alternative forms of political participation and civil society subjectivities that might emerge at EU level. This argument would therefore underpin the not-fixed characteristics of the notions of NGOs and participation, showing that NGOs are not incorporated into the governance settings as pre-given phenomena.

2　*Introduction*

The objective of the critique is not to assess the ECS discourse and activities of the NGO networks against the background of the true nature of civil society – a real or a perfect civil society, if you like. Such analysis, would have concentrated on some aspects that were considered to fulfil the requirements of an ideal civil society subject and then tested whether the case study complied with those criteria. For example, an ideal civil society should be representative and/or inclusive, be linked to the grassroots, preferably have members from most of the European countries, and be sensitive to the interests and wishes of their members and the general public (Armstrong 2002; Kohler-Koch 2010; Kröger and Friedrich 2013). Furthermore, according to an ECS conception, civil society actors should cast a monitoring gaze on the policy processes, making EU governance transparent (Bohman 2004; Sabel and Zeitlin eds. 2010). They could also help in carrying the public discourse to policy processes, thus engaging in creation of a European public sphere (De Schutter 2002; Magnette 2003). As a result, to the extent that a civil society actor has become professionalised (Sauregger 2006) and co-opted by political power (Kohler-Koch 2010), it would have been considered to be violating the voluntary nature of an ideal civil society, thus being exposed to the influence of bureaucracy. If a civil society actor failed in performing those tasks, it would be considered a failure, not an ideal actor, or, at best, an actor in the process of perfecting its handling of the aforementioned criteria.

Previous research has made a great contribution to and offered alternative lines of thought about legitimacy and democratisation. Unsurprisingly, however, most scholars are either disappointed by the elitist nature of NGO networks; their disconnection from the grassroots; or their proximity with policymakers (Kohler-Koch 2010; Sauregger 2006). One could argue that, inevitably with this kind of critical research, most studies concentrated on criticising European NGO networks, but not the lobbying activities of big businesses and consultancy firms, which appear to have great influence on EU policy-making – both on daily issues (Greenwood 2007a) and on long-term projects such as the determination of the form of capital accumulation (Apeldoorn 2002). This book, thus, deviates from earlier research on ECS by not studying ECS discourse against the background of an ideal, authentic and perfect civil society conception. It argues that this literature also contributes to the evolvement of the discourse of ECS and the technologies of that discourse, providing policy solutions as to how to democratise an NGO network by making it more accountable, transparent and efficient, for example.

As it is not concentrating on an ideal civil society, this book also does not consider *critique* to reveal an ideological manipulation of a political and economic class. In this case, the book's primary starting point – the stress on the ways in which the EU invokes participation and develops mechanisms of participation – does not aim to find out something bad or undesirable. This means that encouragement, incitement and guidance of the EU with regards to NGO networks are not regarded here as attempts to mislead, fool or unmask a hidden suppression mechanism. By the same token, NGO networks and civil society activists are not initially considered to be by-products or puppets of the EU institutions or blueprints of a discourse or ideology. The other critiques of NGO networks are, thus, critical in a different sense, in accordance with the theoretical tradition that informs the debate advanced here. That is, the way in which I conceive the critique, a radical interpretation of the social phenomenon and art of discerning, confers to denaturalisation on one hand and the ability to regenerate anew ideas, values and judgments in the sense of Kant (Foucault 1984). Such understanding of the critique that informs this book would suggest depicting the difficulties of resisting or proposing counter-hegemonic subject-positions to hegemonic neoliberal discourse, and of advancing progressive ideas and practices via engagement in current governance settings. Instead of trying to produce alternative ways to legitimise the existing system, it would rather propose problematisation of that system.

However, the point in this regard is not to consider the current participation practices at EU level merely as being inherently negative. Participation was indeed developed as part of a radical democratic alternative to majoritarian kind of liberal democracy during the 1970s (Pateman 1970), aiming to institute mechanisms of participatory mechanisms beyond the electoral processes, such as at work places. A political intervention that aims to engage people in policy and decision-making and their implementation in this sense might take other forms. Such an attempt might facilitate civil society dynamics and enable citizens to pursue their political ambitions, which are often conflicting and agonistic (Mouffe 2005). On this account, one of the ways to position the *criticism* of this book is to think about its focus on the current practices of participation in (EU) governance as an attempt to problematise and denaturalise a concept that was once developed as a means of radical democracy.

This debate is not limited to EU governance, and its implications are much wider. Some commentators have drawn upon the democratising promises of NGOs in the context of global governance (Held 2004; Rosenau 1998; Kaldor 2005; Kumar 2007; Scholte 2002), complex-policy networks at national-level, and economic development (Mercer 2002; Fisher 1997).

Recently, I delivered a seminar in which I presented my research to an audience of development studies scholars who work or have worked on the subject of NGOs in the context of development at the University of Bergen, Norway. The audience underlined similarities between the social process I had described and that of development, suggesting that what I had described was the conduct of the politics of development at European level. These reactions inspired my perspectives and ideas, and they urged me conclude that participation research on different geographical areas might not be considered limited to that particular context.

Governmentality and political phenomena

In order to cast light on how the EU adapted participation discourse to the European context, and how a social actor received and perceived this process, I am inspired by the analytical tools of governmentality and Foucault's other central

4 Introduction

concepts such as discourse and power relations. But, what does it mean to study political science and European politics from the vantage point of governmentality and Foucault's concepts? I would emphasise at least three aspects to this.

First, governmentality applies a genealogical methodology, which suggests observing the ways in which certain concepts and practices are formed, changed or retain their meanings. But, this inquiry is not to be thought of as a method of history, because the research advanced here dates back to the early 1990s. The temporal period under investigation here is therefore still a remembered past, and thus a genealogical approach in this case implies denaturalising, defamiliarising, and problematising the concepts and practices that are taken for granted or in the process of becoming fixed in the sense that their contested nature is forgotten.

The second contribution of governmentality to political science could be to extend its analytical tools and theoretical ambitions to the state (conceived of as an institutional terrain), policy processes and governance networks in order to examine and understand them. This does not mean adapting governmentality to mainstream political science research, but interrogating the political phenomena from the conceptual and analytical tools of governmentality. A governmentality approach proposes studying the state and policy processes internal to the art of government and governmental rationalities. Foucault suggested government is an encompassing notion that includes the government of the self, of the soul, of household and of the state (Foucault 1991). That is, specific ideas and materials, which are always informed and shaped by techniques and rationalities of certain governmentality or governmentalities, make the management of political institutions and the interactions among them possible.

A third contribution of governmentality studies to political science, if they aim to advance critical insights, is to challenge the current state of the art in mainstream political science – meaning rational-choice methodology and consensual aspects of politics (Walters 2012). The impact of governmentality on political issues thus suggests different analytical lenses for the understanding of politics and political. Governmentality in this case appeared to be more in dialogue with social constructivists (Walters and Haahr 2005), governance theory (Sending and Neumann 2006), and the researchers of critical theory including neo-Marxists (e.g. Jessop 2011, 2007; Dean 1994; Rose et al. 2006) and neo-Gramscians (Sum 2009).

How can these aspects reflect on the present discussion of this book? The use of Foucauldian concepts in political analysis, and particularly in terms of European integration and European civil society, is not common. A few commentators – and really a few scholars – developed overlapping assessments about the way in which European integration creates subjectivities (Walters and Haahr 2005; Parker 2012; Haahr 2004). However, they have not specifically concentrated on the notions of participation and civil society, which constitute the conceptual niche of the book.[2] I elaborate on these here from a global perspective by discussing their contemporary theoretical and practical genealogy.

The present work aims to open a new narrative in European civil society and contribute to governance by exploring the origins of the discourse of civil society and participation in the context of development, global and good governance, and new managerialism. The broader spatial and conceptual contextualisation suggests an encompassing discussion about the current use of the concepts of participation and civil society in European governance. Engagement with the literatures of governmentality, European governance, European civil society, theories of civil society, international theory, and discourse analysis provides a multiperspectival outlook for such a research agenda, which aims to investigate the use of the participation and civil society discourses and their implications in constituting certain types of subjectivities at European level.

In the light of this focus, I examined institutional discourses and their perception by an NGO network that has emerged as an effect of those discourses. I took into account the marginal institutions in EU institutional settings, and this proved to be helpful in showing their neglected discursive influence in setting the parameters of civil society discourse. I examined the discourse in documents and webpages, but also in mundane practices such as guidelines, manuals and management frames to understand how they influenced individuals by shaping their cognitive and practical frames, thus relating to the social phenomena and providing intellectual and material tools to govern those phenomena.

The analytical approach advanced here, though, is not limited to the discursive formation of governmentality – appearance of particular rationalities and techniques in the texts – but also the empirical influences of these policies. In the present analysis of the book, this means taking into account the ways in which civil society subjects that are subject to those rationalities and technologies receive and perceive governmentality. The book thus aligns with realist governmentality (Stenson 2005 and McKee 2009), which also suggests that the role of the state is not minimal or epiphenomenal, and that resistances, incoherencies and failures should be considered inherent to governmental projects and programmes.

That said, the implications of this research and how it differs from and contributes to other literatures can be summed as follows.

First, this research might have implications on a critical normative account, because colonisation of the knowledges and practices of civil society suggest that the authentic 'reason' presumed to emerge from civil society for systemic legitimation is hindered in governance settings because of bureaucratisation and the dominance of corporate management mentalities. Habermas in the 1980s and Weber in 1920s addressed the ramifications of bureaucratisation. However, their admonition was largely neglected in the current literature in favour of transcending their argument in the new era of post-national constellation. Habermas (2001b) has been optimistic about the reproduction of values from civil society. Yet, the very mentality of corporate NGO management fostered by transnational governance structures, think tanks and the scholarly community hinders this potential, as economic rationalities and formal rationalities of bureaucracy dominate over the 'rationalisation' processes within civil society. In other words, the means-ends relationship inherent in instrumental rationality and the project of creating homo-economicus subjects penetrate into organisations of civil society.

A critical normative approach might take the repercussions of this process described here seriously, even though my assessments differ from a Habermasian analysis, which suggests that colonisation distorts the authenticity of civic discourse. A critical approach, on a Habermasian account, aims to depict the true and genuine nature of civil society. Although I agree that political intervention shapes knowledge and practices among NGOs, and, in this sense, colonises the domain of civil society, I disagree with an assessment that without such an intervention and the influences of the economy we would have an ideal civil society.

Second, this research might have implications on social movements literature, as, from a liberal-cosmopolitan perspective that is inspired or compatible with Habermas, social movements literature had high hopes in transnational NGOs in terms of their potential of contention and restraining political power (Della Porta and Caiani 2009). If social actors internalise and normalise a hegemonic discourse, then the potential of NGOs are hindered because of the process mentioned above, which restricts and 'colonises' the authentic action and reasoning (such as the ways of framing problems, seeing things, managing issues) because they are shaped and formulated external to the very dynamics of civic action (such as by political intervention and proliferation of bureaucratic rationalities) and due to clear co-optation structures. My argument, however, differs from this perspective along the similar lines to how it differs from Habermas' approach.

The third implication of this work might be on European studies, highlighting from a different theoretical point that European integration is not *sui generis*, and the influence of larger dynamics should be taken into account. This could be observed in the example of the current participation discourse. The discussion of the evolvement of the participation discourse in terms of its role in good governance and neoliberal restructuring of state-society relationships enables us to challenge the presumed sui generis character of the European politics. Methodologically, this focus also helps to observe how the rationalities that emerged in one context (e.g. in the development and transnational governance) are carried to another (in the case the Europe), and adapted to the context of the new locale.

Furthermore, governmentality offers a different interpretation of European governance. In arguing that state power is allocated between many entities and scales, different disciplines have endeavoured to elaborate upon the democratic promises of recent reconfigurations of political power – a composition of which has been conceptualised in order to suggest a democratic polity beyond the nation-state and a general public. This process is conceptualised, for example, as democratic experimentalism (Eberlein and Kerwer 2004), direct deliberative polyarchy (Cohen and Sabel 1997) and reflexive right-based polity (Eriksen ed. 2005). Due to limitations of collective will formation through the mechanisms of representative democracy at EU level (such as general public and political parties), some of the scholars within the aforementioned conceptualisations stressed the democratising potential of the organised actors of civil society in decision-making processes (Schmitter 2003b; De Schutter 2002). They, therefore, argue that states (and the EU) should actively encourage, mobilise and support civil society (Schmitter 2003b; Cohen and Rogers 1997). Pragmatic philosophy has also supported this view by claiming that political power should not necessarily wait for the emergence of public spheres around the governance structures. In this view, politics can play an active catalytic role by creating its own publics (Bohman 2005). This book is critical of these arguments, for governance is not a zero-sum power game in the sense that loss of state power is equally distributed among actors (defined as stakeholders), including civil society organisations (Sending and Neumann 2006). As an alternative to the governance paradigm, I propose integrating power relations with the study of the effects of a politically constructed discourse – in this case ECS.

Foucault illustrated how certain types of subjects might be created as intended and unintended effects of power relations (Heller 1996). Here, power differs from an instrumentalist understanding, i.e. direct and determining control of the person or institution 'A' on 'B'. Foucault's understanding refutes this casual explanation by rejecting that power cannot be possessed (Foucault 1982), for it is not a thing. Against this backdrop, governmentality, which stems from Foucault's later writings, lectures and interviews, as a form of power – other that and in addition to other forms of power, such as disciplinary power and sovereignty – sheds light on *how* political power subjectifies and renders its subjects as both the object and subject of government, as well as *what* kind of subjectivity it creates. I will turn to this point and elaborate on it below in this chapter and Chapter 1. But, to continue with the present debate, when governance is defined as a form of governmentality (Shore 2009, 2011; Walters and Haahr 2005; Haahr 2004) it is necessarily embedded within power relations, with the latter implying the open ended process of subject formations (i.e. forming, reforming and even dissolving) as well as concerning the possibility of shifting power positions. In other words, neither power nor power relations are static and closed concepts; thus they are seen as intrinsic to social control, sociological transformations and social evolution.

Central to this interrogation are concerns such as the interrogation of power, knowledge, discipline and the formation of subjects in relation to political programming. Having related the constitution of the self to state formation, Foucault conceptualised these aspects of inquiry as governmentality (or the art of government) (Foucault *et al.* 2009). This provides theoretical and analytical tools for examining the relationship between the EU's venture of empowering some NGOs, management of the institutions of the EU governance, and the post-Maastricht (1992) political arrangements on the economic and social governance of Europe by the EU. Such an analysis takes into account the context in which the discourse of civil society's involvement evolves, which technologies and strategies this discourse entails, what this discourse aims to achieve, which strategies it employs, and how the objects of this discourse perceive and receive this process.

Governance as a performative act: contribution to Foucault and governmentality studies

In terms of its contribution to Foucault and governmentality studies, this study, first, concentrates on the proliferation of neoliberal rationalisation within civil society. Second, it advances its argument through a process of 'relational subjectification'. This suggests that subject formations do not necessarily emerge as a result of the dominant power/knowledge that has as its target the subjected (e.g. prisoners, pupils, soldiers). Rather, the subjects and objects of government are mutually related, reflexive and *subject* to the same process that influences the ideas and practices shaping societies, including the individuals, organisations, and the state. Subject formations presuppose the interactions between the subjects and objects of government, and subject positions form and re-form during these interactions, which are conducted on the basis of a common frame of knowledge and rationalisation. In the case of system of governance, it abstracts (or universalises) the knowledge and practices of both public administration and extra-governmental participants of governance (including the NGOs). For instance, the designer (the formulators and disseminators of the discourse, such as the US Aid agency, the World Bank, and European Commission, and public sector at national level) often works on similar principles and a similar 'rationalisation frame' as that of the NGOs (Roberts *et al.* 2005).

What is the agency or are the agencies that perform the action of system of governance? To answers this, I avoid two traps – an agency-centred and structured-centred approach. In an agency-centred approach, social phenomena would be understood and explained by the sheer interests and actions of the agents. In this case, the agency of the EU would short fall in explaining the dynamics and implications of governance and participation of NGOs to governance by reducing the explanans (that explain the phenomenon) to the institutional interests of the EU. There are multifarious actors involved in forming and re-forming the participation phenomenon, including the scientific community, other national governments, international organisations, and NGOs. However, explanandum (that is explained) would be incomplete if we would not question the context in which participation and NGO phenomenon emerged and evolved. That is, what are the conditions leading to the emergence of governance and participation? To answer this, we might need to look at larger dynamics, discourses, practices and materials. The structural trap here is to conceive of governance or neoliberalism as a monolithic and self-consciously behaving *subject* that is able to calculate, frame and actualise its own goals and ambitions. A relational approach, however, critiques the Cartesian relationship between structure and agency, suggesting that they should, rather, be conceived of as mutually related. In turn, both the EU and NGO networks are conceptualised as the agents that form, perform, carry and translate the tenets of the discourse. The way in which I elaborate the subjectification process therefore navigates, between discourse, governance and social policy, and political economy.

I also argue that political programming might well be conceived as a performative utterance, having the effect of forming subjects (in this case the European NGOs) and a subjectivity (as a form of NGO categorisation). Thinking of the NGO phenomenon in terms of a constituted civil society subject refers to 'an identity instituted through a stylised repetition of acts' (Butler 1988: 519). If NGOs are instituted via acts (policy initiatives, scholarly discourse, manuals, guidelines, etc.) that have emerged at a particular historical instance, then the materialisation of an NGO as a civil society subject is dependent on the performative acts of certain NGOs and the larger audience (policymakers, academicians, and the public) who internalise and normalise those acts and behave accordingly.

Along these lines, an association between an NGO and the notion of civil society is thus a verbally and practically constructed one. This association is not predetermined, but informed and shaped by mundane practices that, in turn, render such association possible. As Butler suggests, 'these possibilities are necessarily constrained by available historical conventions (Butler 1988: 521)'. If we try to think about governance, and particularly the NGOs from Butler's suggestions on gender identity, then we might confer that an NGO is 'not a self-identical or merely factic materiality; it is a materiality that bears meaning, if nothing else, and the manner of this bearing is fundamentally dramatic' (Butler 1988: 521). One can find such an attempt to interpret political phenomena such as the relationship between governance, civil society and the NGO in terms of post-structural argumentations, like that of Butler, provocative. But the assertion is straightforward: An NGO is not self-identical because it has *meaning* when it is thought of in reference to other NGOs, scholarly arguments about the relations between the NGOs and civil society, and the roles that the policymakers prescribe to them. Furthermore, an NGO is not a merely factual organisational materiality, for it has *meaning* and practical use when it is considered from the scope of a part of an abstraction: civil society.

The dilemma here is that an NGO might participate in governance settings and act with its intentional choices. Nonetheless, this neglects the fact that policymakers – as we will see in the example of the EU – might execute a certain type of organisational knowledge upon that NGO, while setting the *stage* (consultations, forums, seminars, conferences) and inscribing the *script* (rules of policy conduct, appropriate civil society engagement). But, this still does not confer determination, domination and enforcement, for an NGO is not by definition a passive recipient of a bureaucratic project or neoliberal ideology, even though its existence and performances do not precede the political projects and programmes or the contemporary neoliberal reforms that have aimed to restructure the state. 'Actors are always already on the stage, within the terms of the performance. Just as a script may be enacted in various ways, and just as the play requires both text and interpretation' (Butler 1988: 526). Thereby, an NGO operates in a restricted (but not determined) organisational space of governance and 'enacts interpretations within the confines of already existing directives' (Butler 1988: 526).

NGO reality, and its association to the notion of civil society as performative, suggests that 'it is real only to the extent that it is performed' (Butler 1988: 527). If we consider characteristics prescribed to an NGO as performative, they then 'effectively constitute the identity they are said to express or reveal' (Butler 1988: 528). Consequently, if we adapt the conclusions of Butler on gender identity to NGOs: then 'there is no preexisting identity by which an act or attribute might be measured; there would be no true or false, real or distorted acts' (Butler 1988: 528). This holds true for the NGO reality so that an NGO phenomenon is created and reproduced via recursive performances at the stage of governance settings. The argument advanced here matters because the views and policies that foster a true or an idealised nature of NGOs, civil society and participation might hide the performativeness of the NGO identity, European civil society and notion of participation. Although particular kinds of acts are often associated with an NGO as the expression of a core civil society identity, these acts are often derived from presumed expectations from an ideal civil society identity. Its performances are then evaluated according to those expectations – that is, an identity of an NGO is not rigid but processual, one that is shaped and reshaped by expectations and evaluations.

In this book, I take up performative utterances of a political programme and performances of actors in relation to Foucault's insights on discourse, for they are endogenous to power/knowledge relations. As Hall (Hall 1997: 72) argues, discourse

> constructs the topic. It defines and produces the object of our knowledge. It governs the way a topic can be meaningfully talked about and reasoned about. It also influences how ideas are put into practice and used to regulate the conduct of others.

This does mean that, Hall continues (1997: 73):

> things can have real, material existence in the world ... the concept of discourse is not about whether things exist but where things comes from ... Foucault argues that since we can only have a knowledge of things if they have a meaning, it is discourse – not the things-in-themselves – which produces knowledge.

On this account, civil society, participation, social capital and democratisation only exist meaningfully within the discourses about them.

1 Statements about participation, civil society or democracy provide a particular form of knowledge about them.
2 The procedures that prescribe certain ways of talking about these topics and exclude other alternatives regulate what is 'sayable' or thinkable about participation, civil society, social and economic governance, ethics and democracy.

3 Subjects that in some ways actualise the discourse (activists, social actors, participants, active citizens) are informed and guided by 'the attributes we would expect these subjects to have, given the way knowledge about the topic was constructed' (Hall 1997: 73).
4 This knowledge about participation and civil society obtains or lays claim to authority, in way engaging in determining the 'truth' about participation.
5 Policymakers invent and execute practices to organise participation, creating spaces, formulating rules of conduct, devising criteria about the representativeness of the NGOs, formulating and circulating NGO management guidelines.
6 The discourse is historical and might transform in time, and this statement recognises the power of the agency to reverse the discourse.

Production of a political discourse, its performativeness and its circulation by and within the institutions to other locales is thus here conceived of as a form of power and inherent to governing practices. Foucault's definition of power is not by definition repressive, even though it might be exercised often in that vein. Rather, he suggests a neutral interpretation of power, a medium of social relationships (Heller 1996). The characteristics of EU power in this case are to *define* and *prescribe* appropriate notions of participation and civil society and to *induce* and *sponsor* some NGOs. Such institutional power is both intentional and de-centred (or non-subjective).

It is intentional, because it has been implemented in accordance with a project that can be traced back to Delors. It is also de-centred, because when I refer to subjectivity of the EU institutions, for example, when I suggest that the EU does this or that, this does not mean that the subjectivity of the EU is unified or fixed. For instance, when the EU defines participation and civil society, the explanatory power for the act of definition is not reduced to the intellect of the EU. The EU is also informed by and *subject* to the discourse of participation, because the rationalities and practices about participation have been already defined and implemented elsewhere before the EU took up to realise participatory practices.

Object of inquiry and methods

I examined the evolvement of the discourses on ECS and participatory democracy within the EU since the 1990s, as well as their implications on the emergence of a certain kind of NGO categorisation, by focusing on the Social Platform (hereafter the Social Platform or the Platform), which is one of the prominent umbrella organisations of European NGO networks (hereafter EU NGOs) that emerged after the 1990s to lobby the Commission (or do advocacy services) in the social policy field. This survey does not aim to measure the impact of the Platform's work within the NGO community, both at EU and national level. Rather, this empirical scrutiny first and foremost focuses on how a political institution strategically employs a political project to enhance its power and mobilises certain instruments to rationalise and operationalise that project; and on how this project is being reformed according to failures, confrontation and changing contexts. The Platform is investigated as both the effect and the agency of this project, thus it is not studied as just any other organisation, but because of its double role of being the main interlocutor of the Commission vis-à-vis the social actors organised in Brussels and functioning like a trainer of the NGO community (the latter concerns its role in capacity building and reshaping the sector). With respect to European social policy, the Commission (particularly the Directorate-General for Employment, Social Affairs and Inclusion – the DG EMPL) refers to the Platform as a partner.[3]

Within the scope of this research, I tried to combine different methods. First, I conducted documents analyses of the policies, white and green papers, leaflets, guidelines, toolkits, brochures, reports and websites of the EU institutions and the Social Platform, though I also examined the documents produced by other NGO actors such as those of the Civil Society Contact Group, where it was found to be relevant.[4] In order to examine the EU's civil society and participation discourses, I focused on its governance and identity programmes (*White Paper on European Governance*, communication policy, Plan D, Europe for Citizens), and the procedures of policymaking (interest regulation and consultations).

Interviews with the headquarters (secretariat) of the NGO actors constitute the second main method of this book. In 2009, I conducted six interviews: two with secretariats of the Social Platform, three from the European Network Against Racism, and one from the Civil Society Contact Group in Brussels. The third method is the participatory observation, and in this respect I attended a two-day conference – Civil Dialogue: How can we shape the Europe we want? – which was organised by the Social Platform in December 2008. Since 2006, the Platform has concentrated on a single issue each year as part of its working strategy, and the 2008 conference explored the notion of 'shaping an effective dialogue at national and European level – with people, for people'. Bringing together bureaucrats from the EU institutions, academics and the NGOs, along with their networks, this conference explored how to influence EU decision-making and strengthen ties with European networks. This conference thus provided the opportunity to observe how the NGO community perceived the concepts of civil society, participation and European governing. Indeed, this conference was crucial in shaping my views.

A survey on the Social Platform aimed to observe the following. First, it examined the texts produced by the Platform in order to trace the ways of seeing and perceiving the governing rationalities and technologies. This involved detecting the frameworks for representing aims and goals, such as through graphs, flow charts etc. Second, the survey inquired as to how the Platform perceived and received the participation discourse of the EU. The analysis also took up how the Platform related to the EU's policies during the 2000s, including the adoption of new modes of governance, preparations for the EU constitution, enlargement and the Commission's motto of bridging the gap with citizens. Third, the survey examined the Platform's working methods and communication instruments in order to delineate the relationship between knowledge and action. This analysis implies that practice is endogenous to knowledge. Knowledge, in this case, refers to expert knowledge of the *way of doing things*, such as running an organisation, developing negotiation skills and communicating with other stakeholders in the EU governance system. Practice and action, on the other hand, refers to the translation of knowledge into practice, including the strategy of working and representing aims and achievements. I will therefore endeavour to show how the Platform's way of *thinking* and *doing things* has been grounded on an economic rationality, with the latter leading to performance-oriented action, results-based management, evidence-based practice and producing quantifiable and calculable outcomes. In arguing that the Platform's management structure can be related to a broader perspective about the contemporary debate on governance and new managerialism, I will also suggest this process also establishes a surveillance mechanism.[5]

This inquiry does not, though, cover the members of the Platform: it does not aim to shed light on the intra-network relations of the Platform. This is a relevant and important issue that deserves to be investigated, so it can be seen as the most important limitation of this survey. However, my major concern is not how an NGO network such as the Platform achieves collective action or maintains horizontal consensus between its members. Rather, the question is how it performs as both a subject and object of governmentality. I will delve into the Platform's interlocutor role in the EU, underscoring its role in conveying to the NGO community (it can have access to) and actualising policies on participation.

Spatially, this survey concentrates on Brussels. It takes on an analytical investigation of the EU's initiatives and inquires into their effects on the Brussels-based Social Platform. Nonetheless, and within the limitations, it considers environmental influences as well. For instance, it detects the origins of the NGO participation and good governance discourse in the World Bank. Having focused on the Social Platform's capacity building activities in the European countries, it points out that the Platform also aims to shape (and reshape) the social actors in the national space. In the meantime, with respect to development of this discourse, it takes into account the contribution and confrontation of other EU institutions, including the European Economic and Social Council, the Parliament and the Committee of the Regions. Therefore, our survey is not necessarily a closed-system analysis.

The Social Platform has been established with regards to social policy. However, a debate on European social policies is not the main concern of this survey. The current investigation touches upon these within certain confines. The literature on the governmentality approach to European social policy is rudimentary, and when I attempt to make some evaluations, I refer to studies that have applied a governmentality perspective to social policy in the national realm (Clarke 2005; Dean 2006; McKee 2009). Political economy conceptually and analytically supports the main argument of this book, given that in the case study of this book, as we will see, the NGO networks in European governance initially emerged in relation to the EU's changing attitude towards the economic and social policies in the post-Maastricht era. In this sense, I attempt to connect discursive formations (meaning-making mechanisms) and the larger systemic dynamics, such as the transformation of statehood and trends towards neoliberal capital accumulation. This argument is expanded in Chapter 2.

Finally, a word should be devoted to defining our concepts. European civil society has attracted attention from several different disciplines, with each applying its own notions regarding the societal organisations and associations that operate within and constitute European civil society. Political science scholars who have studied these groups, in terms of their role linking the public reason to decision-making (Magnette 2001, 2003; Armstrong 2002; Eriksen 2001) and their role in European governance (Finke 2007; Kohler-Koch and Finke 2007) have given preference to the civil society organisation concept. Whereas scholars of public policy are inclined to speak of 'interest groups' (Greenwood 2007a), the sociological approach, which studies these groups in terms of collective action and mobilisation, tend to use 'movement advocacy coalitions' (Ruzza 2004; Ruzza and Salla 2007) or transnational coalitions (Cullen 2005; Imig and Tarrow 2001; Della Porta and Caiani 2009). I will continue refer to them according to the way they define themselves, as the platform of European NGOs, throughout the book. Second, I should note that the use of the term 'governance' differs from the European art of government and European governing. While the former can be defined as a certain type of political system in which the problems of society are resolved by allocating responsibilities among many actors, government refers to a broader conception that encompasses the rationalities and mentalities of how nature, society and even selves are governed. Third, the difference between the most common use of the notion of neoliberalism and the neoliberal governmentality (and neoliberal political rationalities) should be underlined. The former entails the process of the economic liberalisation, de-regulation (and re-regulation), hollowing out the state and dominance of the market mechanisms. The latter examines the underlying 'rationalities' and 'practices' of this process. Hence, it does not aim to replace the contemporary use. Rather, it investigates the philosophical foundations and sociological implications. 'Neoliberal governmentality' was first used by Foucault (see Lemke 2001). This usage has been largely applied in the literature.[6] Chapter 3 elaborates on this usage; the reflection of neoliberal rationalities in social policies is addressed in Chapter 5.

The outline

The first chapter critiques the discourse of participation, with a particular focus on the Foucauldian interpretation of Europeanisation. It endeavours to deconstruct the symbiotic relationship between the NGOs and democracy that is far too often taken for granted. It explains how the discourse on NGOs relates to the consolidation of political power, as well as how power constitutes subjects. It draws inspiration from the governmentality perspective, which stems from Foucault's later writings, lectures and interviews. Foucault shows how power relations create certain types of subjects. In this respect, governmentality – as a form of power – sheds light on how political power subjectifies and renders subjects as both the object and subject of government. Chapter 2 contextualises the present argument beyond the European context by referring to the contemporary debates over how participation relates to political economy and re-structuring of capitalism. Here, particular emphasis will be given to the link between Third Way policies, social capital and associational revolution.

Chapter 3 investigates the extent to which the Commission is embedded in the emergence of EU NGOs and shapes their values, aims, and organisational structures. The European Commission has shown an interest in societal organisations and civil society discourse since the early 1990s. The Commission has referred to the societal organisations in different contexts of EU politics. They have appeared in the following EC initiatives: (a) the regulation of 'interest politics' and 'interest intermediation'; (b) the restructuring of EU governance; and (c) discussions of the EU's 'democratic legitimacy crisis'. The Commission's relevant policy programmes and projects, which aim to cultivate legitimacy through the ECS discourse, have been developed in accordance with the motto of connecting with the citizens and consultations with EU NGOs. This chapter focuses on the development of the Commission's discourse on ECS, i.e. from the EU NGOs' incorporation into EU decision-making under the Commission's intermediation policy to their integration into administrative reform and the legitimacy crisis of EU governance. With respect to the latter, Chapter 4 evaluates the Commission's motto of connecting with the citizens, which has been introduced as a remedy to the legitimacy crisis of European governing, i.e. Plan D (Com 2005), Communication Policy (Com 2006), and Europe for Citizens (Com 2007). While the first of these comprises the Commission's documents specifically related to the role of NGOs in EU governing, the second seeks the extent to which and how EU NGOs are embedded in the Commission's technologies of bridging the gap between EU governing and the citizens.

Chapter 4 explains how the platforms of EU NGOs conceive and define the Commission's discourse on ECS and participation. It sketches out a debate on the Social Platform by concentrating on how it receives and perceives these policies (defined as the European art of government). The inquiry into the Social Platform aims to understand how the actors of civil society that are subject to EU governance reflect upon these policies. This chapter, first, explains how the Social Platform perceived the major developments of EU politics during the 1990s, including the introduction of new modes of governance, the convention on the future of Europe, enlargement, the motto of bringing the EU back to its citizens, and social policies. It then examines the Platform's decision-making processes, working methods and communication tools. This chapter also explores the Platform's relations with its constituencies, with a particular focus on capacity building and training activities. Finally, it analyses how the Platform perceives the Commission's discourse on participation and participatory democracy. The final chapter aims to conclude the debate by outlining several implications of the research.

Notes

1 Since the early 1990s, the European Union's legitimacy has been a major concern of EU studies and EU institutions alike. Several suggestions have been advanced to reinforce the EU's legitimacy, such as strengthening the European Parliament (Horeth 1999), enacting a European constitution (Habermas 2001a), searching for a European public sphere (Habermas 2001; Eriksen 2005; Schlesinger 2007; Trenz 2008; Grimm 1995; Nanz 2007; Trenz and Eder 2004; Van de Steeg 2002) and involving civil society organisations in European governance (Kohler-Koch and Finke 2007; Smismans 2006; Fossum and Menendez 2005; Greenwood 2007a and 2007b; Heritier 1999; Schmitter 2003b; Lord and Beetham 2001; Magnette 2003; Curtin 1999; Steffek, Kissling and Nanz 2007; Kendall and Anheier 1999).
2 Although Foucauldian concepts have not been used in European civil society, some commentators applied them in transnational civil society (Sending and Neumann 2006; Jaeger 2007).
3 See for instance: Com (2000) *'European employment and social policy: a policy for people'*, prepared by the DG Education and Culture.
4 The CSCG is a prominent actor in the EU NGO milieu in that it prepares for EU NGOs toolkits and strategic guidelines for lobbying the EU institutions.
5 The Commission launched the *White Paper on Governance* in 2001 as an administrative reform proposal for the EU institutions. Despite other institutions being doubtful about this, the Commission had already started an administrative reform in 1999, which resulted in an activity-based management structure in 2004.
6 See Allen 1998; Barry *et al.* 1996; Burchell *et al.* 1991; Clarke 2005; Cruikshank 1999; Dean 1999; Haahr 2004, 2005; Lemke 2001, 2002, 2007; MacKinnon 2000; Mitchell 2006; Morrison 2000; Moss 1998; Patton 1998; Rose 1996; Rose and Miller 1992; Shore 2006, 2009; Simons 1995; Swyngedouw 2005; Yeatman 1997; O'Malley *et al.* 1997 etc.; Springer 2012)

1 Theoretical perspective

Governmentality and discursive formation of European civil society

The introduction has offered insights into how a governmentality approach could study a political phenomenon and it debated how the present study could differ from other works on European civil society (ECS), governance and NGOs. This chapter expands and applies those insights to European governance and its relationship to the NGO phenomenon. It starts with a critical review of the ECS literature and then advances a theoretical and analytical argument on the governmentalisation of the EU and discursive formation of ECS.

Supranational intermediaries of European civil society (ECS) have been studied by three schools of thought: there is the normative approach (Armstrong 2002; Magnette 2001, 2003; Eriksen 2001; Curtin 1999; Smismans 2006; De Schutter 2002); the social movement approach (Della Porta and Diani 1999; Della Porta and Caiani 2009; Della Porta 2007; Imig and Tarrow 2001; Cullen 2005, 2010); and the governance approach – including the third-sector and interest intermediation (Kochler-Koch and Finke 2007; Eising and Kochler-Koch 1999; Obradovic 2005; Finke 2007; Zimmel and Freise 2006; Mahoney 2004).

Drawing inspiration from the tenets of critical theory, the normative camp argues that there is a new type of political system emerging in Europe, a reflexive polity (Eriksen 2005). Since substantial power has been transferred to supranational institutions in this new setting, national democracies fall short in translating will formation to this new type of decision-making and law-making process. The more difficult it has become to scrutinise supranational institutions, the more they have gained political power. Based on this, the normative approach considers European civil society and the European public sphere to be crucial agents that can carry the public use of reason and articulate societal deliberations to political public spheres. Furthermore, these organisations could apply a critical gaze to decision-making processes, thus rendering governance processes transparent and accountable.

The normative approach to civil society argues that what makes a political system democratic is the articulation of the discourses that emerge *from within* the life-world of civil society to the decision-making and law-making structures through public sphere(s). The tendency of the normative approach in ECS studies has, therefore, been to conceive of the EU NGOs as the nucleus and

18 Theoretical perspective

medium of the emerging European civil society and the agents of trans-European participation beyond national territorial boundaries. In this view, NGOs could function as a transmission belt between citizens and EU governance. For instance, the Convention method, which involved the NGOs during the preparations of the European Constitution, is seen as a successful experiment (De Schutter 2002). Thus, the normative approach assigns the role of linking public deliberations to EU decision-making to the medium of Brussels-based EU NGOs (Curtin 1999; Smismans 2006; Magnette 2001, 2003; De Schutter 2002). This suggests that EU NGOs could function as the public sphere of civil society by incorporating public reason into governance structures (Magnette 2003; Curtin 1999). In Kantian terms, this also asserts that EU NGOs embody the burden of *authentic public reason* articulation on behalf of all affected. In other words, EU NGOs function as the intermediary of European civil society (defined in a broader sense than, but not referring to, the institutional actors), thus reflecting the discourse of opinion-forming publics (Habermas 1996a) and anonymous societal discourse (Benhabib 1996). However, an exceptional conceptualisation of ECS – beyond an actor-based focus – was developed by Fossum and Trenz (2006), who define ECS as a realm, a social constituency of the European polity.

The literature on social movements has studied EU NGOs from the vantage point of supranational contention and the promise of these organisations in fostering European collective identities (Imig and Tarrow 2001; Della Porta 2007; Cullen 2005, 2010). In parallel to the normative approach, this school also focuses on the articulation of societal concerns to decision-making processes. Imig and Tarrow (2001) maintain that EU NGOs perform 'excellent work' in interest representation. However, the scholars draw a pessimistic conclusion: these organisations are unlikely to mobilise civil society in Europe, since they are disconnected from the grassroots. Cullen's survey (2005) also supports Imig and Tarrow's assessment of the EU NGOs' success in lobbying, but she conceives of the Social Platform as an agent that resists the neoliberalisation of EU integration. However, social movements literature on ECS does not limit itself to the policymaking milieu, also examining other forms of collective action such as European Social Forums.

It is the governance approach to ECS that advances a focused research agenda on the involvement of NGOs in EU policymaking structures, diverging from the normative and social movements approaches. Governance has placed great emphasis on the involvement of NGOs in these newly emerged policymaking structures, because the latter's democratic features and legitimacy have been questioned on the grounds of their accountability, inclusiveness and representativeness (Swyngedouw 2005). Governance suggested that NGOs could offer a legitimising function, but this would differ from that of a normative approach. As suggested by Scharpf (1997), for example, governance separates normative considerations of democracy (i.e. input-oriented legitimacy) from its results (i.e. output-oriented legitimacy). With respect to the latter, it explains the legitimacy and legitimising roles of the actors in terms of their efficiency in producing satisfactory results in solving the social issues and generating wealth etc., accordingly. This finds ground also in the notion of good governance, which has been introduced by the World Bank and United Nations with respect to economic development since 1990s. Good governance complements the notion of efficiency with other norms such as openness, participation, effectiveness and transparency – norms that have been incorporated into European governance. Furthermore, good governance gives particular importance to the roles of NGOs in activating the grassroots (Weiss 2000).

There has not, however, been an agreement on the conception of governance. As Rhodes (1996) demonstrates, it has least six different meanings, including the minimal state, corporate governance, New Public Management (NPM), good governance, social-cybernetic systems and self-organised networks. The flexibility of the meaning of the concept makes governance for practitioners (including the politicians, civil servants and civil society actors) and scholars a versatile concept (ibid.), a floating signifier (Shore 2009) and in most cases a buzzword. Notwithstanding its several possible connotations, governance in its broadest terms is defined as the participation of public and private actors in 'intentional regulation of social relationships and conflicts', as well as 'non-hierarchical forms of decision-making' (Kohler-Koch and Rittberger 2006: 28).

The governance turn in EU studies (Jachtenfuchs 2001; Kohler-Koch and Rittberger 2006) has developed against the intergovernmental (Moravsick 1995) and neo-functional theories of integration (Haas 1958; Schmitter 2003a), with an aim to provide an alternative to state-centric interpretations of EU politics. One interpretation has applied the concept to European governance at large, and defined the EU as a polity of multi-level governance (Hooghe and Marks 2001). This political entity is characterised as having more competencies than an international organisation, but less than a state, wherein the governance responsibilities are shared between the supranational entities and member states, along with the non-state actors. Defined in this way, the governance approach to ECS concentrates on the role of NGOs in effective problem-solving of common concerns in partnership with other political, economic and social actors (Kohler-Koch and Rittberger 2006; Jachtenfuchs 2001; Kooiman 1993). In this sense, NGOs might take on responsibilities for delivering welfare services (Kendall and Anheier 1999; Zimmel and Freise 2006). Another interpretation of European governance separates from the multi-level approach: it restricts the application of the term within the EU decision, policy and law-making processes; focuses on the implementation of EU laws; and applies the notion to the institutional structure and performance of the EU institutions (Smismans 2006; Shore 2009; Obradovic 2005). This viewpoint has been inscribed in the *White Paper on European Governance* (Com 2001, 428 final), a document introduced by the Commission to boost the legitimacy of the institutions, increase the accountability of European executive bodies to the elected assemblies and open up the Union's decision-making procedures to allow citizens to participate in making decisions that concern them. Elaborated in this way, the governance approach to ECS primarily studies the influence of organised civil society actors (notably based in Brussels and called European NGOs) on EU decision-making processes (Kohler-Koch and Finke 2007). Put in this way, this scope is also covered by interest group research, including the corporatist (Balme and Chabanet 2008) and neo-pluralist (Greenwood 2007a; Bouwen 2004) explanations to interest-intermediation at EU level.

In the assessment of one of the prominent scholars of governance, the theoretical relationship between governance and democracy is presently taking shape (Kohler-Koch 2009). However, the governance approach to ECS does not question whether NGOs are linked to the grassroots or not, the condition of which is seen as their fundamental promise for democratisation, i.e. in acting like a transmission belt between political power and European citizenry (Steffek *et al.* 2007; Smismans 2006). Hence, governance seems not to have an explicit problem with the autonomisation of European NGOs, in the sense that they act as external to their local constituents. Governance, therefore, does not propose a substantial strategy that aims to build a connection between the public and the EU. Prioritising efficient and effective problem solving, it prefers a stakeholder and partnership democracy (Schmitter 2003b). Normative and social movements approaches on European NGOs, on the other hand, seemed to agree they institutionalise the articulation of public judgement; however, these approaches do not question whether the actors of civil society could manage this task by lobbying and consultations.

In this book, I will try to advance and propose a different research agenda from each of the three literatures – normative, social movements and governance. In the introduction I explained general theoretical and methodological reasons of this. The normative approach often takes for granted the moral credentials of EU NGOs in articulating the public use of reason to decision-making processes (Armstrong 2002; Magnette 2001, 2003; De Schutter 2002). Here, I avoid any normative orientation about involving NGOs in EU decision-making processes. Therefore, I do not attempt to study the Commission's ECS discourse and the Social Platform in terms of their potential democratising and legitimising effects. A study of this kind would orient answering the question of whether they are democratising or not, and then conclude that: 'yes' they are democratising, or 'no' they are not democratising; they are democratising, but not sufficient; or they are gradually democratising. I also do not attempt to consider their work as contention, thus differing from social movements literature.

Among these studies, governmentality has some overlaps with governance theory, for compared with the normative and social movements approaches, it does not conceive of civil society (organisations), or NGOs, vis-à-vis a sovereign power. Ascribing governing functions to civil society organisations, it dismantles the boundaries between the public/private and state/civil society (Rhodes 1996). Governance, however, has limited theoretical and analytical tools for a critical inquiry. It abandons the very feature that is intrinsic to the conceptualisation of civil society: being the domain from which a critical rationality has emerged (Cohen and Arato 1992). Limiting the function of civil society organisations as effective problem-solving actors, governance occludes any opportunity for the emergence of communicative rationality, counter-hegemonic movements, or liberty to deny the requirements imposed by political rationalities *from within* civil society. For example, to Habermas, civil society is the space in which the communicative rationality – as opposed to the rationalities of the market and bureaucracy – flourishes (Habermas 1996). For Gramsci, it is the space in which counter-hegemony is built (Cox 1999). Foucault also argues that the resistance to the governing rationalities and counter-conduct emerge from within civil society (Foucault 2009).

As highlighted, here I concentrate on the Foucauldian critique. Through this critique I aim to interrogate whether and how political programming defines and constitutes the performative actors of governance before (and during) incorporation into the governance mechanism. In other words, this book starts from the argument that civic actors are not necessarily incorporated into the governance mechanism as fixed identities, *as they are*; rather, they are formed because of the effects of political programming, which endeavour to create certain types of subjects – such as through incitement and guidance of their actions – and make them subject to political power. Though this does not imply that political programming is necessarily operationalised without any failures and confrontation, it may well be thought of as a process between successes and failures (O'Malley *et al.* 1997).

The abovementioned perspectives do not question the process of civic actors' becoming lobbying actors. This book differs from governance literature in that it does not aim to discuss the extent to which NGOs contribute to EU governance. Rather, I suggest interrogating the role of political programming (in this case, the Commission's initiatives) in shaping and guiding the very practices of the Platform (including its organisational structure, administrative method, reporting framework and tools of communication). I also propose examining the content of lobbying, and inquire into whether the relationship between formal and procedural mechanisms frames the qualitative aspect. By integrating the interplays between power, knowledge, subject and discipline in the analysis of the Social Platform, I advance a critical survey. In this respect, I argue that governance, as a new form of governmentality, results in forming subjects (and subjectivity) that have the capacity and willingness to participate in the new setting. According to this reading, governance is not necessarily an improvement in our understanding of democracy, but a reconfiguration of power relations. Therefore, supporting civil society actors does not necessarily promote democracy and create public spheres.

In the following pages, I will clarify the main concepts of a governmentality approach, and advance my interpretations of them and how they relate to the concerns of this present study.

Governmentality, governance and NGO phenomenon

Foucault's interest in governmentality is related to his earlier work on power, discipline, knowledge and the subject. With this concept, he emphasises the linkage between the processes of state-formation and the constitution of the self. There are three usages of governmentality (Walters 2012: 11–12).

First, it is a form of power that differs from strategies and domination – two other forms of power that Foucault compares with government: 'In contrast to sovereignty, government has its purpose not the act of government itself, but the welfare of the population, the improvement of its conditions, the increase of its wealth, longevity, health etc.' (Foucault 1991: 100). Foucault detects two distinguishing doctrines of this new form of power: reasons of state and the theory of police (Moss 1998: 3). The former concerns the shift from the way sovereign power is defined: political power is no longer considered to be the ruling and securing territory. Rather, according to new doctrine, political power governs things and men. The theory of police, on the other hand, implies that art of government should extend to all aspects of the individual, i.e. body, soul, wealth and health (ibid.: 3).

As Moss (1998) relates, Foucault explains this form of power as being pastoral power, which originated in the institutions of Catholic Church before being implemented more efficiently by the state:

> Unlike ancient forms of power, pastoral power was concerned with the salvation of everyone in the 'flock' on an individual level, requiring, ideally, a thorough knowledge of the subject's 'soul' and officials who could monitor and account for each and every individual. It was an individual power in that it sought, through supervision, to structure the life of the individual, both through confessional technologies and techniques of self-mastery. As the ecclesiastic institutions declined and the modern period began, Foucault argues, the function of pastoral power spread from the monastery to the state and its institutions.
>
> (Moss 1998: 3)

Governmentality, then, refers to conduct and the 'conduct of conduct', including governing of the self, governing of others and governing the state (Foucault 1991). As Dean (1999: 10) explains, 'conduct' as a verb 'means to lead, to direct or to guide, and perhaps implies some sort of calculation as to how this is to be done'. As a noun, 'conduct refers to our behaviours, our actions and even our comportment, i.e. the articulated set of our behaviours' (ibid.: 10). Under this meaning, governmentality draws attention to 'reciprocal constitution of the power techniques and forms of knowledge' (Lemke 2001: 191).

Walters suggests Foucault described the 'techniques of government' or arts of government, because 'to speak of a technique or art presupposes that the practice in question has been subjected to a certain degree of investigation, critical reflection and calculated refinement'. (Walters 2012: 11–12). In this respect, Walters continues, 'governing become the subject of more or less formalized bodies of knowledge, and mediated by guidebooks, manuals, webpages, and the like'. He illustrates this assertion with the instantiation of childbearing, where parents are not imposed a particular nurturing frame, but follow their own free choices among the available knowledge in the market.

Theoretical perspective 23

How does this relate to our case, European governance and NGO phenomenon? Arguing that practices of governing an organisation become the subject of formalised knowledge shaped by an organisational theory and managerialism and rational choice, we will show that these practices are mediated by guidebooks, toolkits, consultancy agencies, webpages, communication tools and the activities of NGO networks. When I suggest that conducts of NGO networks are informed and shaped by managerial knowledge, I mean that they are autonomous to act, decide and perform, but within a pre-defined frame of management. However, unlike the childbearing example given by Walters to illustrate the free-choice aspect of the art of government, management practices in the case of NGO networks are imposed and coerced. Due to the requirements of funding, they cannot decide how to govern themselves. But, still, a method of conduct by guidelines and manuals is a form of government, because it acts upon the actions of the NGO networks, but does not tell them what to say and what to do apart from framing their management. Management practices such as project cycle management (PCM) and log-frame analysis (log-frame) are means of such conduct – that is, NGO networks follow these frames and EU institutions can evaluate their actions. These frames are based on a rationality of evidence and activity-based management, solidifying a frame of a governmentality on which both its rationalities and technologies are entangled. Institutions of global governance, the EU and the national public administration process also privilege managerial knowledge and managerial organisational forms.

The conduct of NGO networks is not limited to their organisational forms. They also target their micro-behaviour in governance settings, including their relationship with policymakers and other stakeholders with the principals of ethical conduct. We will elaborate on this in Chapter 3, but the point is to give early insights on how new governance settings emerging in the EU shape and aim to shape individual and organisational form in order to make the individuals and organisations amenable to government. This assertion shall be related to the critique of this book – a critique of an idealised notion of civil society agency – because it shows that individuals and organisations are made up and invented.

A second usage of govermentality, Foucault applies in his earlier writings – about power relations and subject formations – to explicate how state power is exerted, or what we should understand from the very notion of 'state power'. In this respect, Foucault does not necessarily endeavour to explain the state as such, i.e. from a perspective à la political science. Rather, Foucault problematises the role of the state (power) in constitution and evolution of social relations and subject-formations. Therefore, he relates a constitutive and productive understanding of power to explicate the relationship between the state and the self. As Foucault and his followers inform us, in most cases, this involves the creation of certain subjects and subjectivities (Rose and Miller 1992; Dean 1999; Barry *et al.* 1996). Yet, the latter concerns a form of power that endeavours to make subjects amenable to taking part in a certain task, not necessarily by coercion or force, but through mobilising their *willingness* and empowerment to adapt *skills*, and enabling them to *access* power.[1] Although this form of power empowers and gives

24 Theoretical perspective

certain liberty to subjects, it also brings mechanisms of control and surveillance. Thus, Foucault delineates that after the eighteenth century, the issue in the western world was not the statisation of society, but *governmentalisation of state*. In this case, Foucault compares the art of government with sovereignty and discipline, to elucidate that state power does not merely concern the security of the territory, but the population. Bob Jessop (2007, 2011) asserts that Foucault thus questions state-initiated projects with regard to the analysis of 'micro-physics' of power.

Despite the fact that Foucault integrated the state as a category into his analysis, he draws a clear distinction between the juridico-political use of power and the microphysics of power (Jessop 2007). For instance, his interpretation of power differs both from 'Liberals and Marxists, both of whom see the state as a unity and as the dominant locus of power' (Bevir 1999: 353). Whereas liberalism considers state power to be a threat to the 'autonomy and freedom of individual within civil society' (ibid.), for orthodox Marxists, the state is an apparatus of the ruling class (and bourgeois interests) to reinforce the capitalist mode of production and in turn suppress and control the proletariat.[2] Foucault, however, portrays the state as a polymorphic entity (Bevir 1999), analysing governance beyond the bureaucratic institutions in an assemblage of plural actors, ideas and things (Dean 1999). To Foucault, 'the modern state [...] has come to be through the development and adaptation of various techniques of government, none of which are integral to the state nor necessarily products of intentional activity. Techniques of government are not tied to a centralised state power but rather at work in diffuse and varied ways throughout society' (Bevir 1999: 353).

Suggested in this way, governmentality discovers *'the conditions of possibility of the modern state'* (Walters 2012: 12). The genealogy of EU governance would also try to understand its reality and survival in reference to particular practices and techniques, which are initiated at EU level to conduct micro-behaviour of individuals. Governmentality then in this case examines *the conditions of possibility of European governance*. These conditions here include: proliferation of New Public Management (Bevir 2010), a tendency towards neoliberalism at a global level (Jessop 2002a, 2002b; Harvey 2005; Hall 2011), dispersion of the ideas about the benefits of associational life such as with regards to social capital (Putnam 1995), discursive formation of (good) governance at a global level (Walters 2004) and incorporation of participation as a constituent dimension of that discourse (Swyngedouw 2005; Gaventa 2004).

The third usage of governmentality refers to one particular family (Walters 2012: 12). Foucault and his followers in this case refer to liberal and neoliberal governmentality as a 'family of arts and techniques of governing state and their subjects' (Walters 2012: 12–13).

Some commentators examined the European art of government along these lines (William and Haahr 20005; Haahr 2004). Larner's (2000) discussion of three different interpretations of neoliberalism can be fruitful in grasping how a neoliberal form of governmentality differs from other interpretations of neoliberalism. To Larner, neoliberalism can be interpreted as public policy, ideology and governmentality. As a policy, its discourse encompasses the 'hollowing out of the state, privatisation of public services, deregulation and liberalisation, flexibility of labour markets, expansion of the private sector, the promotion of new doctrines of 'good governance', and the spread of New Public Management techniques and practices' (Shore 2009: 11). As an ideology, governmentality implies a 'form of rhetoric disseminated by hegemonic economic and political groups' (Larner 2000). Nonetheless, Larner argues that 'there is a short distance from ideology to discourse'. For example, he claims, Stuart Hall's (1988) analysis of neoliberalism as a hegemonic project draws more inspiration from discursive analysis than a traditional base-superstructure model. What Larner adapts from Hall's analysis is that neoliberalism has not been a unique ideology that was put into action by a specific class, or an alliance of several segments of society. Rather, the conflict and confrontation of different segments of society, both hegemonic and non-hegemonic groups, played a role in constituting hegemony. However, Larner (ibid.) argues that this step from ideology to discourse 'requires us to move from Gramsci to Foucault'. It is not only Larner who addresses the proximity between ideology and discourse, following Gramsci and Foucault. In particular, the scholars who work in critical social policy (Dean 2006; Clarke 2005; McKee 2009) and critical public management (McKinnon 2000) have also endeavoured to mingle both perspectives. Having interpreted neoliberal governmentality more as an ethics and ethos, these analyses concentrate on the constitutive aspects of governance. Although they acknowledge the structural change in capital accumulation (from the Keynesian welfare state to a Schumpeterian workfare state), they try to explain the effects of this process on society and the self through a postmodern understanding of power. Thus, they have distanced themselves from structural determinacy and base-superstructure analyses.

Rationalities and technologies

In this analytical framework, governmentality sets political reason itself as its object of inquiry, and studies the mentalities of politics along with the devices that it invented to exercise its rule. It examines the impacts of the mentalities and governing practices on those that are subject to them (Barry *et al.* 1996: 2). Hence, the art of government considers knowledge (rationalities and the systematisation of a certain set of rules), principles, frameworks and visualisations to be intrinsic to a discursive field that renders society governable (Barry *et al.* 1996; Rose and Miller 1992; Rose 1996; Dean 1999). Central to this argument is that political power is rationalised through this connection between rationalities and practices (Lemke 2007, 2002; Rose and Miller 1992; Rose 1996; Barry *et al.* 1996; Dean 1999). Elaborated in this way, governmentality traces the connections between political rationalities and the strategy of governing society with knowledge.

Rose (1996: 42), in this respect, details three features of political rationalities. First, they entail a moral form of selecting the appropriate ideals and principles of governing. Dean (1999: 12), in a similar vein, argues that the art of government is an 'intensely moral activity', in that it constitutes a telos of 'making oneself accountable for one's own actions'. Dean further argues that the policies and practices of governments are also moral in the sense that they 'presume to know, with varying degrees of explicitness and using specific forms of knowledge, what constitutes good, virtuous, appropriate, responsible conduct of individuals and collectivities' (ibid.: 12).

The second feature of political rationalities, Rose stresses, is that they embody an epistemological character – they generate particular conceptions of the objects (nation, population, economy, society, community) and the subjects (citizens). However, political rationalities are not pure and neutral knowledge that simply 're-present' the governing reality. Instead, they are intrinsic to the 'intellectual processing of the reality' (Lemke 2001).

Third, they employ a certain style of reasoning in order to 'render reality thinkable and practicable, and constituting domains that are amenable – or not amenable – to reformatory intervention' (Rose 1996: 42). Political rationalities, therefore, are not ideational structures: they are exerted in daily practices, they guide actions and they motivate our ambitions, intentions and desires. Hence, governmentality examines mentalities of rule in the empirical realm, i.e. how they are put into practice; and how they are translated into technologies, defined as political technologies. The latter comprise the instruments, procedures, mechanisms, vocabularies and techniques that endeavour to enable the political rationalities practicable (Dean 1999: 31). In other words, power manifests itself through these practices (Merlingen 2003, 2006).

The governmentality approach, however, assert that these are not the mere instruments of the political authority that serve to consolidate its power. Rose (1996: 41–2), in this respect, argues that

> the 'power of the State' is a resultant, not a cause, an outcome of the composition and assembling of actors, flows, buildings, relations of authority into relatively durable associations mobilised, to a great or lesser extent, towards the achievement of particular objectives by common means.

Rejecting the interpretation of the practices of political power as domination, Rose elucidates the process through which the political rationalities are rendered into certain practices by the concept of *translation*:

> The translation of political programmes articulated in rather general terms – national efficiency, democracy, equality, enterprise – into ways of seeking to exercise authority over persons, places and activities in specific locales and practices. The translation of thought and action from a 'centre of calculation' into diversity of locales dispersed across a territory – translation in the sense of movement from one place to another.
>
> (Ibid.: 41–2)

Yet, neither political programmes, nor power relations by definition, refer to a smoothly progressing process; rather, they can be seen as a process between successive implementations, failures and evaluations (O'Malley *et al.* 1997). In turn, the constructive role of contestation, and the failures can be interpreted as the source for further reform.

Government sets political reason itself as its object of inquiry, and studies the mentalities of politics along with the devices it invented to exercise its rule. It examines the impacts of those mentalities and governing practices upon those that are subject to them (Barry *et al.* 1996: 2; Simons 1995). Therefore, it considers knowledge: the rationalities and systematisation of certain sets of rules, principles and frames, the visibility of knowledge and techne of governing, and the forms of subjects that it aims to create as the constituents of governing practices (Barry *et al.* 1996; Rose and Miller 1992; Rose 1996; Dean 1999). As Foucault argues (1991) governmentality research studies the rationalities in relation to certain historical contexts that are embedded within social relations. As noted above, this runs counter to the Kantian perspective, which conceives of reason as a transcendental phenomenon, a faculty of mind that exists prior to empirical relations. Hence, governmentality studies 'political rationality not as an exterior instance, but an element itself which helps to create a discursive field in which exercising power is rational' (Lemke 2002: 55). For instance, political rationalities create certain truths about a particular domain, e.g. madness, citizenship, and medicine, in order to render society governable. These truths, and the mentalities of rule, are endogenous to the constitution of certain forms of subjectivity, which entail the *ethos* and *mores* of ethics of self-government.

Power and subject

The art of government revises the relations between power, knowledge and subject in *Discipline and Punish* (Foucault 1977) and *History of Sexuality Vol. 1* (1976). Whereas, in these studies, Foucault concentrated on the repressive power that is exerted on bodies, a power that limits the autonomy of agency, in his later works he emphasises the productive consequences of power and freedom of the subjects. He relates the techniques of governing individuals to the production of knowledge, tracing the connections between constituting people as subjects and governing them with knowledge. In this respect, governmentality is a re-conceptualisation of power and knowledge relations: it merges how power shapes the conduct of self and how this new rationality entails an understanding that 'everything and everyone be managed' (Allen 1998).

The way Foucault conceptualises power originates from his post-structural methodology. He keeps a distance between structural interpretations of power (such as Althusser) and analytical concepts of Marxism (Bevir 1999). He escapes the reductionist approach of reducing the explanation of social phenomena to a monolithic political project (structural explanation), or to the autonomous actions of the actors (voluntarist explanation). Though he never fully appreciates the realist ontology of science (Bevir 1999: 347), he elucidates power relations in terms of its totality, embedding the state in a network-like configuration:

> Power relations are rooted in the system of social networks. This is not to say, however, that there is a primary and fundamental principle of power which dominates society down to the smallest detail.... It is certain that in contemporary societies the state is not simply one of the forms or specific situations of the exercise of power – even if it is the most important – but that in a certain way all other forms of power relations must refer to it. But this is not because they are derived from it; it is rather because power relations have come more and more under state control [...] power relations have been progressively governmentalised, that is to say, elaborated, rationalised, and centralised in the form of, or under the auspices of, state institutions.
>
> (Foucault 1982: 793)

Foucault makes explicit how we should understand power relations in the art of government: 'What defines a power relation is that it is a mode of action which does not act directly or immediately on others. Instead it acts upon their actions: an action upon action, on existing actions or on those which may arise in the present or the future' (Foucault 1982: 788). Foucault continues and makes it clearer how individuals (also groups and institutions) exercise this form of power: 'It is a total structure of actions brought to bear upon possible actions; it incites, it induces, it seduces, it makes easier or more difficult; in the extreme it constrains or forbids absolutely; it is nevertheless always a way of acting upon an acting subject' (Foucault 1982: 789). This description is similar to that of Mitchel Dean, who provides insights for using Foucault's concepts and analytical tools in the field of public administration and governance. Consider the following definition:

> Government is any more or less calculated and rational activity, undertaken by a multiplicity of authorities and agencies, employing a variety of techniques and forms of knowledge, that seeks to shape conduct by working through our desires, aspirations, interests and beliefs, for definite but shifting ends, and with a diverse set of relatively unpredictable consequences, effects and outcomes.
>
> (Dean 1999: 10)

As this definition underscores, government is apposite to power relations. The main focus in such analysis is to investigate how individuals become (certain forms of) subjects. Foucault (1982: 781), there conceived of governmentality as 'a form of power which makes individuals subjects'. By referring to two meanings of the word *subject*, he draws an identical relation between the freedom and autonomy of subjects and subjection in power relations:

> There are two meanings of the word "subject": subject to someone else by control and dependence, and tied to his own identity by a consciousness or self-knowledge. Both meanings suggest a form of power that subjugates and makes subjects to.
>
> (Ibid.)

Theoretical perspective

Hence, Foucault's concern with subject and power relations in his later work, particularly *The Subject and Power* (1982), suggests that power acts upon free subjects – and only as far as they are free; 'in order to act freely the subject must first be shaped, guided and moulded into one capable of responsibly exercising that freedom' (Dean 1999: 165).

Foucault's revisions of his approach to power in his later work, therefore, leads to differing readings about how he interprets the autonomy of agency. Some of his proponents argue that the later Foucault places more stress on the premise of free agency, not just reacting to power, but altering power relations (Moss 1998). They argue that Foucault's interest in ethics enables him to posit the freedom of the subject to work on itself, i.e. capable of rejecting unwanted forms of identity (Moss 1998) and in conscious control of its capacities (Patton 1998). In this respect, Foucault develops a contingent notion of autonomy that differs from Kant's universal, ahistorical and metaphysical notion. According to some, however, Foucault did not abdicate his 'hostility to the subject': 'Foucault vehemently rejected the idea of an autonomous subject, that is, of the subject as its own foundation, of the subject as capable of having meaningful experiences, reasoning, forming beliefs, and acting outside of a particular social context' (Bevir 1999: 354).

In sum, governmentality focuses on 'how certain identities and action orientations are defined as appropriate and normal and how relations of power are implicated in these processes' (Sending and Neumann 2006: 657). It analyses the 'relation between the individuals and the political order from the perspective of the different processes whereby the former are objectified as certain kinds of subjects through the ways they are targeted by political power' (Burchell 1991: 119). Furthermore, the governmentality approach provides an analytical tool to study the government of the self in relation to the government of society, as well as the constitution of the subject in relation to the formation of the state (Lemke 2002: 51). We have focused on the constitution of the self; the following will endeavour to elaborate how technologies of the self are pertinent with respect to the political programmes of rendering society governable.

Governing the EU and EU governance as a new form of governmentality

Along the lines of this conceptual debate, I propose studying the constitutive impacts of this political project – constitutive in the sense of how power, intentionally or unintentionally, may create certain types of subjects and make them amenable to governance. Governmentality can help us investigate how the EU, particularly the Commission, constitutes actors of governance. This project is rendered through rational means, tactics and procedures. It is not a mere act of directing the interests of the actors towards the EU. Rather, it targets the conduct of the self with itself, with others and with society. Thus, it is a moral activity in the sense that it renders a certain form of governmentality appropriate. In sum, I argue that governance is rendered as the new art of government, and sponsored civil society is both the subject and object of this new form of government: governing civil society and governing through civil society.

The governmentality approach to EU governance is a recent, but steadily growing interest. Scholars who study European politics in terms of governmentality have concentrated on different aspects. The initial argument, among these scholars, is to conceptualise EU governance as a new form of governmentality (Shore 2006, 2009; Swyngedouw 2005). The point of departure for this perspective is in a critique of the governance approach. Although the governmentality approach shares the main argument of the governance perspective by explaining governance beyond the administrative units of the state apparatus, it develops a critical and different understanding. First, according to governmentality, governance does not necessarily result in a distribution of power between extra-state actors, a process that is generally associated with a zero-sum explanation of the reconfiguration of political structures. The latter connotes a new constellation of politics – to the extent that the state has shared its sovereign power with new actors, the sclerotic bureaucratic features of traditional governance evolve into a more democratic and innovative regime. The contribution of the governmentality approach to EU studies, however, is not in finding something bad about the governance approach. The criticisms of governmentality are, in fact, more substantial, and were explicated earlier in this chapter and in the introduction. Second, the governmentality approach originates from a postmodern interpretation of power, which itself originates from a post-structural understanding of social phenomena. This understanding stresses the constitutive impacts of language. Third, therefore, one of the main tenets of governmentality – governance at a distance (Rose and Miller 1992) – should not be confused with the central argument of governance: allocation of administrative responsibilities. Both suggest the governance of society beyond the state by the sharing of responsibilities between many different actors and the rescaling of governing practices. However, one of the primary differences between the governance and governmentality approaches is that the latter concentrates on ethics and morality. Government is concerned with political programmes: it focuses on the episteme, morality and style of reasoning involved in these programmes. It is concerned with how these political programmes are *translated* into certain technologies and practices, and how these are received and perceived by the actors who are subject to these programmes. In other words, government is not merely interested in the policy framework (or public policy); it depicts the underlying *ethos* and *mores* of these policy frameworks. Finally, in contrast to governance discourse, governmentality is not a contemporary phenomenon – Foucault traces the appearance of governmentality as a new form of power back to the seventeenth century. Hence, it would be misleading to assess how politics has followed a chronology from the government to governance, and then to governmentality.

Having compared government with governance, we can continue our reflections on the former in EU studies. Government addresses the disciplining and productive impacts of EU governing; it studies the EU's role in shaping the conduct of conduct, for instance, through the new modes of governance. Haahr (2004) asserts that the Open Method of Coordination (OMC) (a method of governance the EU has employed since the early 2000s to coordinate most of its social policies in the member states without political and legal sanctions) has been developed as a calculative and disciplinary project to shape the conduct of the states via the techniques of benchmarking, best practice and national action plans. His approach concentrates on the constitutive impacts of the OMC, i.e. the pertinence of the techniques of representation (such as annual performance graphs) and identity. Furthermore, the governmentality approach in EU studies also deals with the constitutive impacts of language. For instance, Walters (2004) tracks a genealogy of the EU integration by examining the role of the political and theoretical discourse in the establishment of the European Coal and Steel Community (1951) and the European Economic Community (1957). He argues that the dominant functionalist discourse formulated by Haas, Jean Monnet and Schuman was reflected in the Treaty of Rome (1957), and this mentality had implications for the further development of EU integration. The governmentality approach, moreover, intervened in the EU democracy debate (Walters and Haahr 2005b; Haahr 2005). However, instead of concentrating on democracy in itself, it has rather focused on the discursive field of the problematisation of democracy. In other words, the latter does not endeavour to democratise a system by devising normative models, but studies policies and scholarly debates as constitutive elements that make government possible.

The governmentalisation of European governance has similarities with the understanding that defines the EU as a norm-building polity, e.g. Linklater's approach, which considers the EU a norm-building project (Linklater 2005, 2007). The EU as a norm-building entity is standardising, normalising and homogenising daily life (Walters 2004). The abolition of genetically modified food in Europe and the establishment of a minimum level for the amount of lead in oil are among the many examples of how the EU standardises the relation of the self to itself and to its social, physical and biological environment. As a consequence, the art of government transcends the spatial and institutional configuration of the 'government' beyond the nation-state.

European Integration has transcended the 'know how' technologies of government beyond the nation-state (Rose and Miller: 1992). As Rose and Miller (ibid.: 6) argue, 'knowledge does not simply mean "ideas", but refers to the vast assemblage of persons, theories, projects, experiments and techniques that have become such a component of government'. As a matter of fact, the episteme of the recent era, the power to produce knowledge, has transcended to a beyond-nation-state realm to such international organisations as the World Bank, IMF and EU – what Jessop (2007) would call institutions of meta-governance. Following these features of the political rationalities of government, this book argues that the discourse on the ECS and participatory democracy constitutes a moral form, arranging the division of tasks in the governing of society while delineating the ethos of government of the self. This moral form is manifested in political programmes and policy indoctrinations such as the *White Paper on European*

Governance (Com 2001, 428 final), the European Employment Strategy (1997) and Active Citizenship. This moral form is further transmitted into other locales, i.e. Eastern Europe and neighbouring countries. While several notions, such as civil society, NGO, active citizen and participating citizen constitute the epistemology of this discourse, its style of reasoning renders the consciousness of European citizens as an object of government. As we will see in Chapter 3, the latter is due to the Commission's diagnosis that the legitimacy crisis of the EU stems from citizens' lack of information about the EU's benefits. Therefore, the EU policies can be interpreted as attempts to create an imagined social constituency (Fossum and Trenz 2006), defined as European citizenship. The EU, then, endeavours to make this imagined collective identity aware of its own existence, while rendering itself knowable. In other words, political programming plays a constitutive role in two senses: on the one hand, it delineates the style of reasoning, episteme and morality of government; on the other, it forms subjects by acting upon their actions, ethics and consciousness. Concerning the European art of government, the subjectivity that has been promoted is not merely a concern of individuals – it also applies to collective identities, such as NGOs.

Political programming and addressing the consciousness of an imagined European citizenry are matters for the epistemology of the EU's political power: how to render the EU knowable. Political power reinforces itself to the extent that it is knowable, and its knowledge of governing is being practiced. The knowledge of governing – the art of government – is intrinsic to the constitution of political power. Political power is exercised and reproduced in each space where its rationalities and technologies are translated to those who are subject to it. Put another way, the art of government does not only shape the actions and frame of mind of the people, but also enables the reinforcement of the political power in daily interactions. This covers a broad range of aspects, such as the imperatives of how the governing of society, the environment, the economy, one's own organisation and even the people becomes possible. In this respect, government of Europe cannot be thinkable without the rationalities through which Europe is rendered governable. The EU presents itself as a governing power an entity that acts on behalf of Europe; it also exposes itself as knowable not only to the states, but also the people. For instance, technologies of connecting with citizens aim, on one hand, to present the EU as a legitimate governing entity, and on the other, disperse the aforementioned imperatives of governing.

It is here argued that agencies of ECS that now engage in European governance NGO networks), as we will see in the example of the Platform, *translate* the knowledge of political power to those who are subject to EU governing. The very act of translation does not, necessarily, suggest being instrumentally used by the EU institutions to inform people about the benefits of the EU. In this case, NGO networks would be regarded as if they were puppets of political power, doing whatever tasks and missions were given to them. However, this is not the point. The argument advanced in this work, rather, focuses on representation of political power in this case representing the restructuring of Europe as new political order through language – or new word order (Jessop 2002b) – and through certain technologies. European civil society and its agencies are then, here, considered inherent to both a semiotic construction of Europe and to technologies of government.

It is an empirical question about the extent to which particular NGO networks, *inter alia*, engage in transferring the new knowledge systems of European government to Europe's imagined civil society in their capacity building and training activities. In the case study of the Social Platform, we will be able to portray an illustration of the way in which an NGO network carries and normalises the art of government and new knowledge systems while being their effect and embodying their generic features in its organisational form. There is also good reason to expect that other networks engage in similar practices and are financed by the EU, because they are also administered by the same frame of NGO administration.

Against this backdrop, therefore, I will examine how political programmes are *translated* into certain technologies and practices, and how these are received and perceived by the actors that are subject to these programmes. According to this reading, governance is not necessarily an improvement in our understanding of democracy, and a political project of empowering civil society actors as part of an *ideal* model of state-society relations does not by its own nature promote democracy. Governmentality, instead, suggests studying the constitutive impacts of this political project, examining how power projects to create certain types of subjects and make them amenable to control. Constituting actors involves action upon action – shaping, forming, and manipulating conduct and the conduct of conduct. Governmentality, therefore, provides analytical and conceptual tools for interrogating the Commission's civil society discourse and its implications on the Social Platform. I will, then, argue that political programming, e.g. the Commission's initiatives of funding the NGOs, developing a consultation regime, enshrinement of participatory democracy as a norm in the Lisbon Treaty, fostering a discourse on civil society and active citizenship in order to close the gap with the citizens have the effect of forming subjects observed in this case as the Social Platform and a subjectivity as a form of NGO categorisation that have the capacity and willingness to participate in the new setting. This process is associated with the notions of governance, NPM and good governance.

I should, however, note that although this survey focuses on the Commission generated discourse on ECS, the aforementioned notions have not been created from within the Commission. NGOs emerged by deliberate political intervention in Europe, but in a context where the discourses on civil society and participation had already become key terms elsewhere. Yet, to some extent, the Commission itself is exposed to this process, considering it conducted an administration reform during 1999–2004, one that can be associated with NPM (Kassim 2008). The Commission, therefore, is not necessarily seen as the intellectual centre of governance; rather, as an actor playing a certain role in carrying it into the European context, while adopting it into its institutional concerns. Therefore, rationalities behind the constitution of subjects (in this case the Social Platform) are not, necessarily, reduced to the Commission's projects.

Post-national government of the social

NGOs in Brussels initially emerged in relation to the EU's social policies, and the case study of this work – the Social Platform – works in this policy field. We will also examine how the Social Platform has received governance of social policies at EU level. Social policy is one of the terrains in which the governmentality approach applied on EU governance has been limited so far (Daly 2006). In order to close this gap, however, we will refer to other studies that have searched for the possibilities of studying social policies at national level while engaging with political economy (see Chapter 2). These studies emphasise the transformation from the ethos of welfare to workfare, and from employment to employability: 'advanced government is now concerned to draw individuals into accepting individual responsibility for aspects of social protection once governed by the welfare state, but to do so according to appropriate or approved ethical techniques of the self' (Dean 2006: 10). We have already mentioned that current policies and discourse on social policies foster individualisation, self-responsibility, empowerment, continuously upgrading skills and activation. Active society, according to this perspective, 'can be linked to a particular politics of self in which we are all encouraged to "work on ourselves" in a range of domains' (Larner 2000: 13).

Foucault's later focus – which he developed in line with governmentality – his interest in ethics, particularly ethics of the self, can be illuminating to debate the relationship between subject formations and social and economic governance through the EU. Dean (1999) names four aspects of 'ethical government of the self, or of an attempt to govern the self': ontology, asceticism, deontology and teleology. The ontology of government pertains to what we seek to act upon; to Foucault (1976), this substance was flesh in Christianity, and pleasure in ancient Greece. The current substance on which the individual ought to be working can be considered his or her own abilities; therefore, the activation, lifelong learning and empowerment policies – which have been central to the European social policies since 1990s – might constitute an ethos of the new man (human being), eternally upgrading his or her skills, or the active citizen even working on him or herself when unemployed.

The second aspect of ethics, the asceticism of self-government, concerns how we govern this substance (Dean 1999). For Christianity, it meant abstaining from the normal pleasures of life or denial from material satisfaction. In antiquity, the concept of *askētikós* meant hard working and subject to rigorous exercise and self-discipline. The contemporary implications of an ascetic morality, then, are closer to the ancient concept, since neoliberal rationalities necessitate a hectic self, not necessarily active when involved in the modes of production, but in working on the self (e.g. to become an active citizen). The constituents of governance, including those that constitute the supply-side of policy-making, can also be thought of as hectic subjects that are oriented to constant performance. This perspective informs how I characterise the functioning of the EU governance mechanism after the publication of the *White Paper on European*

Governance (2001, 428 final) and conceive of the NGOs participating in governance settings as performance-machines.

The third aspect of ethical self-government involves deontology, which is concerned with the moral obligations that guide how we relate to ourselves and to others. This has been explained above in terms of the moral aspects of political rationalities. Deontology, a branch of ethics, derives obligation from rule (*deon*); therefore, the analytics of government seek those rules and norms that are conceived of as good, appropriate and normal. It is these rules, or regimes of truth that Foucault argues play a role in constituting the self. This term relates to our present discussion because governance presupposes and promotes those rules and norms, namely – as Chapter 3 will expand on – codes of conduct, requirement to provide constructive and useful information, and engage in networking activities.

These three aspects set the ground for the fourth aspect of ethical self-government, its *telos*, which is concerned with 'why we govern or are governed, the ends or goal sought, what we hope to become or the world we hope to create, that which might be called the telos of *governmental or ethical practices*' (Dean 1999: 17). A rational-choice perspective would answer these questions according to subjective perspectives and interests of each individual or institution. However, one might question how those atomistic interests manage to engage in a dialogue in governance settings. A constructivist view, to which this work is closer, would stress the importance of ideas and norms in shaping behaviour. However, the question in this case is how they manage to regulate both micro-behaviour of individuals and macro-practices of institutions. In this sense, governmentality suggests a genealogical inquiry of the ideas and practices of governance, aiming to cast light on how a particular form of public administration requires a certain form of subject.

The EU, particularly the Commission, started to intervene in social policies in the late 1990s. Its interest involved the abovementioned dimensions of neoliberal governmentality. The Commission's social policy was based on an understanding that established a link between work and social protection. It comprises elements of activation, empowerment, adaptability and fostering an entrepreneurial spirit among the citizens (Jessop 2006). It has emphasised the role of training and education in the development of personal skills in relation to the emerging style of government at EU level. Education policy is a case in point, and Mitchell (2006: 398) assesses the Commission's discourse in this policy field in relation to the retrenchment of the welfare paradigm:

> With the rhetoric of globalisation, competition, and lifelong learning there is a strong underlying message of the necessity for constant personal mobilisation and entrepreneurial behaviour on the part of the individuals while at the same time the emphasis on structural and institutional constraints to these goals is generally downplayed. Further, the inexorable emphasis on the *individual* and on his or her learning choices interpellates rational, atomised agents responsible for their own life paths in lieu of groups or classes

experiencing collective dislocation as the result of widespread socio-economic structuring under laissez-faire capitalism. This accompanies a more general abdication of welfarist responsibilities in providing truly viable economic opportunities for workers.

We will develop this in Chapter 4, but this quote is illustrative of the form of government that the EU has been fostering and how the aspect of training is a key technology in such government frame. The quote also shows the rationality of reinforcement of an entrepreneurial and responsible self, the norms of which also informed the behaviour of NGOs in the sense that they encourage them to act as initiative-taking and implementing groups for the benefit of Europe and Europeans. We will return to this topic in Chapter 4, but now I would like to continue with how we can locate the NGOs in government.

Governing through NGOs

The governmentality approach has been criticised for focusing on policy initiatives, but neglecting the impact of these compacts on those who are subject to governing. Thus, a few studies have examined NGOs in terms of governmental rationalities. While Morrison's work (2000) concentrates on the compacts signed between the British government and representatives of the voluntary sector, Sending and Neumann (2006) discuss the role of Norwegian NGOs within the frame of a global governmental rationality. Therefore, despite the main trend in governmentality studies of examining the public policies, our knowledge of how the actors perceive and receive these rationalities is still limited. Further, neither European NGOs nor other international NGO networks have yet been studied in terms of the governmentality approach. The work of Morrison and that of Sending and Neumann are, however, illustrative.

Morrison (ibid.) develops three main arguments. First, the compacts reflected the reconfiguration of the state by incorporating civil society organisations to the public administration. Second, the ethos of the NGOs shifted from welfarism to economism, and professionalism and managerialism replaced the traditional volunteer ethos. Third, civil society should no longer be defined as a space external to state, but as a space where government happens. Morrison's work is promising in the sense that it shows how NGOs can be studied through Foucault's conceptual frameworks. The first argument is a global trend and we see its implications at the EU level, and we will open the managerial dimension below. Morrison's third argument on the other hand, has conceptual and practical implications, which we aim to advance throughout this book.

Compared to Morrison, Sending and Neumann's concern (2006) is not the New Public Management structures and transformation of social policies, but the global governance structures. In this respect, the latter prioritises the critique of the dominant governance approach. Our analysis has to involve both insights, because they augment our argument on two main dimensions: the shift from a welfarist understanding to economism, and the incorporation of NGOs to EU governance structures. The challenge is to discuss the two together and within the same analytical framework. It involves elaborating the administrative reform of EU governance within the framework of the transformation of the art of government. Such analysis draws on several aspects of governance-beyond-the-state, such as technologies of agency, technologies of performance and contractual relations. Whereas technologies of agency render individuals and collective action (such as NGOs) responsible of their actions, technologies of performance have a results-based orientation toward effectiveness, efficiency and strategies of benchmarking (Dean 1999; Rose 1996). The actors are, then, made amenable to subjection to political power through technologies of contract, which also allow for a disciplining mechanism. To illustrate, initially actors are subjectified in accordance with an ethos of self-responsibility, self-esteem and self-care. The performance of the subjects, then, can be measured through the indicators of efficiency and the quantification of success, whereas contracts create mechanisms through which the subjects are controlled by the former. In this approach, 'the role of non-state actors in shaping and carrying out global governance-functions is not an instance of transfer of power from the state to non-state actors. Rather, it is an expression of a changing logic or rationality of government (defined as a type of power) by which civil society is redefined from a passive object of government to be acted upon and into an entity that is both object *and* a subject of government' (Sending and Neumann 2006: 652).

Now we can address the managerial dimension, mentioned above as the second argument of Morrison. The main characteristic of the emerging civil society subject in governance milieu confers to two interpretations of managerialism. First, it suggests a larger social change. It was Burnham (1942) who first advanced the notion of a *managerial revolution* that unfolded during the nineteenth century, and his assessments still may shed light on the ongoing debate. Burnham claimed that not only were businesses, enterprises and corporations governed according to the tenets of managerialism, but also other sectors of society, including parliaments:

> The actual directing and administrative work of the bureaus [in the parliament] is carried on by new men, a new type of men. It is, specifically, the *managerial* type, the type we noticed also when considering the structural developments in 'private enterprise'. The active heads of bureaus are the managers-in-government, the same, or nearly the same, in training, functions, skills, habits of thought as the managers-in-industry.
>
> (Ibid.: 150)

These observations might hold true for the new governance settings, as they privilege the transfer of the organisational knowledge of the private sector to public administration, while promoting a managerial regimen. The second usage of managerialism in public administration aims to cover this development, in a way to describe all organisational changes that have happened in the public sector since 1979 (Considine and Painter 1997). Succinctly, it referred initially to corporate management, with its intentional focus on the unified and hierarchical decision making and knowing *how* rather than knowing *what* (ibid.). New managerialism emerged to depict the changes in the 1990s, and stressed the dominance of economic rationality within bureaucracies; contracting out responsibilities of the state to private sector; orientation to efficiency and utility maximisation; separating policy-making from policy-implementation; and prioritising scientism (Yeatman 1997). The organisational changes in this era – the early 1980s and onwards – has also been defined as New Public Management – which has also been considered in relation to proliferation of the notion of governance and neoliberal reforms (Rhodes 1996; Bevir 2010). Some of these characteristics of NPM can also be found within the mentality of the new modes of governance, such as Open Method of Coordination, which focuses on the best practices, benchmarks and measurements of the performances (Haahr 2004). The Commission (Com 2000) also requires that NGOs should organise according to managerial principles, and the Platform helps circulate these norms within the NGO community with respect to capacity-building and training activities about NGO management.

Thus, one of the central arguments of this book is the subjectification of an NGO in reference to a managerial understanding, in a way that it has that capacity and willingness to participate in the new settings, in a way associated with the notions of governance, NPM and good governance. Given that managerialism does not merely imply the adaptation of management practices and values from private sector, and given that managerialism suggests a model of social governance through which multiple and diverse areas are *managed* by professional managers (Burnham 1942; Parker 2002), managerialism suggests a form of governmentality conducted through management.

Managerialism is a key concept because it has a tendency to engage in a relationship between other governmental rationalities and technologies by coupling and colonising them. First, the agencies of government, namely those of the EU institutions, NGOs, and other constituent of policy networks, have a tendency to adapt the tenets of managerialism. Therefore, the agencies of governance processes are governed by managers. Management knowledge, on the one hand, creates managers; on the other, agencies adapt to an environment wherein management prevails. Second, their performance is defined, steered and observed on the basis of managerial norms and practices, including outcomes, results, project management based on SMART criteria (specific, measurable, attainable, relevant and time-bound), activity-based management. Third, management emerges as a mediating system between the market, political power and civil society, coupling the structurally-differentiated systems by providing institutions of the respective domains shared norm and values.

Up to this point, I have described the central concepts of government and elaborated on how they can be related to the notions of governance, European governance and ECS. Below, I would like to illustrate a conceptual model for an analysis of an NGO participating in governance settings, which will be used in Chapters 4 and 5.

Application of governmentality to empirical research on NGO phenomenon

The governmentality approach can guide our study by deciding the methods of inquiry and empirical material to be selected. It informs the limits of investigation as well as how we should make sense of the materials we have access to. Our survey, then, tracks the imprints of the Commission's ECS discourse on the Social Platform by examining how it perceived and reacted to the discourse of participation, new modes of governance and the reconfiguration of power relations.

To recapitulate, governmentality (or art of government) involves a project (and/or assemblage of different projects) that constitutes a mentality, morality, style of reasoning and an epistemology. As shown, Foucault and his followers argue that the art of government has the goal of explicating the link between the state-formations and constitution of the subjects (e.g. Lemke 2002). Constitution, in this case, is explained by the implications of an action upon action, one that shapes, forms and manipulates the conduct and the conduct of conduct. The analytics of government, thus, examines the rationalities and the techniques through which the political programmes are exerted. Governmentality research has stressed that the recent rationalities involve the domination of market rationalities over the political; liberalisation of the markets are explained in relation to concerns such as autonomisation and responsibilisation of the actors, and their orientation to (better) performance. Devolution of the responsibilities of the state to private actors, particularly through contractual relations, is considered as related to this process.

Government concerns the link between rationalities and practices, prioritising questions that delineate four characteristics of power: (1) how the hermeneutics of visualising, i.e. ways of seeing and perceiving, is linked to subjectification; (2) how the genealogy of thought and constitutive impact of language and discourse (e.g. the knowledge produced in science) explicates subject formation; (3) how knowledge and action are pertinent; and (4) how techniques of subjection create collective identities (Dean 1999). An analysis of the Platform through these four parameters will help us observe what kind of a subject the Platform has become – that is, how it thinks, how it operates, how it represents its activities, and what kind of an identity it represents.

Dean explains the first parameter, fields of visibility, as follows: 'An architectural drawing, a management flow chart, a map, a pie chart, a set of graphs and tables, and so on, are all ways of visualising fields to be governed. These all make it to be possible to 'picture' who and what is to be governed, how relations of authority and obedience are constituted in space, how different locales and agents are to be connected with one another, what problems are to be solved and what objectives are to be sought' (Dean 1999: 30). Dean's second parameter, the technical aspects of government, involves questions of 'by what means, mechanisms, procedures, instruments, tactics, techniques, technologies and vocabularies is authority constituted and rule accomplished' (ibid.: 31). Third, the *episteme* of

40 Theoretical perspective

government – the art of government as rational and thoughtful activity – concerns 'the forms of thought, knowledge, expertise, strategies, means of calculation, or rationality employed in practices of governing' (ibid.: 31). Finally, Dean's governmentality approach focuses on the processes of subjectification and subjectivation and the formation of identities. Subjectification implies how power constitutes, creates, forms, and re-forms subjects, whereas subjectivation concerns the practices and the processes through which the individual makes herself a subject. This final aspect of the analysis of government thus asks:

> What forms of person, self and identity are presupposed by different practices of government and what sorts of transformation do these practices seek? What statuses, capacities, attributes and orientations are assumed of those who exercise authority ... and those who are to be governed?
> (Ibid.: 31)

An analysis of the NGO phenomenon through these four parameters will guide our investigation, i.e. what kind of a subject an NGO involved in Europe might become. With respect to the aspect of visibility, the Platform's documents, including its yearly reports and working strategies, may help investigate how and which fields it aims to govern. Further, the methods of inscription and representation that are used by an NGO can also be discussed in relation to the rationalities of governance and subjection of the Platform to the Commission's civil society discourse. This concerns the inquiry of how an NGO receives the general trend on the management techniques (e.g. NPM) and which issues it visualises.

With regards to Dean's second parameter, the technical aspects of government, in our analysis, we will delve into these questions as they relate to an NGO in the fourth chapter. It will be demonstrated how the concepts of civil society and participatory democracy have been related to the changing contexts by the Commission (such as to social policy competences, legitimacy crisis, the motto of bringing the EU back to its citizens, and the project on governance). It will also be shown that the Commission has fostered civil society discourse through green, white and discussion papers; supported NGOs, though sometimes unlawfully, with funding mechanisms; introduced certain norms and principles about consultation; and a common database. As a final point, 'participatory democracy' has been legalised, since it has been enshrined into the Lisbon Treaty. Chapter 4, then, examines how the Platform perceives this vocabulary that has been so far fostered by the Commission.

To continue with Dean (ibid.), third, the *episteme* of government, to trace episteme generated by an NGO, the survey in this case examines working logic and how an NGO relates this logic to the theme of participation. Finally, with respect to power's impact on formation of identities, Chapter 4 inquiries into the process of subjectification (i.e. how power constitutes, creates, forms, and re-forms subjects) and (subjectivation) the practices and the processes through which the individual makes herself a subject. This final aspect of the analysis of government examines the implications of a political project on persons, self and identity, including the 'statuses, capacities, attributes and orientations' that are devised and imposed on the subject (ibid.: 31; and see also the introduction and this chapter for a broader explanation for the theoretical foundations).

This analytical frame can be applied to examination of the relationship between an NGO's activities and the notions of governance, including 'good governance' and new modes of governance, from several aspects of governmentality. First, this might be thought of as being pertinent with the moral and ethical aspects of governmentality (Rose 1996), e.g. with its implicit premise that the involving of an NGO to the Commission's decision-making processes is intrinsic to a 'good' and appropriate way of doing politics and mobilisation of collective action. Second, the analysis of an NGO should entail the power/subject and power/knowledge relations, as governmentality leads to examine the ways in which political power subjectifies, the agencies through which power is exerted, and how the agency is empowered and made responsible for its own life. Third, the governmentality approach portrays what kinds of subjects are constituted. As it relates to our concerns, this aspect concentrates on the symbiotic relationship between technologies of performance and managerial organisational structures of an NGO. For the guiding ethos behind recent governmental rationalities suggest goal-orientation and outcome achievement, and these rationalities would likely project a *performance machine*-like NGO, which in turn would be subjugated to the control, guidance and surveillance – even though advanced forms of liberal government promise liberty and autonomy to the subjects. Therefore, the survey of an NGO that has been involved in governance mechanisms would expect it to act like a performance machine, while exerting its double role of being object and subject of governance. This anticipation entails the fulfilment of the requirement of conforming to a set of goals that are planned, carefully calculated, and inscribed into documents. The overall activities of an NGO, its reports and its tools of communication can be seen as constituents of its technologies of performance. The evaluation of the performance would then determine the success (and probably the survival) of a given NGO in a governance context. The latter would be seen as both the technique and the means of performance in achieving contractual obligations between an NGO and the EU, considering the financial support of the EU (Com 2000) and the milieu of European governance needed to organise and work via managerial knowledge and practices. The managerial-bureaucratic features of an NGO can be examined through its decision-making structures, working methods and techniques of communication, such as its reports, website and newsletters.

Fourth, governmentality research can help us detect the underlying mechanisms through which power relations are exerted, authority is built and political obedience enforced. An analysis of power relations between an NGO and the EU can be sought primarily in the sponsorship. A funded NGO must fulfil obligations of the funding, meeting certain yearly objectives. The donor and benefiter relationship between the donor and the recipient thus, can be thought of one of the crucial mechanisms through which an NGO is subjectified and made an object of governing. This has, in fact, been pointed out as a major critique to NGOs, considering it would threaten the autonomy of civil society.

The fifth aspect of governmentality research concerns interrogation of the audit, or postmodern patterns of surveillance within the interactions between an NGO and European governance. Related with the fourth aspect, as a condition of funding an NGO is required to perform certain activities and in turn report them to the EU. The question in this case concerns whether reports as well as the very system of reporting and evaluation create both a mechanism of surveillance and discipline. Argued from a Foucauldian-inspired perspective, reporting is not a mere practice of documenting set of outcomes, but it might shape actions and create a certain cognitive frame to relate to the social phenomenon (i.e. leading the actors to interpret social phenomena as calculable *things*). Therefore, a certain form of inscribing the methods for meeting objectives and the representation of end results may structure actors' relations to social reality. With respect to this, it should cautiously be noted that this process does not naturally lead to colonisation: some can treat reporting as a mere act of satisfying the donors. Nevertheless, the reports make the performance visible; thus enable the audit and surveillance possible.

Up to this point, the analysis has taken the NGO phenomenon as its object of inquiry; it has suggested interrogation of an NGO as a new form of NGO category. In contrast, the sixth aspect proposes studying the implications of an intermediary or an international NGO's capacity building and training activities on the NGO community, both at EU and national level. This implies considering this kind of an NGO acting as an interlocutor of the political power (i.e. in this case transmitting the Commission's messages) and shaping its members and the local NGO community via technologies of capacity building. Governance discourse – as inscribed in the *White Paper on Governance* (Com 2001, 428 final) – proposes integrating civil society as a stakeholder in the EU decision-making processes and participating in the new modes of governance (such as the OMC). The influences of NGOs on the EU decisions and in the implementation of the EU regulations nevertheless are, in practice, trivial (Obradovic 2005; Smismans 2006). The focus on an NGO's training activities towards the NGO community might reveal that it has more substantive effects in this field; yet, this subject matter has been so far neglected. Therefore, training activities can be studied as, on one hand, intrinsic political socialisation of the EU (i.e. representing the EU as a legitimate ruling entity), on the other, an endeavour to constitute a certain NGO type, a collective action style. At the final stage, an NGO engaged in European governance can be seen as an actor that is *constituted* and in the meantime *constituting*: *the nuclei* of a new NGO categorisation, one that *directs* the growth of this categorisation and *transmits* its generic characteristics. In other words, this role can be seen an attempt to create Platform-like entities within civil society. How this might happen? The following suggests a conceptual illustration.

As the training practices strive to achieve, the communication between NGOs fosters learning among them. European NGOs explain the norms the procedures

Theoretical perspective 43

of governance for other NGOs, and this fosters a process of norm and rationality shifting by conducting their behaviour. Such conduct has an effect on *leap in mentality*, one that suggests transformation from one *normal* to another one. The normal here involves the totality of ways of doing things and ways of thinking. Posed in this way, the argument is that the mind is contingent on the institutional structuring; it internalises *what exists* as the normal. Unless interacting with another normal – i.e. a discourse and practice in some other context – or initiating a critical attitude that questions the dominant discursive equilibrium (i.e. why it has become the normal, and whether it is possible to imagine a different equilibrium) in order to extend the horizon of the mind, the mind would not problematise the philosophical question of *what can be known* above and beyond the existing. In the case of the network communication, this creates an infrastructure to find an answer to the ontological question of *what can be known* via intersubjective epistemology (in this case networking interactions are used to render the EU and governmental rationalities knowable). In other words, epistemology and ontology are interrelated, because government is only made possible by practice. The networking interactions that aim to foster a *leap in mentality* problematise or aim to problematise prior normal(s), triggering a process that generates a new normal equilibrium. In this process, *the normal of the self* is detached from its previous normal condition, due to power relations between the discourses. Hence, the self realises that what it used to know and practice, that what belongs to itself as subjective truth, was in fact a reflection of a particular truth. The mind (here that of the member of the NGOs) then modifies its subjective equilibrium beyond the previous one.

EU governance prescribes some intermediary NGOs (such as the Social Platform) to train other NGOs about organisational knowledge and the norms of EU governance, guiding in *what is to be done*. Thereby, a discourse on organisational knowledge, EU governance and a particular view of liberal police (read: social policies) circulate in different national spaces, via the channel of intermediary NGOs such as the Platform. This model is illustrated in Figure 1.1.

This model suggests how network communication can illustrate dialogical norm reproduction beyond the nation-state. European NGOs can play a crucial

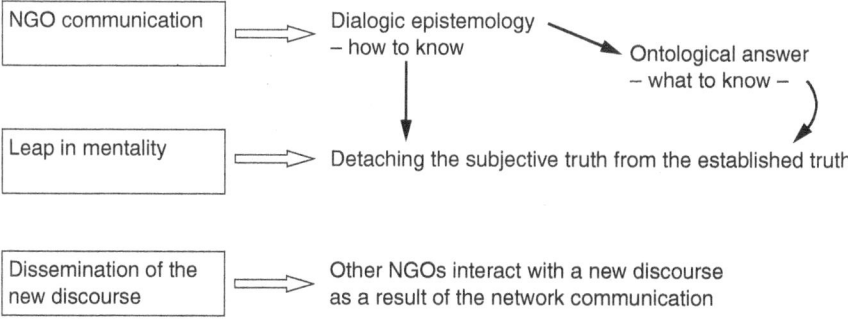

Figure 1.1 Network communication and dispersion of discourse.

role, as outlined above, because EU governance invokes them to link the EU to the EU's presumed civil society. The model can also illustrate on subject formation processes, in the sense of how one becomes a certain type of subject. Argued in this way, the discourse on participation and active citizenship is brought into the agenda of NGOs as a technology of government. In this respect, the European discourse has had an impact on self-ethics, i.e. what the self aspires to become, how it should act (empower itself in order to able to negotiate with decision-makers), and how it should run its organisations. Hence, the EU NGOs articulate the knowledge of the system of governance to the NGO sector, from the power centres to the ruled.

The following pages will problematise the discourse and the role of the European NGOs, particularly the Social Platform, in European governance from the perspective of the European art of government. By examining the Platform from the perspective of the governmentality approach, I mean to examine the constitutive impacts of the European art of government within European space. We should understand the constitutive impacts as the forms of knowledge, subjectivity, morality and technologies that are created by the EU in order to render European space governable. To illustrate this, in the following chapters, we will examine the constitutive impacts of European governance, i.e. how the EU institutions' policies shape a certain form of subjectivity. Accordingly, we will conduct an inquiry into EU institutions' pertinent policy initiatives, namely white papers and procedures of interest intermediation. Following this inquiry, we will elaborate a debate on the Social Platform by concentrating on how it receives and perceives these policies (defined as the European art of government). The inquiry into the Social Platform aims to discuss how the actors of civil society that are subject to EU governance reflect upon these policies.

Notes

1 See Avelino and Rotmans (2009) for a theoretical discussion of different interpretations and Detel (2005) for a Foucauldian account of power.
2 For a discussion on state power, see Jessop 2002a and 2007.

2 Civil society participation in governance
A global project?

This chapter focuses on the connection between participation and the proliferation of NGOs, and a global project. Here, 'Project' refers to the policy initiatives of different political institutions and governmental agencies that are articulated as a coherent policy frame at a global level. This project is informed by structural changes in the regimes of capital accumulation and statehood, which lead to political intervention within the scope of governance reforms. The focus on larger social processes puts the NGO phenomenon in a spatio-temporal context, suggesting the reasons for the spread of the participation discourse at this particular time, not before. This global perspective also indicates that European NGOs and their functions in European governance cannot be examined merely by looking at Europe and the sui generis nature of European integration. To be sure, the EU policy environment has its own dynamics and peculiar conditions that are influenced by the European integration process. To unpack these peculiarities and the ways in which participation and civil society have developed in the context of the EU is the task of the following chapter. In arguing that the EU shapes and is affected by trends in global governance and in political economy, the present chapter suggests that the EU, in fact, has borrowed and reproduced certain aspects of a globalised participation discourse, adapting it to the European context.

NGOs and other organisations in civil society have significantly increased in number since the 1990s, and some commentators even call this process an associational revolution comparable to the emergence of the nation-state in the nineteenth century (Fisher 1997). The evidence of this growth

> includes the increased numbers of officially registered associations, the thousands of NGOs represented at international conferences, the increased proportion of development funding directed through NGOs, the attention paid to cooperation with NGOs by the World Bank and other international agencies, the highly publicized success of lobbying efforts of NGO coalitions, and the growing support provided to NGOs through global networks, including hundreds of World Wide Web sites.
>
> (Fisher 1997: 440)

46 *Civil society participation in governance*

Political intervention and guidance within a policy frame is one of the explanations for the growth of NGOs after the 1990s. NGOs have been promoted within the policy initiatives and via the political programmes of international agencies, as the above quote underlines. Their political encouragement, however, is not limited to the context of development; advanced countries also actively encourage the emergence of the associations and their involvement in policy processes (Anheier 2004). This chapter tries to show that, particularly since the 1990s, invoking civil society actors to engage in governance has been a common practice across the globe – in both the North (developed countries) and the South (the post-colonial states or in the context of economic development).

Political economy of civil society participation: neoliberal rationalities and government of the social

Jessop (2002a, 2007) casts light both on the changes in the regimes of capital accumulation (that is, from Fordism to post-Fordism) and the transformation of the statehood – what Jessop calls a transformation from a Keynesian National Welfare State (KNWS) to a Post-national Schumpeterian Workfare State (PSWS), with the latter extending to EU governance. While KWNS straightforwardly refers to the characteristics of the traditional welfare state and Fordist production, the PSWS emphasises horizontal and global dimensions of political rule, innovation and the arrangement of welfare in the context of human resource management.

This has widely affected the advanced democracies and one of the ways and components of this transformation, Jessop (2002a, 2002b) argues, is appealing to and reinvigorating civil society and communities. As a point of alignment of governmentality with political economy, Jessop does not intend to examine ideas or political projects by reducing them to necessary reflections of a ruling or vested capitalist class or political institution. The focal point of Jessop's political economy is the transformation of the regimes of capital accumulation and concomitant changes in state formations. This focus informs this book because it offers a theoretical perspective to locate participation as a social process and underpins the changes in the notion of statehood. The processual dimension and non-fixed features of the state, market and civil society are important because when we talk about rendering and actualisation of rationalities and technologies – including participation of NGOs – regarding how to govern societies, we always refer to a particular spatio-temporal fix (Peck and Tickell 2002). Therefore, the statehood and the subjectivity of the state implied in KWNS and PSWS amount to different organisational phenomena. Rose and Miller (1992), in their powerful argument, elaborate on how political power is rendered beyond the state in a 'decentred' manner. Some commentators (Jessop 2011; Stenson 2005; Meckee 2009) criticised them for undervaluing state power, suggesting the state was still an important power despite it sharing its traditional responsibilities with several actors and scales. Rose and Miller

(2008) later replied that they did not imply underestimating the state, but rather showed the ways in which governing society was made possible beyond continuous control of the state. In our discussion, political power contained within the state and transnational governance organisations is a key theoretical and operational issue, because the central argument of this book is the definition and constitution of participation and civil society discourses within a policy frame by the institutions. In my opinion, the change in statehood suggested by Jessop offers a different kind of subjectivity – that is, the state as a subject of an activity formulating and encouraging the participation of the NGOs, invoking them to participate in governance processes as characters of the recent form of the statehood. As stated in different occasions throughout this book, restructuring statehood is operationalised via the *devolution* of the responsibilities of the state to private actors in the context of (good) governance (Springer 2012; Lemke 2002; Power 2011). The political economy account offers a nuanced and historicised understanding of this re-structuring, linking the changes occurring in regimes of capital accumulation, public administration and social relations.

Non-state actors in this process share the traditional (welfare) responsibilities of the state, namely delivery services, and engage in the supply side of policy processes by providing knowledge and information for policymakers. That is, the growing number of civil society actors – appearing under different names in different contexts, including NGOs, non-profit organisations, third sector, civil society organisations, community-based organisation – and the importance given to them, relate to changes in state structures and capitalism. Despite this global tendency, my argument does not suggest totalising and generalising its implications, as if all states, economies and civil society actors experience this transformation in a similar vein without resistance. The stress on political intervention also does not suggest that we live in a totally controlled and programmed world. Rather, as Rose and Miller (1992) suggest, we live in a world of political programmes. Plurality of the programmes also indicates their alterability, temporality and potential for failures.

One of the arguments suggested by scholars of political economy to explain the growing emphasis given to participation is the need to embed the changes to capitalism in society. Porter and Craig (2004), referring to Karl Polanyi argue that the Third Way governments and the World Bank have supported and reinforced the participation mechanisms to ameliorate the deleterious effects of neoliberalism and put on it a so-called human face.

> Our thesis is that for a range of reasons and in a fabulous range of ways we are moving into a re-embedding, securing phase in contemporary liberal hegemony. Contemporary liberalism has moved beyond a previous disaggregating, deregulatory and 'more market' phase (frank, rationalist 'neo'-liberalism), and has turned toward embedding, legitimating and securing liberal reform.
>
> (Porter and Craig 2004: 391)

48 *Civil society participation in governance*

Porter and Craig (2004: 391) explain this embedding move with two turns:

> The 'inclusive', embedding turn, we think, has two vital, formative dimensions: the first, a defensive or reactionary one best understood via Karl Polanyi (1944), and the second, an 'expansion of inclusions', best seen as both a project of re-framing and reconstitution of society and political economy as a series of plurally institutionalized and 'joined up' liberal domains, programmes and subjects.

The first phase constitutes reactions to and protests against the liberalisation of markets and structural adjustment programmes (SAPs) in the context of development and the developing world from the late 1980s to late 1990s. For instance, anti-SAP riots in Caracas in 1989, Tunis in 1984, Nigeria in 1989 and Morocco in 1990. SAPs included 'privatisation, denationalisation, and elimination of subsidies of all sorts, budgetary austerity, devaluation, and trade liberalisation' (Leal 2007: 542). This was followed by a series of economic crises: in the Asian tigers in 1997 and, in the early 2000s, Turkey, Brazil and Argentina. As the argument of Porter and Craig suggests, in times of crises with the SAPs and marketisation, procedural market-correcting reforms were not enough to assuage the growing frustration of the masses. Participation and the social inclusion policies, Porter and Craig continue, have appeared in such a context, helping to embed economic relations into society. What does this mean?

> We like others currently find Polanyi's (1944) 'double movement' progression in market/society relations instructive. The first movement, economic liberalization and integration, involves the breaking up or disembedding of traditional and local social regulation by market relations, enabling increased, unfettered penetration of market forces.... This is followed by the second, embedding moment, where, acting almost intuitively a range of what Polanyi called 'enlightened reactionaries' rally to mitigate the social disruptions of market-led liberalization. In the current case, the enlightened reactionaries are as likely to be functionaries within international financial institutions or central governments seeking to restructure social services, as activists within increasingly engaged NGOs, seeking partnership around poverty issues. They might equally be framers of competition and trade regulation, ordinary left voting constituents, or public health activists, aware of rising health inequalities and clients falling through service gaps. Each in various ways contests and regulates the market orientation, giving it a human face or policy limit.
>
> (Porter and Craig 2004: 391)

Others concentrated on the emergence of the discourse as a strategy by the World Bank to suppress resistance to the IMF's economic policies. In this respect, Leal (2007) argues that the World Bank created the discourse on participation and supported NGOs in the Third World in the late 1980s, when people reacted strongly against SAPs:

[Given] the fact that SAP politics of 1980s and 1990s would only serve to heighten popular resistance throughout the Third World, it would become imperative for the global power elites to seek some kind of palliative solution, to put a 'human face' on inhumane policies; at the very least, to create the illusion that they were not indifferent to the suffering inflicted upon the poorest of the poor by the new neo-liberal treatment. Consequently, a 1989 World Bank Report entitled *Sub-Saharan Africa: From Crisis to Sustainable Growth* advocated creating new institutions and strengthening civil society organisations (CSOs), inclusive of groups such as NGOs and voluntary organisations such that these might create channels of participation, by establishing links both upward and downward in society and voicing local concerns more effectively than grassroots institutions.

(Leal 2007: 542)

Against this background, international organisations, not least the World Bank, have been actively involved in promoting governmental programmes for participation in the global South, relating those programmes to good governance schemes. From an optimistic account, these have focused on the potential of NGOs in 'delivering welfare services, implementing development projects, and facilitating democratization; and instrumental treatises on building the capacity of NGOs to perform these functions' (Fisher 1997: 441). However, NGOs have also been critiqued – the most serious attack on the discourse of participation has been advanced by development studies.

Development agencies and international NGOs, in particular, support local NGOs for their effectiveness in pursuing the goals of what some have called a 'new policy agenda,' a heterogeneous set of policies based on a faith in two basic values neoliberal economics and liberal democratic theory (Biggs and Neame 1996; Edwards and Hulme 1996a; Moore 1993; Robinson 1993). As these proponents envision them, NGOs have the capacity to efficiently transfer training and skills that assist individuals and communities to compete in markets, to provide welfare services to those who are marginalized by the market, and to contribute democratization and the growth of a robust civil society, all of which are considered as critical to the success of the neoliberal economic policies (Fowler 1991; Frantz 1987; Hyden 1998).

(Fisher 1997: 443)

These critiques align with double movement argument of Porter and Craig, suggesting that NGOs engaged in rendering political programmes about governing development within the scope of neoliberal structuring. Arguing that either political power (states or global governing institutions such as the World Bank and IMF) or economic interests manipulate NGOs as agencies for social stability and popular status quo (Cox 1999; Leal 2007; Demirovic 2003; Petras 1999), these scholars thus provided a critique of the democratising role of the NGOs. This neo-Marxist approach suggests that 'dominant hegemonic forces' have strategically

50 Civil society participation in governance

created a discourse and mechanisms for integrating the associations emerged from civil society and engage citizens to new political restructuring organised around ideas of neoliberalism in order 'to create and maintain a social consensus around the interests of the dominant power' (Cox 1999: 111; see also Leal 2007: 543).

Others portrayed participation as a new tyranny, the new form of social control and reproduction of hegemonic relations (Cooke and Kothari 2001). For example, Leal (2007) argues that with this strategy, the World Bank aimed to incorporate the counter-ideology into the system, since political power has learned that any frontal attack only strengthens and legitimises the resistance in the eyes of society. Therefore, political power prefers to involve the negating voices in the ruling bloc as part of the dominant ideology (Leal 2007: 542). Defined in this way, counter-ideology does not threaten neoliberal policies. Though it addresses the needs of 'the excluded, the powerless, extreme poverty, gender or racial discrimination', it does not go beyond and challenge 'the social system that produces these conditions' (Petras 1999: 435). According to Petras (1999: 440), NGOs, as a constituent of the counter-ideology, form the radical wing of the neoliberal establishment. Parallel with this statement, Leal (ibid.: 544) further claims that the World Bank uses the discourse on participation instrumentally as a 'justification of the removal of the state from the economy and its substitution by the market'. In this sense, he opposes the views that consider it to be a form of popular government. To him, this entails 'depoliticised versions of participatory action [which] inevitably serve to justify, legitimise, and perpetuate current neo-liberal hegemony' (ibid.: 544). This is why, to him, participation has become a 'buzzword' that places emphasis on 'the *techniques* of participation, rather than on its meaning' (ibid.: 544).

Notwithstanding these critiques, another variant of critical scholars have concentrated on emancipatory dimensions of participation, finding or trying to formulate something good within it.

> Activists and revolutionary theorists attribute significance to local voluntary associations not because they see these groups as part of a growing civil society that engages with the state but because they see them as part of a process that is capable of transforming the state and society. They envision the emergence of alternative discourses and practices of development and anticipate the contribution of NGOs to an 'insurrection of subjugated knowledges'. Seeking alternatives to development, rather than development alternatives, and sceptical about so-called democratization processes, these analysts, activists, and radical critics of neoliberal development agendas value NGOs for their ability to politicize issues that were not formerly politicized or that were ironically depoliticized through the discourses of development or 'democratic' participation.
>
> (Fisher 1997: 445)

Among these discussions, a governmental approach takes a distance of the instrumental approach to NGOs because it might be associated with an understanding that regards the agency as merely a by-product of political power. It might also be inclined to reduce explanations of social phenomenon to the actions of an agency of political institutions. The second camp, interrogating alternative discourses and emancipatory dimension of participation, is closer to our argument (see also Hickey and Mohan 2004). However, this research might neglect how power relations refer to political institutions, and might imply that there is a true nature to the notions of civil society and participation that is rendered via political programmes. As we will see in the case of the Social Platform, social actors might claim and enjoy autonomy, but their knowledge and practices are always informed by particular discourses. I will discuss a Third Way approach to participation with this regard.

Returning to present debate, Porter and Craig's argument is important and pertinent to our discussion for a number of reasons. First, they show how the discourse of participation has been linked to the changes in global economy, a debate that started with Jessop in this chapter. They also show neoliberal economic policies initially detached the economy from society, giving capitalist relations a purely rationalist interpretation. What they argue is that economic transformation must be socialised via social inclusion-oriented welfare policies and participation. This assertion is valuable to understanding the dynamics of capitalism, but it also helps us contextualise the background of participation discourse and its relationship to the reform in welfare policies. Second, Porter and Craig's argument, which they substantiate with an examination of the Poverty Reduction Strategies in the World Bank's documents and social inclusion policies, and in the New Zealand government's Third Way-oriented policies, offers a nuanced interpretation of the ways in which participation discourse is connected to larger social dynamics. Nuanced, because it is not suggesting that participation discourse has mobilised a couple of NGO organisations simply in order to sell neoliberalism or as agents of propaganda to conceal a hidden truth behind neoliberalism. Neither are they are regarded as blueprints of an ideological strategy implementing a social engineering plan formulated at the headquarters of the IMF, World Bank or the EU. Because of this, Porter and Craig's analysis is not contradictory, but complements the critique of the totalisations, generalisations, and meta-historical accounts inherent in a governmentality approach. Below, we will see how Mitchell Dean (2002) interprets the contemporary relationship between the political/civil society and market from a Foucauldian perspective. Before that, as a final note about Porter and Craig's analysis, I should emphasise that what they have found in the documents of the World Bank and the New Zealand government also reflects how participation was discursively formed, appearing in different texts and connected to narratives such as putting a human face on neoliberalism via social inclusion policies. In the next chapter, these narratives re-appear, but this time connected to a different issue – that of legitimising and democratising European governance and connecting the EU to its citizens. This does not mean that the economy aspect was absent in the European context; indeed, the idea of engagement of organised actors of civil society appeared right after the Maastricht Treaty (1992), and

Jacque Delors mentioned his vision to create a 'European social and economic space'. The extensive literature on European governance and European civil society in particular has focused largely on the democratising potential of NGOs, making a great contribution to the field and enlarging our knowledge. What I suggest is that the political economy aspect of participation may also be pertinent in the European context, not only in the sense that it has been used to embed the changes in European economy to European society at the level of language, but also to relate participation discourse to the changes in social policies at practice level. Practice, here, refers to activation and creation of entrepreneurial individual-oriented social policies fostered by the EU from the 1990s onwards. We will expand this discussion in the next chapter, but it might be necessary to make these early remarks for European researchers to relate the present discussion to the overall argument of the book and the European context.

Now I would like to proceed with Mitchell Dean's argument, then I will return to the relationship between the Third Way and Third Way policies. Dean (2002: 45) elucidates the changing interplays between the state-society with the notion of folding, which he borrows from Deleuze's reading of Foucault (Deleuze 1988):

> [L]iberal police works by three distinct but related operations: an unfolding of the (formally) political sphere into civil society; an enfolding of the regulations of civil society into the political and a refolding of the real or ideal values and conduct of civil society onto the political. The first marks the path of connection to what lies outside the state. This is illustrated today by the linkages, networks, partnerships and 'joining up' of state organizations with the commercial, local and voluntary bodies found in civil society. It is found in the analysis of public administration and governance theorists (Kooiman 1993; Minogue *et al.* 1998) and the prescriptions of advocates of Third Way politics (Giddens 1998) and the augmentation of social capital (Putnam 1995). This is the *unfolding of the formally political sphere upon non-political agencies* – a line of 'explication'.

This quotation provides a succinct summary of our argument, drawing a connection between governance, the emphasis given to civil society organisations due their potential fostering of social capital, and Third Way policies. Dean thus reveals the possibilities of using the analytical tools of governmentality within the scope of political economy, at least according to the way I interpret it. Unfolding of the political into civil society shows parallels with the second movement of embedding neoliberalism, because in both cases the domain of political is conceived of as conceptually and operationally flexible, adapting to the contextual changes. In Dean's first moment there is not any emphasis given to the changes in economy, because changes in liberal police (read: social police) occurs due to real and presumed values and expectations of civil society. This offers another line of connection with governmentality approach and political economy, because Porter and Craig also explain this *unfolding* with the reactions of civil society to isolation of economy from societal bases. Even though the focal point of political economy is to understand this operation inherent to structural changes in capitalism, a focus on economy is not absent in a governmental approach either. This is more clearly presented by Dean when he explains the second operation of liberal police, enfolding:

> The second operation follows a line of 'implication' by which the operations of civil society are folded back into the operations of the state – the *enfolding of the processes of civil society into the political sphere*. This is readily illustrated by the market constructivism of neo-liberalism...
> (Dean 2002: 45)

The second operation might be considered as a part of governance processes, because the state does not merely only share its responsibility with non-state actors, but also receives new functions and new roles that it executes in different ways. The qualitative changes in statehood I mentioned at the outset of this chapter aimed to indicate this aspect. That is to say, the political sphere also transforms between unfolding and enfolding processes. Transition from top-down management to non-hierarchical or heterarchical governance processes from the 1980s onwards in advanced countries of North aimed to underline this change in the political sphere. Institutions of global governance then aimed to transfer this frame of particular governmental rationality to the context of development, or post-colonial states, and good governance discourse, which involves strong emphasis on participation and the bourgeoning of a strong civil society as preconditions of effective governance.

The third operation of liberal police, refolding, with this regard appear to be unique to western societies, because it argues for an already established civil society that can affect state formations, even though this might lead to authoritarian leanings (Dean 2002: 45):

> The third is the line by which values, expectations and conducts of civil society, real or ideal, form the means and objectives of governmental programmes. This is the line of 'replication', of modelling, of mirroring what occurs or is supposed or presumed to occur within civil society – a *refolding of the values of civil society into the political sphere*. This is illustrated by Mead's 'authoritative policy', which overrides the inclinations of its subjects, to reinforce and revive the 'dense, reliable networks of mutual expectations' already found within civil society.

Third Way as a governmental rationality

In my attempt to draw theoretical and analytical connections between a governmentality approach and political economy, I have reflected upon an alternative way of conceiving of the state, market and civil society and the ways in which their relationships change in a non-reductionist fashion. With this, I tried to problematise the subjectivity of the statehood. We can now proceed to the relationship between Third Way and third sector, elaborated by one of the key figures in global civil society literature, Helmut Anheier (2004), who illustrates how this new subjectivity of the state takes up actions in a policy frame.

> [It] is difficult to identify what the Third Way is, in particular its ideological core. In many ways, it is still an emerging political vision to modernize 'old-style social democracy' that rested on solidarity and state led welfare, and seeks to develop a comprehensive framework for a renewal of both state and society to counteract neo-liberal policies that are regarded as socially blind, simplistic, and unsustainable.
> (Anheier 2004: 111–12)

This definition, more or less, covers all the aspects we reflected in our previous debate: it suggests a political vision offered by the Third Way for changes in the form of state and society in order to govern society and underlines that the Third Way offers an alternative to socially disconnected neoliberalism – an argument we have already seen in the double movement of neoliberalism. Anheier in this quote – and others, not least Giddens (1998), elsewhere – advocates a Third Way, though not as an alternative, but a market-correcting approach, as we have seen in Porter and Craig's argument. Some commentators even consider the Third Way to be a guise of neoliberalism (Anderson 2000; Hall 2011), which is mirrored on its perception of the change in statehood:

> The role of the state changes from welfare provider to risk manager and enabler – a fundamental redefinition from the social democratic welfare state, and one that is complemented by a change in the notion of citizenship that stresses individual rights and responsibilities alike (Giddens 2000; Mulgan 2000).
> (Anheier 2004: 112)

On the other hand, the rationalities proposed and rendered by the Third Way aim for the re-organisation of the state in such way as to establish links with civil society with necessary intervention:

> The Third Way foresees a reorganization of the state that requires a renewal and activation of civil society, social participation, the encouragement of social entrepreneurship, and new approaches to public–private partnerships in the provision of public goods and services. Specifically, the framework involves a renewal of political institutions to encourage greater citizen participation; a new relationship between government and civil society that involves an engaged government as well as a vibrant set of voluntary associations of many kinds; a wider role for businesses as socially and environmentally responsible institutions; and a structural reform of the welfare state away from 'entitlement' towards risk management (Giddens 1998, 2000).
> (Anheier 2004: 112)

Anheier makes the point regarding the close affinities between the Third Way and third sector even more strongly: 'Clearly, the Third Way and the third sector are in close policy vicinity of each other, especially in the areas of civil society and welfare reform' (Anheier 2004: 112).

Third Way policies then, Anheier suggests:

> expect third sector organizations to be efficient providers of services in the fields of health care, social services, humanitarian assistance, education, and culture, *and* agents of civic renewal by forming the infrastructure of burgeoning civil society. The fact that Third Way and neo-liberal approaches alike harbour such expectations basically suggests that the growing economic and political role of the third sector is somewhat independent of 'new politics' and part of more fundamental changes taking place in post-industrial societies.
> (Anheier 2004: 113)

As the above quote indicates, the point is that neoliberalism and the Third Way, which was initially proposed as an alternative social-democratic project, coincide with neoliberal and Third Way expectations about the functions of organised actors of civil society. As Porter and Craig argue, Third Way policies might in fact be helping to reinforce neoliberal policies, and the promotion of participation discourse is considered part of this process. An interpretation of the European context, namely the post-Maastricht Treaty (1992), European Employment Strategy (1997), Lisbon Strategy (2000), the *White Paper on Governance* (2001), may provide new lenses for investigating social phenomena from a global perspective. Given the growing tendency for the social sciences, disciplines and sub-disciplines to be highly professionalised, with each creating their own codes of communication, if not a particular paradigm, organised actors of civil society appear in different contexts and under different names, and are connected to diverging focal point. To reconcile different disciplines or to suggest a synthesis might be too heroic an intellectual action to attempt. In fact, I do not aim to engage such an activity in this book. As part of a genealogy of participation, I aimed to show that its somewhat hegemonic conceptions and definitions circulate globally. In doing so, and by extending the debate on European civil society to a global level, I aimed to denaturalise, defamilarise, and problematise an issue that has been found problematic within the scope European governance and European civil society by policymakers and scholars. The European context may not be thought of as external to the processes – namely the way in which, by whom and under which circumstances the issue of participation is problematised at a global level. Critical studies about NGOs have not developed along the lines of development literature in European studies, mostly concentrating on the impediments that hinder NGOs realising their democratising functions. It can be argued that hegemonic academic discussions in European studies in this respect have been teleological, perceiving NGOs to be part of an everlasting democratisation project. It is, therefore, necessary to unpack the institutional dimension of power, as we are trying to examine how the EU exercises its power to conduct and constitute certain form state, civil society and market relations. This underlines a *non-reductionist*, and *non-fixed* aspect of power and institution, interrogating which conditions make the EU governance launch and render a project programmatic action on governance entailing non-state actors, including the NGOs. This perspective is concisely described as follows:

> These modes of governance have been depicted as a new form of governmentality, that is 'the conduct of conduct' (Foucault 1982; Lemke 2002), in which a particular rationality of governing is combined with new technologies, instruments and tactics of conducting the process of collective rule-setting, implementation and often including policing as well.
>
> (Swyngedouw 2005:1992)

Limits of the normative expectations of NGOs

Before proceeding to next chapter where we begin to examine the evolvement of participation discourse within the EU institutions, we should also reflect on how problems observed when NGOs are engaged in governance settings relate to power relations. With the contribution of the critique of governmentality, we can draw several assessments. First, Swyngedouw (2005) points out five aspects that threaten the democratising credentials of governance-beyond-the-state: status; inclusion or exclusion; the system of representation; scale of operation; and internal or external accountability. Concerning status, Swyngedouw attacks the notion of 'stakeholder'. He argues that although the concept is discursively inclusive and allows many different actors in governance structures, in fact, the 'internal power choreography of systems of governance-beyond-the-state is customarily led by coalitions of socio-economic, socio-cultural or political elites' (p. 1999). In this respect, the governance structures are 'limited in terms of who can, is, or will be allowed to participate' (ibid.: 1999). Swyngedouw further emphasises that the very act of assigning stakeholder status is an exercise of power: on the one hand, it is conditional on other participants' readiness to accept new groups to the existing structures, and on the other, on the new groups' willingness to participate. Furthermore, transnational governance structures have to deal with the structure of representation. Although some deny the existence of such a problem (such as Moravsick 1995), other scholars endeavour to entrench a relation between governance structures and all affected (Habermas 2003; Eriksen *et al.* 2005). According to the former, there is no democratic deficit, while the latter claim that not only transnational governance, but also national democracies, suffer from a democratic deficit. Therefore, modes of democratisation beyond the state are of particular importance for the latter group: deliberative democracy. By claiming that national parliaments cannot respond to changing circumstances, scholars have tried to find new configurations of collective will formation: that is, extra-parliamentary actors and processes should also be considered within the scope of democracy. In this respect, scholars of deliberative democracy have formulated new insights into representation, wherein civil society and its organisations attain a crucial role, such as discursive representation (Dryzek 1999) and functional representation (Cohen and Rogers 1997; Cohen and Sabel 1997; Hirst 1994).

Having sketched the new insights into representation, we can turn back to our main focus, the promise of the role of NGOs in establishing a representative link. It proves difficult in a traditional meaning of the concept, i.e. representing through a certain kind of authorisation (voting or membership). On the other hand, the new insights on representation would also face crucial difficulties in fulfilling its promises due to the other four aspects that threaten the democratising credentials of governance. The third aspect that Swyngedouw (2005) mentions concerns the accountability of governance. He claims that accountability is 'very poorly, if at all, developed', thus resulting in a more autocratic and non-transparent power (ibid.: 2000). As an accumulation of the former, he concludes that governance structures experience legitimacy problems. He emphasises that the recent formulations of legitimacy rely on 'the linguistic coding of the problems and strategic actions' and 'postmodern theories of political consensus formation [...] which implies a reliance on the formation of discursive constructions (through the mobilisation of discourse alliance) that produces an image, if not ideology, a representation of a desirable good, at the same time ignoring or silencing alternatives' (ibid.: 2001).

We have mentioned that critics of development have studied participation and civil society discourse in the context of attaining the consent of the public for political transformations. It can also be argued that this is in parallel with the emergence of the ECS discourse, i.e. to attain the consent of the ruled. Put another way, the discourse first emerged in a different locale, in this case the World Bank, and for a specific context, in relation to developing countries. The Commission then borrowed this discourse and adapted it to its own discourse on the legitimacy crisis. Similar to the World Bank's discourse, the Commission suggested that the involvement of CSOs would bolster the legitimacy of the EU. Nonetheless, our argument here is that the discourse on participation and civil society does not correspond to a situation in which the discourse is instrumentally used by the political power. While the latter enunciates the tactical use of the concept in order to tame public reactions, as a tool for social control, the governmentality approach investigates the discourse as a constituent of the art of government. The stress on the constitutive impacts of discourse and the productive consequences of power are the two major aspects of government. It is a slight move from ideology and hegemony to discourse formation; in this sense, it is a move from Gramsci to Foucault. For instance, Shore (2006) argues that the Commission used the concept of participation symbolically, in such a way that it created the illusion of entailing measures of popular participation, i.e. government by the people. However, this symbolic use of the term does not merely serve as a means to achieve a certain end, in this case attaining consent and masking repressive dynamics of social control. The very success of the discourse is that it goes beyond an instrumental use and renders the rationalities of neoliberal forms of governmentality – such as New Public Management, supranational elitism and managerialism – amenable and practicable in a prescriptive normative discourse, i.e. participatory governance and active citizenship. Moreover, the discourse is concerned with constituting the NGOs according to the imperatives of a certain kind of subjectivity. It is also concerned with making NGOs the subject of government by ascribing to them the role of translating these rationalities to the local NGOs through technologies of capacity-building and training. The latter is of particular concern for our argument. The proponents of the current form of participation emphasise the positive consequences of associational life, including the development of civic virtues, improving social trust, and promoting public deliberation. However, political rationalities may well be articulated through associational life – in particular, coordinated interactions of NGOs from different countries may result in a dispersion of discourse.

In sum, we elaborated a critique of the relationship between the Third Way, NGOs, third sector and neocommunitarianism (Jessop 2002b; Fyfe 2005; Anheier 2004; Morrison 2000; Cooke and Kothari 2001). It is argued that the emphasis given to civil society participation has been articulated as a global project. This project – despite its deviations in the implementations in a given country, and despite its failures and resistances it has encountered – has been reinforced by institutions of global governance (World Bank, EU and donor institutions) and has been rendered by governments in a major endeavour of political structuring. Civil society participation in World Bank policies has been integrated into the 'good governance' discourse, and associations of civil society have been central in implementing and monitoring Bank-driven projects and policies, such as Poverty Reduction Strategies (Porter and Craig 2004) and Country Assistance Strategies (CAS). Some commentators criticised the Bank's policies, given that they were, mostly, inefficient to provide solutions to poverty, and reinforced local elites (Gaventa 2004). Porter and Craig (2004), for example, from a Polanyian perspective, argue that participation policies helped embed neoliberalism socially in late 1990s, meaning that they gave neoliberal policies a 'human face' and presented these policies as naturally acceptable, after the harsh face of SAPs during the 1980s and early 1990. Some critiques concentrated on positive aspects of participation, emphasising the fact that these policies might bring in social transformations by empowering human agency and opening political spaces to civic engagement (Gaventa 2004). However, some argue that the potential being sought by scholars within the Bank driven projects should not be exaggerated, and researchers should continue seeking power structures within it (Bebbington 2004).

3 European governance and civil society

Previous chapters have advanced the theoretical and conceptual tools that inform how we can interpret European governance and the emergence of a civil society discourse in the European context. This chapter develops this debate by examining the European policies that have been launched since the 1990s. Central to this investigation is observing the coherences, inconsistencies and the changing meanings of civil society in the EU institutional context. The aim is to debate the programmatic and fluid nature of the participation and civil society discourse. The chapter starts by stressing on the historical role of the European Commission as an institutional centre for Europe to develop projects and programmes, considering that the Commission has been a key actor in promoting participation in the post-Maastricht era. This is followed by an overview of the relationship between European social policies and civil society, because the NGOs have emerged initially in this policy field. The chapter continues with a discussion about specific policies that particularly concentrated on NGOs, in terms of governance and communication strategies. It then examines the ways in which participation is actually performed, and how this has been defined and re-defined by the EU. This is followed by an inquiry into how different EU institutions reacted to participation and civil society discourses, and how the EU attempted to carry these within Europe, particularly to Central and Eastern European countries. This chapter concludes with some remarks and assessments.

European Commission and proposing political projects

This chapter concentres on the Commission in the development of ECS and participation discourses, since it has played a central role in their definition and execution. Furthermore, the NGOs have to engage primarily with the Commission because of the EU's policymaking structure. The chapter therefore starts with an overview of the Commission's project designer role for Europe then looks at particular proposals with regards to civil society and participation.

The Commission, within the scope of the Monnet tradition, has endeavoured to act as the motor of integration, while claiming to represent the principles of unity, efficiency, responsibility and impartiality throughout the European integration process. Thus, it has developed some projects to further European integration, though sometimes pushing legal boundaries. Some of these projects have been successful in time – for instance during the most dynamic, and arguably most successful, periods of Walter Hallstein and Jacques Delors.

The Commission played a pro-active role in European integration during Hallstein's two-term presidency (1958–67) and pushed the limits of its roles, which were constitutionally determined by the two treaties of Rome (1958), which establishes the European Economic Community (EEC) and the European Atomic Energy Community (EURATOM). Although the two treaties of Rome recognised certain decision-making powers of the Commission (which replaced the preceding High Authority of the European Coal and Security Community), its power to impose its decisions on member states was restricted (Nugent 2010; Gillingham 2003). Hallstein, the first Commissioner of the EEC, achieved some success, such as in reconciliation of cereal prices despite the veto by France. Yet, substantial proposals by the Hallstein Commission, such as the establishment of a European constitution; a common social policy requiring a single European welfare state and common citizenship; and regional policy and foreign policy-making capacity for the Commission, were met with deep suspicion by the member-states at the time (Gillingham 2003). The Hallstein Commission's proposal about financing the Common Agricultural Policy (CAP) through Community funding deepened these suspicions. This proposal suggested that the Community should have its own financial resources, independent of member states, as well as enhancing the budgetary powers of the European Parliament. The Commission managed to secure the Parliament's support in this proposal since it concerned discarding the threat of veto by member states, thus strengthening the supranational features of the Community. Nonetheless, France opposed the idea of further supranationalism because the Commission's plan was seen as a threat to its national interests. While these debates were continuing, France took on the Presidency of the Community and the tension between France and the Commission grew. The French Presidency marginalised the Commission, yet the Council became the centre of debates. As consequence of this tension between the Commission and France, France recalled its representative from Brussels – known as 'empty chair' crisis. This crisis was resolved by the Luxembourg compromise in 1966, which granted member states power of veto for any decision considered to be a violation of their national interest (though it was not clearly defined what 'national interest' entailed). The practice of unanimity in Council decision-making was abandoned with the Single European Act (SEA) (1986). However, after two decades of marginalisation, the Commission endeavoured to play a dynamic role under Delor (1985–94).

Delor's Commission was considered to be a successful period (Gillingham 2003). He started his role when European integration was in a period of stagnation – from the 1960s through the 1970s. This became known as a period of 'eurosclerosis'. One of the greatest achievements during this time was the SEA, which has been described as the 're-launching' of European integration. It was designed to give the Community a broader policy responsibility, and involved provisions altering aspects of Community decision-making. On one hand, the capacity of the Council of Ministers to take decisions by qualified majority vote (QMV) was strengthened to complete the internal market by 1992. On the other, the influence of the European parliament was strengthened via the creation of a two-stage legislative procedure – 'the cooperation procedure'. After 1986, regulations drafted in Brussels had the force of law in the member-states. SEA brought new competences to the Commission in the fields of environmental, social, regional and monetary policy.

Although Delors' period concentrated on the completion of the internal market and single currency, he also wanted to merge the social aspects of Europe to the economic liberalisation policies that were in progress. Thus, he introduced the notion of the 'European social and economic space', which resulted in involvement of the representatives of trade unions (ETUC) and employers (UNICE) in the decision-making process through the 'Social Dialogue'. This practice did not have any binding force when it commenced after 1985. However, the social protocol annexed into the Maastricht Treaty provided social dialogue legal grounds. There were also critiques of this initiative. Gillingham (2003: 259), for instance states that:

> if central Brussels provided an intimation of it, the zone in question would be filled by lobbyists rather than 'solidaristic' workers or virtuous peasants bound 'organically' to the soil. The policy networking that took hold at the Commission during the 1980s would serve only special interests; the tax-paying public had no influence over it.

The Treaty of Maastricht, entailed by the SEA, brought the three pillars: the European Communities; Common Security and Defence Policy (CSDP); and Justice and Home Affairs (JHA). It also included a Social Chapter – from which UK opted out – and brought forward the notion of European citizenship. The Treaty of Maastricht furthered the policy and institutional deepening by introducing a timetable for economic and monetary union; specifying the economic and budgetary criteria; and creating a new legislative procedure, co-decision, which gave the European Parliament the power of veto over some legislative proposals. The three pillars method was abolished and the phrase of the European Community was replaced by the European Union in the Lisbon Treaty, signed in 2007 and ratified in 2009.

Treaty of Amsterdam (1997) was not seen as ambitious as the SEA or the Maastricht Treaty (Nugent 2010). It was expected that the treaty would finalise the restructuring of the EU's institutions before the Eastern enlargement. Rather, it brought relatively modest attempts, strengthening the EU's decision-making capacity in JHA and extending the co-decision procedure to more policy spheres. It also expanded the competence of the EU to the area of employment, which resulted in the launch of the Employment Strategy and governance of this strategy via new methods of governance, such as the Open Method of Coordination.

In 1999, the Commission experienced the most damaging incident of its institutional history. The Santer Commission had to resign due to evidence of corruption, with some of the Commission officers involved. The Commission was then seen to be in permanent decline (Gillingham 2003). In order to recover its damaged image and maintain its legitimacy, the Commission engaged in decisive institutional reform between 1999 and 2004 (Kassim 2008). This brought new provisions to the Commission's recruitment and career policies, but also moved the Commission's administrative methods towards a techno-managerial style and activity-based management (Kassim 2008).

Central developments during the 2000s were the failed attempts at a constitutional treaty and its replacement with the Lisbon Treaty, and the enlargement of the European Union. The legitimacy of the EU has been intensely debated since the Maastricht Treaty (1992), with the claim that the 'permissive consensus' – the traditional grounds on which the EU indirectly attained legitimacy – has been inadequate in supporting the growing competences of the EU. The Treaty of Nice (2001) dealt with the institutional composition of the EU, but did not satisfy expectations. After the Nice Treaty, national leaders agreed to convene another Intergovernmental Conference (IGC) in 2004. To facilitate the debate and help prepare, the December 2001 European Council meeting issued the *Laeken Declaration on the Future of the European Union*, which provided for the establishment of a Convention on the Future of Europe (European Council, 2001) (Nugent 2010). The Laeken Declaration (2001) suggested that the soon-to-be enlarged EU needed to be more democratic, more transparent and more efficient. The Union also needed to resolve three basic challenges: 'how to bring citizens, and primarily the young, closer to the European design and the European institutions'; 'how to organise politics and European political area in an enlarged Union'; and 'how to develop the Union into a stabilising factor and a model in the new, multipolar world' (European Council, 2001).

The Convention comprised 105 members. The dominant presence was of parliamentarians rather than governmental representatives. The final text, formally presented to the Italian Council Presidency on 18 July 2003, took the form of a Draft Treaty Establishing a Constitution for Europe. The constitutional treaty would have replaced the existing treaties – the TEU (Treaty on European Union, 1992), TFEU (Treat on Functioning of the European Union, 1957), EURATAM Treaty (European Atomic Energy Community, 1957), in their post-Nice forms – with a single treaty. It comprised 448 articles, 35 protocols, two annexes and 50 declarations (Treaty Establishing Constitution for Europe, 2004).

The constitutional treaty could not come into force until it had been ratified by all the member states. The treaty was signed in October 2004, and all member states were obliged to ratify it by October 2006. Most member states ratified post-accession treaties by parliamentary vote. Referendums had been used in Ireland for all four treaties from the SEA; in Denmark for the SEA, Maastricht and Amsterdam treaties; and in France for the Maastricht Treaty. Yet, the constitutional treaty was more than 'just another' amending treaty (Nugent 2010: 74). Ratification referendums were held in France on 29 May 2005 and in the Netherlands on 1 June 2005. By 1 June 2005, ten member states had ratified the treaty – only Spain via referendum. France and Netherlands were negative about the treaty, considering it an elite rather than a popular project that entailing Anglo-American social and economic values (Nugent 2010). Political opposition to the government and projected Turkish accession to the EU were other claims that affected the result of the ratification process (ibid.: 74). The results of the French and Dutch referendums were negative. Two alternatives were discussed after the treaty. The first suggestion, advocated by the Luxembourg President of the Council Jean-Claude Juncker, as well as by French President Jacques Chirac and German Chancellor Gerhard Schroeder, was to continue ratification in the remaining countries, since the treaty was not necessarily lost. The treaty itself could enable this with the statement that if four-fifths of the member states ratified the treaty, but one or two failed, 'the matter would be referred to the European Council' (Nugent 2010: 73). The second view, supported by British prime minister Tony Blair was to put the treaty on hold.

A Council summit was held one week after the referendums. Member states that were planning to hold a referendum were cautious after the results of the French and Dutch cases, in that they thought it would be more difficult to win public consent. The summit's resolution was to freeze the issue until the first half of 2006 for a 'period of reflection [which] will be used to enable a broad debate to take place in each of our countries' (European Council, 2005; also see Nugent 2010: 74). Member states that planned to hold referendums could proceed with their plans. This only happened in Luxembourg, where the treaty was ratified. During the 'period of reflection' some initiatives were introduced to close 'the gap between the citizens and the EU'. Plan D, Active Citizenship, and Europe for Citizens – the policies we will look at in this chapter – were launched after 2006 to allow the EU to explain itself to people (in EU talk, 'its citizens') by presenting the benefits of the system of EU governance, explaining how the EU works, and allowing citizens to take part in EU politics. After 2006, web consultations were also opened to citizens, with the aim of creating a cyberspace for public reflection (Hueller 2010).

The reflection was in practice, however, restricted to exchanges between EU practitioners (Nugent 2010). The constitutional aspects of the treaty were dropped, and the more reformist aspects remained. For this purpose, an Intergovernmental Conference was convened in June 2007. Poland pressed for the use of Nice voting rules until 2017 in the treaty, with an accompanying protocol. UK pressed for an opt-out from the JHA and said CFSP issues would be beyond the reach of the European Court of Justice. The revised treaty was formally agreed by the heads of state and government at an informal meeting on 18 October, and was signed in Lisbon on 13 December 2007. Ireland was the only member state that held a referendum – on the first attempt, the treaty was rejected; on the second it was endorsed, after Irish expectations were fulfilled. Originally the treaty had reduced the College of Commissioners to two-thirds of the number of the members, and this could have resulted in Ireland not having a Commissioner. After the revision, the structure returned to the Nice system: one Commissioner for each country. Ireland was also concerned about some taxation issues, military neutrality, ethics (especially abortion) and social matters, and was assured that the treaty would not affect its position on these (Nugent 2010). In sum, the Lisbon Treaty was a long and tedious period of preparation, negotiation and ratification (Nugent 2010).

Evolution of civil society discourse in EU

Kohler-Koch and Finke (2007) categorise the history of the Commission's relationships with social actors into three stages: consultation (1960/70s); partnership (1980/90s); and participation (2000/onwards). *The first generation*, in EU decision-making processes can be traced back to the establishment of European Coal and Steel Community (Armstrong 2002). The Paris Treaty (1952) enshrined the establishment of advisory committees, which would comprise the representatives of producers, workers and consumers. The Treaty of Rome institutionalised the advisory role of functional groups with the establishment of the European Economic and Social Council (EESC). This can be seen as related to the Monnetist 'neo-functionalist' understanding that characterised the early years of the integration (Walters 2004). Yet, the attempts to foster functional representation were not successful: that is, the EESC was marginalised in the EEC/EU institutional set up.

The *second-generation*, the idea of involving social actors in EU decision-making processes, has been one of the priorities of the Commission, during and after the Delors Commission. Underpinned by the motto of the European social and economic space, this vision led institutionalisation of 'Social Dialogue' – between representatives of trade unions and employers – with the Social Protocol attached in the Maastricht Treaty (1992). Organisations of citizens – also known as non-profit organisations, NGOs, civil society organisations and organised civil society – however, appeared in the Commission's agenda in the post-Maastricht era, though not formalised as social policy. Kohler-Koch and Finke (ibid.) explain that this was because of the Commission's perception of fading permissive consensus and the failure of the Maastricht referendum in Denmark. Therefore, the consultation policy of the Commission was no longer only based on the epistemic quality of the external advisers, but also public consent. Accordingly, 'bringing the EU closer to the people was propagated [by the Commission] at the 1996 Turin Summit', and as Kohler-Koch and Finke (ibid.: 210) underline, 'this became the norm to follow by all EU institutions'. Against this backdrop, 'Civil Dialogue' – which will be further elaborated on in this chapter – was introduced in 1996 in the field of employment and social affairs.

The *third generation* in the relations between the Commission and social actors, as defined in Kohler-Koch and Finke (ibid.), commenced in the early 2000s with the launching of the *White Paper on Governance* (Com 2001). In this era, the Commission connected its ongoing (and prospective) consultations with social actors to a broader project of an administrative reform of the EU institutions, a reform that it planned to realise within the limits of the treaties. The motto, 'bringing the EU back to the people' has also continued in this period – although, in contrast to the 1990s, the Commission has introduced several standards, norms and procedures with the aim of democratising the contributions of social actors, particularly in the Commission's consultation and interest intermediation regime. These initiatives are also associated with the principles of 'good governance' (Kohler-Koch and Rittberger 2006; Kohler-Koch and Finke 2007), promoted by the World Bank and United Nations (Weiss 2000).

Civil society discourse initially evolved within the scope of social policy. Since the early 1970s, the European Commission has been trying to intervene in the social sphere with directives and regulations, including environmental protection, consumer rights, women's rights and health and safety at work. Nonetheless, the power of the Commission in executing the directives have been limited – as the Community's law stipulates, they are executed by member states, not the European executives. The competences of the EU in the social sphere have comparatively increased with the Maastricht (1992) and Amsterdam (1997) treaties. However, this has not necessarily translated into the transfer of competences to supranational bodies. In turn, member states disagreed on harmonisation, unification and supranational control, but concurred with coordination of social policies via new modes of governance (also known as Open Method of Coordination or OMC), which is based on voluntarism, non-sanction and soft-law mechanisms. It has been seen as unlikely that member states would transfer their sovereignty to supranational bodies. Yet, the Commission has endeavoured to advance supranational intervention in this field, despite the sovereignty of member states being recognised with the introduction of principles of subsidiarity and the introduction of new modes of governance (e.g. in social policy, environment and tourism). The OMC allows the Commission to propose guidelines, and frame and monitor their implementation, though without any legal binding mechanism, because the responsibility of implementation rests with the member states.

As a result, the manoeuvre space of the Commission has been restricted; it has tried other strategies such as action plans (three social actions plans have so far been introduced in 1974, 1989 and 1995). Cram (2006a) claims that the Commission, particularly the DG for Employment, Social Affairs and Inclusion (DG-EMPL), uses another strategy, which is mobilising the social actors to form European NGOs and in turn involving them in the Commission's consultation regime. Cram's main argument is that the Commission has tried to foster an understanding that social policies are regulated at EU level, and democratically. Cram, however, acknowledges that the strategy of activating social NGOs has been relatively successful. First, the DG-EMPL started financing social NGOs in the early 1990s, but via unlawful methods until 1999. The treaties of the EU ascribe the Commission the role of using the Union's resources, while giving the auditing responsibility to the Parliament and the Council. Based on the request of the British parliamentarians, with claims that the Commission's support of social NGOs had no legal basis, the Parliament decided to suspend the Commission's funds in 1998. The social NGOs organised a collective protest and these funds were released by a Council decision in 1999. Thus, the Commission's *extra-acquis* behaviour was justified after the Council's decision. The second success of the Commission, according to Cram, was the enshrinement of the principle of participatory democracy into the draft constitutional treaty (2004), and later in the Lisbon Treaty (2007).

Meanwhile, however, the Commission has seemed to advance the resolutions of the Amsterdam Treaty (1997) about social policy, i.e. connecting employment policy to social policy. The Amsterdam Treaty for the first time recognised employment policy as a common European concern. Consequently, at the Luxembourg Summit (1997), the heads of states and governments decided on an employment guideline with the aim of creating an active labour market: this entailed the four principles of *employability* of the labour, *entrepreneurship*, i.e. alleviating the conditions for the business (such as reducing the tax and contribution costs on labour, and fostering new jobs in the third-sector); *adaptability* of business and labour to the new technology and so-called 'changing market conditions'; and creating 'equal opportunities' for men and women. The Lisbon Strategy (2000), adopted by the heads of states and governments, furthered these goals, by agreeing to make Europe 'most competitive and knowledge-driven economy by 2010'.

The changing roles and discursive shifts of European civil society in EU governance

As mentioned, the European Commission has shown a growing interest in social organisations and civil society discourse since the early 1990s. The Commission referred to social organisations in different contexts of EU politics. They have appeared in the following EC initiatives: (a) the regulation of 'interest politics' and 'interest intermediation'; (b) the restructuring of EU governance; and (c) discussions on the 'democratic legitimacy crisis' of the EU. Social organisations first emerged in the agenda of the Commission in 1992, within the interest politics regulation frame (Com 1992). In this context, they were defined as 'special interest groups', together with the economic groups and firms that were lobbying in Brussels. Afterwards, the Commission never lost sight of its appeal to social organisations, and it tried to adapt its discourse on the social organisations to the context of the EU politics of the day (Smismans 2007). In the second half of the 1990s, for instance, the Commission tried to increase its regulative role in social policies, such as through the European Employment Strategy (EES) and the Open Method of Coordination (OMC) (Mosher and Trubek 2003). In this respect, in 1997, the Commission published a discussion paper about which voluntary organisations were active in the social sector. Smismans (2007) argues that the Commission has used the civil society discourse to justify its growing intervention on social policies as a strategy to respond to the nation-states' reaction. Besides, the Commission did not only highlight the roles played by social organisations in the economy, such as creating jobs, and their increasing responsibility in governance in this document. It also, for the first time, elaborated the political implications of the social organisations, such as their role in the creation of European citizenship and the emergence of a European public sphere.

At the beginning of the 2000s, the Commission broadened its focus from social organisations that were active in social policies to all groups. Consequently, it introduced the NGOs as a new concept. This shift was a great advantage for the Commission, in that it could use the social groups to legitimate its policies and the EU at large. Furthermore, the limited focus on the use of social groups in legitimising social policies shifted to the general legitimacy of EU governance (Smismans 2007; Kohler-Koch and Finke 2007). *The Commission and Non-governmental Organisations: Building a Stronger Partnership* (Com 2000, 11 final) was the second and final paper in which the Commission specifically elaborated upon the social groups. Just one year later, the social organisations were mentioned in the *White Paper on European Governance* (WPEG) (Com 2001, 428 final), under the category of civil society organisations (CSOs). The WPEG repeated the Commission's previous position about the roles of social groups in governance and EU politics. The WPEG, however, placed CSOs within the context of EU administrative reform and EU governance, in which CSOs were defined as partners and participants, contributing to the efficiency of European governance. In addition to this, WPEG related the CSOs to the legitimacy of EU governance and the issue of creating a European public sphere.

During the 2000s, the European Commission detailed the political roles of social organisations under the mottos 'bringing the EU back to its citizens' or 'closing the gap between the EU and the citizens'. In this respect, it initiated Plan D for Democracy (2005), Debate Europe, the Communication Policy (2006), and Europe for Citizens (2007). One of the components of 'bringing the EU back to its citizens' was Civil Dialogue – incorporating NGOs into the Commission's decision-making structures through consultations. Civil Dialogue started in 1996 after the first European Social Policy Forum convened by the Social Platform. To regulate interest politics, after 2000 the Commission launched standards and principles (Com 2002, 704 final), established a database for civil society organisations, prepared a code of conduct and broadened the database for all interest groups.

The European Commission and the discovery of the civil society discourse

The Commission tried to regulate its relations with social organisations by (a) considering them within the context of interest politics at the EU level, (b) engaging them in the EU governance structure, and (c) relating them to the centre of the EU legitimacy debates.

In 1992, the Commission published a paper about its regulation policy for interest politics with non-governmental actors (Com 1992). In this paper, the Commission refers to social organisations; it categorises them under the general category of special interest groups, which includes all extra-political groups, namely business groups, consultation firms and civic groups. Nevertheless, the document finds it necessary to distinguish social groups from business groups through the practical solution of defining them as non-profit organisations.

As the paper specifically focuses on interest groups that try to influence EU-level politics, this categorisation is not intended as a general criterion for the definition of non-profit organisations. The paper illustrates European and (inter) national associations/federations of social organisations as an example of non-profit organisations, with legal advisors, public relations and public affairs firms and consultants as profit-making organisations.

In the second half of the 1990s, the Commission was interested in social groups that were active in the social sector. In this respect it published *Promoting the Role of Voluntary Organisations and Foundations in Europe* (Com 97, 241 final). In this document, the importance of these groups is demonstrated according to the total amount of members of EU volunteer organisations, which was estimated in 1997 to be about 100 million people. This document presents the most detailed views of the Commission on the political and economic roles of social groups with a specific focus on the characteristics these groups should have and the functions they should carry out in social and political life.

While other documents of the Commission focus on the social organisations themselves, *Promoting the Role of Voluntary Organisations and Foundations in Europe* elaborates the role of these organisations in the economy. It strongly stresses the role of the sector in the labour market, creating jobs and training and retraining the unemployed, especially those having problems entering the labour market. This is not surprising, since employment was one of the prevailing issues in the second half of the 1990s. In fact, the Commission launched the European Employment Strategy in 1997, the same year it published this document. Interestingly, the Commission did not emphasise the job-creating potential of social organisations in its later initiatives, since its focus shifted to their potential for identity creation.

In *Promoting the Role of Voluntary Organisations and Foundations in Europe*, the Commission suggests that social organisations should be supported by the state, as these organisations create jobs. It supports this claim with figures, as well as pointing to 'the tendency of governments to engage the voluntary organisations and foundations in the delivery of services of which they were themselves formerly both designers and providers' (Com 1997, 241 final: 4). The document elaborated here specifies some of these new functions that the sector has adopted, such as training and retraining the unemployed, either from their own self-initiative or as a government-led policy. These initiatives concentrate especially on people having problems participating in the labour market. The work of the voluntary organisations, then, could include all possible actions to prevent people being marginalised in the labour market. The document even makes an interesting remark in this respect, pointing out that voluntary work provides career opportunities for people who participate in this sector. Presenting voluntary work as an intermediary stage before entering the labour market, it claims that the experience of voluntary work in social issues could open up career opportunities. Nonetheless, this approach is problematic in that it tries to justify unpaid and non-secure work. For instance, it promises a bright future to those who participate in a voluntary organisation, claiming that a better job often results from first having worked for the community. This entails the understanding that work for the community is at the same time a moral activity.

Although the main focus of *Promoting the Role of Voluntary Organisations and Foundations in Europe* is the role of social organisations in the economy, it also evaluates the possibilities for European identity-building and promoting democracy through social organisations. This was the early imprint of the EU's project of merging the idea of a European citizenship project with the concept of participation. In such a project, the EU would promote participation as the panacea for both the identity and legitimacy crises of the EU. *Promoting the Role of Voluntary Organisations and Foundations in Europe* suggests that participation in an organisation is a democratic experience for people in addition to elections. It emphasises that this project does not compete with representative democracy, and is thus not a challenge to the legitimacy of the European Parliament. Furthermore, the document asserts that social groups function as the *intermediary* between the government and citizens, so that citizens can examine the government's actions and provide advice and feedback to public authorities. These political roles will be discussed in detail along with the further initiatives of Plan D for Democracy, the Communication Policy and Active Citizenship, in order to elaborate the relationship between the normative grounds of the European citizenship and the functional role that the Commission assigned to social actors in this process.

EU funding as a disciplining technology in the creation of a transnational space for voluntary organisations

In *Promoting the Role of Voluntary Organisations and Foundations in Europe*, the Commission also elaborated on the reasons for creating a transnational space for social organisations, starting with a diagnosis of some problems for the trans-European civil society. This is explained as resulting from the lack of trans-European joint work between national and local civic groups. Here, therefore, the Commission expects that intense joint cross-border work between organisations will create a European civil society. The Commission would facilitate this process of interconnecting European civil society, providing funds to social organisations and imposing a legal infrastructure within the European space so that these organisations can act freely among the countries of Europe.

The Commission goes on to list problems that hinder cross-border collaboration, such as cultural differences, the availability of funds, national attitudes towards the EU, and national legal conditions for the activities of a foreign organisation. Cultural and linguistic differences are the most important of these problems, while membership, organisational structure and the objectives of the organisations create further obstacles. In addition, not all countries granted legal recognition to voluntary organisations/civic groups. For this reason, some organisations encountered restrictions when they tried to open an office and work in another country. In order to facilitate the operations of these organisations in Europe, the Commission proposes a statute for European associations that would give a legal personality to an organisation engaging in those activities (Com 97, 241 final: 10–11). Furthermore, to overcome the problem of the countries' different systems of taxation, working methods and administrative procedures, the Commission prepared training programmes for organisations wishing to participate in trans-European collaboration.

The Commission was serious about supporting these organisations, since they were described as the disseminators of information about Europe: 'The Commission recognises the importance of the role that voluntary organisations play as disseminators of information, as bodies close to ordinary citizens, and proposes to involve them more closely in its activities of disseminating information' (Com 97, 241 final: 13). However, the document also details problems inherent to these organisations that could be a barrier to transnational collaboration. These include, for instance, the representativeness of some European networks, the scepticism of some public authorities (at either the national or European level) toward the European work these organisations aim to do, the fact that these organisations are not governed professionally, and a lack of skills needed to establish networks.

The Commission also emphasises that social organisations face problems in terms of financial resources, as they depend on long-term funding for survival. Due to difficulties in obtaining funds at the national level, organisations sought European sources of funding. However, it was not easy to secure EU funding either. Organisations could not follow the information on funding, and some states restricted the access of the organisations to European funding where NGOs have a decision-making role.[1] Furthermore, even if they could access EU funding, any delays in payments could affect the organisations' work.

Another observation is that, implicitly or explicitly, the document applies a categorical separation of European civil society from civil society (organisations) within Europe. Despite the fact that this document examines the economic, social and political roles of social organisations at the national level, it does not include them in its conception of European civil society. Rather, the Commission's conception of European civil society here refers to the Brussels-based lobbying networks. Not all NGOs, for instance the national NGOs, can lobby European institutions, participate in the EU's decision-making committees and follow the European agenda. The umbrella organisations in Brussels, rather, engage in these activities with a claim to represent the claims of their constituents. Thus, we can question whether this can be interpreted as a process of emergence for representative civil society, namely a process that represents those who cannot participate through representative participation. In the document, therefore, the Commission's role is stressed as facilitating the interactions of social organisations in Europe through EU funding. In sum, the document interprets the accelerating volume of cross-border interactions and interconnectedness between the national organisations as the Europeanisation of the national civil society organisations. Nevertheless, the document does not assess this process as the nucleus of the emergence of European civil society, since it appears that it already fills this conceptual and ontological space with the Brussels-based organisations. Table 3.1 summarises the Commission's discourse on civil society,

Table 3.1 The roles, characteristics and functions ascribed to social groups in *Promoting the Role of Voluntary Organisations and Foundations in Europe* (Com 1997, 241 final)

The role of voluntary organisations	Characteristics a voluntary organisation has and should have	The functions of voluntary organisations
• Contribution to employment opportunities. • Being instrumental in the formation of active citizenship. • Promotion of democracy. • Maintaining services. • Representing the interests of the people to public authorities, and protecting human rights.	• To some degree they (should) have institutional and formal subsistence. • They do not (should not) seek profit. • They (should) act independently according to their own rules and be free from interference from public institutions, including governments. • The people who govern these organisations should not seek to use the organisation to their personal advantage, including for profit. • The organisations must be present in the public arena; their actions should contribute to the public good. • The document states that 'being independent is not easy, and the notion of the public good is controversial' (Com 1997, 241: 2).	• They deliver services for their members or the public in social services and health care. Furthermore, they function as trainers and information providers. • They provide advocacy, which is to campaign and lobby to change public perceptions and enact a certain policy. • They function as intermediary bodies that coordinate the activities of, or provide information and assistance to the organisations in a specific sector, or they work to strengthen a particular sector, e.g. social policy. In those cases, the organisations link the sector with the political authorities. To the Commission's definition, it can also be added that these organisations not only link the sector to the political authorities, but also to the governance structures.

which was represented in *Promoting the Role of the Voluntary Organisations and Foundations in Europe* (Com 1997, 241 final)

Extending from the social policies to the EU legitimacy

At the beginning of the 2000s, the Commission instigated a paradigm shift in its approach to civil society by implementing a broadened definition of it in an attempt to legitimise EU governance at large (Smismans 2007). This was a transformation from the earlier approach, in which civil society was restricted to the voluntary sector taking an active role in the social sector. The Commission started to use the discourse of civil society in the context of acceptance of its actions not just in social policy, but in all of its activities, and furthermore, in the context of the raison d'être of EU institutions. However, the paradigm shift was not reflected in the Commission's perception of civil society. Although the Commission broadened its scope with respect to civil society, including all sectors of civil society organisations, it carried over the roles and characteristics that it drew for voluntary organisations in 1997.

The Commission (2000), one year before the publication of the *White Paper on European Governance*, declared its intention to integrate the NGOs into its governance structure, identifying the NGOs as its vital partners for governance because of 'the expertise and dedication of NGO staff and their willingness to work under difficult operational conditions' (Com 2000). It set out five aspects of the *'rationale* [my emphasis] for cooperation with non-governmental organisations': (1) fostering participatory democracy; (2) representing the views of specific groups of citizens to European Institutions; (3) contributing to policy making; (4) contributing to project management; and (5) contributing to European integration (ibid.: 2000: 4–5).

Having been influenced by the European Economic and Social Committee's report in 1999, *The Role and Contribution of Civil Society Organisations in the Building of Europe* (EESC 1999, and see also below in this chapter), the Commission for the first time linked the NGOs to participatory democracy. Emphasising that the EU's legitimacy rested on representative democracy, the Commission stated that NGOs could contribute by fostering participatory democracy in the decision-making processes of the EU. In other words, the Commission equated participatory democracy at the EU level with the involvement of civil society in the decision-making processes. The Commission also related the NGOs to the context of enlargement and the EU's relations with developing countries. Here, the Commission argued that NGOs could 'contribute to the development of democracy and civil society in the candidate countries' by achieving 'the stability of institutions guaranteeing democracy, the rule of law, human rights and respect for and protection of minorities' (ibid.: 4).

Though the Commission linked the engagement of NGOs in politics to the consolidation of democracy in Central and Eastern Europe and developing countries, it attributed an instrumental role for them with respect to EU governance. First, the Commission aimed to integrate NGOs into the EU governance mechanism; second, it aimed to 'win public acceptance for the EU' through the NGOs (ibid.: 5). Regarding the role of NGOs in EU governance, contrary to *Promoting the Role of Voluntary Organisations* (Com 97, 241 final), *Building a Stronger Relationship with NGOs* (Com 2000) does not emphasise the social and economic role of the NGOs, such as the delivery of services and creation of employment and training. Rather, it focuses on the specific function of the NGOs in terms of EU policies, the management of EU projects. NGOs can manage, monitor and evaluate EU-financed projects, such as the projects on social exclusion and discrimination, protecting the natural environment and the provision of humanitarian and development aid.

Second, according to the document, NGOs can be instrumental in winning public acceptance for the EU, since they act according to the 'general interest' of the people, dealing with concerns and issues related to the people's wellbeing rather than pursuing the commercial or professional interests of their members. The Commission prioritises the role of European networks of NGOs as the *catalysing agents* of this process, in that they can mobilise national NGOs and 'make an important contribution to the formation of a European public opinion', which the Commission recognises as the 'pre-requisite to the establishment of a true European political entity' (ibid.: 5).

Third, with this document the Commission makes it clear that it prioritises and reinforces managerial organisational structures to administer its funding, so that NGOs are obliged to comply these structures and finding management frame developed by the Commission (ibid.: 7). Technical and managerial capability of an organisation would then help the Commission to control and evaluate its activities (ibid.: 16–17).

The governance turn and bringing back the citizens of Europe

The *White Paper on European Governance* (WPEG) (Com 2001, 428 final) is an important programmatic text, because it indicates the need to reform the institutional design of the EU, the structure of its policy-making and techniques of policy implementation. It explains the reasons behind the reforms as the extension of the issues the EU is dealing with, especially the expansion of the EU to include new member states and responding to the globalisation process. The WPEG, in line with *Building a Stronger Relationship with NGOs*, specifically emphasises that civil society constituted a crucial part of this process, both in sharing governance responsibilities and legitimising EU governance.

> [The EU] will no longer be judged solely by its ability to remove barriers to trade or to complete an internal market; its legitimacy today depends on involvement and participation. This means that the linear model of dispensing policies from above must be replaced by a virtuous circle, based on feedback, networks and involvement from policy creation to implementation at all levels.
>
> (Com 2001, 428 final: 11)

With the WPEG, the Commission introduced the discourse of involvement and participation to the agenda of the EU as a cure for its democratic legitimacy problem, which, according to its perception, resulted from the gap between the people and the EU.

> Yet despite its achievements, many Europeans feel alienated from the Union's work. This feeling is not confined to the European Institutions. It affects politics and political institutions around the globe. But for the Union, it reflects particular tensions and uncertainty about what the Union is and

what it aspires to become, about its geographical boundaries, its political objectives and the ways these powers are shared with the Member States.

(Ibid.: 7)

The WPEG posited that the participation of civil society in EU politics would play a crucial role in closing this gap. Restricting the definition of participatory democracy to the formal involvement of civil society in policy-shaping processes and consultation, it stressed that 'participation is not about institutionalising protest' (ibid.: 15). In a way, this approach tries to build a European civil society conception that is separate from social movements and grassroots traditions. Rather, it privileges a definition of participation that is compatible with the governance approach. It rests on the definition of interest representation, and corresponds to a pluralist system of decision-making in which all interest groups compete to influence policymaking on equal terms. In sum, the participation discourse is not only related to the technologies of legitimate EU governing, in the sense that the Commission strategically used it to garner public support, it is also the constitutive element of the EU art of government – i.e. how to govern organisations, find solutions and make a better contribution to EU governance.

Further extension of the discourse: European civil society and technologies of EU communication

In line with the motto of closing the gap between citizens and the EU, which was coined in the mid-1990s, the Commission launched new policies during the 2000s, namely Plan D for Democracy, Debate Europe, Communication Policy, Active Citizenship and Europe for Citizens. In the last of these, the Commission's civil society discourse extended from the *agents of governance* turn to *agents of identity and consent builders*. In the late 1990s and in the *White Paper on European Governance*, the main objective of the Commission was to restructure EU governance (Jachtenfuchs 2001; Kohler-Koch and Rittbergen 2006). Thereby, it associated its discourse on civil society with the governance turn. Nonetheless, in the 2000s, the Commission reduced its emphasis on the relationship between civil society and governance. Since then, the Commission has prioritised the discourse on civil society, which included two main aspects: the generation of a European identity and the mobilisation of the public for EU integration. The Commission's new strategies for closing the gap with citizens have focused on European NGOs as a target of this policy, while assigning them an intermediary role between EU institutions and the people, so that EU governance can be better connected to the citizens.

As mentioned above, the strong emphasis on the necessity to connect Europe with its citizens was first reflected in the *White Paper on European Governance*. The White Paper identifies two reasons for the 'alienation of the citizens from the EU'. The first reason, based on the governance perspective, suggests that the citizens cannot build a connection with the EU institutions since they are not 'involved in the governance' of their lives. The argument is that if people can participate in the problem-solving processes, they can become closer to the idea of Europe, and this would strengthen EU democracy. The second reason is the notion that citizens are alienated from the EU because they lack information about the EU and the role EU policies play in their lives. In the 2000s, the Commission prioritised the political socialisation roles of NGOs, which entailed their intermediary function and identity-formation roles. The governance turn literature has discussed the role of NGOs in the first reason given by the White Paper (Kohler-Koch and Finke 2007; Kohler-Koch and Rittberger 2006; Finke 2009). European studies, however, has neglected to examine the second reason, which attempts to embed crucial political socialisation roles in social organisations. One exception is Warleigh (2001). Having examined the European NGOs' socialisation roles, he concludes that they will not be able to achieve these tasks because of their distance from the grassroots. Nevertheless, the analysis of Warleigh is not critical in the sense that he does not problematise the central question of why and how the Commission endeavoured to create a European civil society.

NGO networks as a technology in connecting with the citizens

Plan D, Debate Europe, Communicating Europe in Partnership, Europe for Citizens and Active European Citizenship focused on connecting the EU with citizens, and informing the people about the EU and the role of the EU in their lives. The EC launched these policies in response to the diagnosis that legitimate European governance was not plausible if the people residing in the European territory lacked knowledge of who governed, how it governed, why it governed, where it governed and with whom it governed. Hence, it made available funds to support projects and initiatives that would help the 'dissemination of the idea of Europe (a Union)' in order to mobilise a public discussion, which was assumed to be one of the nuclei of the emerging European public sphere. In these programmes, the Commission stressed the significance of NGOs, considering them to be the interlocutor between political power and society.

Magnette (2003) emphasises that the clarity of the political structure can enhance political participation and political interest. Hence, the Commission's aim of informing the people about EU governing could contribute to its legitimate governing. Nonetheless, the Commission's strategies are problematic: first, it considers 'explaining itself' to be a matter of public relations, i.e. selling a product (Shore 2009); second, it becomes proactively involved in fostering debates about EU governing. The Commission's aim has gone beyond enlightening the people about the EU administrative mechanism. Rather, the Commission has been trying to build a political-ethical discursive field for EU governing, emphasising how good EU governance is, the extent to which it is an inseparable part of human life, and how the subject of EU governing is constituted.

Nevertheless, the Commission's ambition to constitute the political ethics of EU governing faces serious problems. Despite the fact that the EC entails bold normative ambitions, such as enhancing participatory democracy, consolidating legitimacy and creating a European identity, to achieve these, it has rather adopted the technologies of public relations. It focuses on advertising the EU, and in doing so, tries to *convince* the people of its raison d'être. Convincing, however, is different than consent. For example, in the contract theory it is the very act of consent that itself explains the emergence of the state, in this case though it is the lack of communication that explains the legitimacy crises of the EU. If the emergence of political society results from the a priori consent of the people, then the question of whether the state ever faced the crisis of explaining itself as legitimacy problem might be an interesting one.

Moreover, the Commission's preference of *citizens* as a concept in the motto of bridging the gap with the citizens is problematic, too, since it excludes non-citizens as legitimate participants in public debate. The Commission could have chosen any other concept in order to emphasise the people inhabiting the European space, such as individuals, persons, humans, residents, inhabitants or the population. In sum, the EU draws the participation criteria of the EPS with citizenship at the outset and excludes non-citizens, namely the third-country nationals.

Plan D for dialogue, democracy and debate

One of the Commission's initiatives with respect connecting citizens to EU governance was Plan D for Democracy (Com 2005, 494 final). Plan D had the objective of reinforcing a public debate on the future of Europe, and for this task the member states and EU institutions would collaborate in mobilising 'citizens, civil society, social partners, national parliaments and political parties, with the support of the EU institutions' (Com 2008, 158/4 final: 3). It formulated the mottos of the mobilisation strategy as 'listening better', 'explaining better' and 'going local'. In this respect, it particularly concentrated on the role of civil society organisations, particularly NGOs. Six civil society projects were supported by the Commission, which brought together approximately 40,000 people from different countries within Europe in a seminar-like activity. The aim of these projects was 'to test the innovative consultation methods and enable people from the different national public spheres to connect with each other as European citizens and debate the future of Europe' (ibid.: 3).

The innovative strategies of fostering a debate among the citizens included 'virtual and face-to-face communication, deliberative consultation and polling' at 'country-level, cross-border and pan-European consultations'. These were experimented with in civil society projects to determine the extent to which knowledge of the European art of government could be translated in the European space. As a reminder, the discourse on European governance portrays deliberation as the mode of conduct among the different actors (stakeholders) (Papadolous 2002, Eriksen 2005). Plan D attempted to translate this politically limited definition of the mode of conduct between the 'governance' actors to civil society, presenting it as a daily practice of conduct between individuals, and the conduct between the individuals and the political authority. The report prepared by the Commission on these projects concluded that 'the civil society organisations managing the projects served as multipliers and disseminated the views expressed by citizens through their political and media networks, at different stages of the projects' (Com 2008, 158/4 final: 5). On the basis of this statement, it suggested that 'the Plan D civil society projects showed that participatory democracy can usefully supplement representative democracy' (ibid.: 5). At the latest stage, in December 2007, the Commission gathered the six Plan D citizens' projects in a conference entitled *The Future of Europe: The Citizen's Agenda*.

Plan D also introduced other 'innovative ways of communication', such as internet debates on the 'Debate Europe' website[2] and the Plan D visits of the Commissioners to national parliaments, civil society, business and union leaders, regional and local authorities in member states. In this respect the Commission representatives in the member states organised 830 seminars and 4,000 press statements and conferences, and the Commissioners managed a total of 370 visits (Com 2007, 568 final: 9). Compared with the civil society projects, the visits of the Commission's representatives focused on direct interaction between the individual and EU officials.

After 2008, Plan D proceeded under the title of Debate Europe, with the motto of Democracy-Dialogue-Democracy.[3] Debate Europe continued to employ the 'innovative communication' methods initiated by Plan D in order to advertise the impact of EU governance in the daily lives of people, such as on 'internal market-related success stories, roaming mobile charges, low-cost flights, closing the gap in regional development, environmental protection and the fight against climate change' (Com 2008, final 158/4: 6).

Debate Europe is a web portal that comprises EU Tube, which includes videos about EU along with commentaries and blogs; descriptions of EU policies and benefits under the 'EU at a glance' and 'EU activities' page; a call centre for fielding questions about the EU with 'Europe direct'; an online game called Europa Go; and activities oriented towards school children under 'Spring Day for Europe'.[4] The last of these is worth elaborating on, since the Commission's interest in children cannot be explained as an attempt to inform citizens about EU policies to combat alienation from EU governance, or put in terms of the Commission's optimism, to connect citizens with EU institutions. How can the Commission's interest in children be explained? The activities that were put into practice under the interest in schools reveal the Commission's aspirations of building a European political-ethical space, so that children are nurtured as Europeans and develop a political allegiance to EU institutions. For instance, *Spring Day for Europe* encourages such activities as 'playing the role of creative figure' (for the European Year of Innovation 2009), exchanging traditional songs between countries, competitions to create a leaflet for Europe, gathering students' best ideas for Europe, organising games in schools about European decision-making processes, European inventions and inventors, and matching euro coins with the country of origin. More interestingly, the Commission arranges role-playing activities for EU decision-making simulations in schools.[5] In 2007, moreover, 75 Commissioners visited schools in 44 regions in 18 countries, and 400 German European officials visited their former schools during the German EU presidency (Com 2007, 568 final: 9).

The White Paper on Communication

The *White Paper on Communication* (WPC) was an EC policy launched in 2006 in line with the motto of closing the gap between citizens and the EU. The impetus for launching the communication strategy was the communication gap with citizens. The Commission defines this, here and elsewhere, in different ways, such as bringing the EU back to citizens, connecting with citizens, or closing the gap with the citizens. Scholars of governance and democratic theory have taken the diagnosis of a gap for granted, debating whether and the extent to which this gap could be closed. However, the governmentality approach employs a different strategy. It problematises the Commission's problematisation, and therefore examines the technologies used by the Commission in its connecting with the citizens discourse.

The WPC is remarkable in that it introduces communication as a policy in its own right, arguing that the gap with citizens can be closed if they learn more about the EU and feel that their views matter in EU decision-making. The communication policy, in this respect, concentrates on mobilising a 'European debate' in several ways. Some of these overlap with Plan D, such as the visits of the Commissioners and other EU officials to schools and supporting civil society projects. It also introduces such strategies as the Commission's representations in member states; creating new European spaces to bring together different actors; reinforcing the EU dimension in the national educational system; using media technologies to increase the visibility of the EU; bringing together 'European teachers' through a network and a special programme within the College of Europe; digitally connecting European libraries; reconsidering the EU institutions' visitor programmes, and complementing EU websites with online forums – 'virtual meeting places' – and links to external information sources. It also indicates that achieving these objectives depends on a 'partnership approach', the technology of the European art of government, which requires the collaboration of 'EU institutions, the national, regional and local authorities in the Member States, European political parties, [and] civil society' (Com 2006, 35 final: 2).[6]

Having acknowledged that the 'communication strategy' of the Commission in the post-Maastricht Treaty (1992) era was based mostly on relating the EU's one-way communication activities, the WPC declares the intention of bringing change in two aspects. First, the new communication policy will reinforce mechanisms of 'listening to the people', such as support for civil society projects, new European spaces for European debate (i.e. houses of Europe opened in Tallinn, Dublin and Madrid in 2007–2008) (Com 2007, 568 final: 8) and web consultation portals for the people (i.e. *Your Voice*) (ibid.: 13). Nevertheless, interestingly, the WPC does not refer to the Commission's civil dialogue initiative, which aimed to involve civil society in EU decision-making. As a reminder, the

Commission had presented civil dialogue in the second half of the 1990s under the motto of bringing citizens back into the EU, repeating this in the *White Paper on European Governance*. In other words, even though the Commission presents listening to the people as the cornerstone of its communication policy, it avoids mentioning the strategy that has already been put into action on precisely the same grounds. It is difficult to explain why the Commission preferred not to mention the civil dialogue as an example in which NGOs participated in EU decision-making processes.

The second new aspect in the communication policy is explained in the WPC as a shift from the institutional approach to a decentralised one. As the WPC says, this concept was originally explained ambiguously with respect to its specific meaning and which procedures it entailed:

> The European Commission is therefore proposing a fundamentally new approach – a decisive move away from one-way communication to reinforced dialogue, from an institution-centred to a citizen-centred communication, from a Brussels-based to a more decentralised approach. Communication should become an EU policy in its own right, at the service of the citizens.
>
> (Com 2006, 35 final: 4)

Despite the fact that the EC advanced ambitious proposals – in fact, a fundamentally new approach – it could not provide solid grounds for this radical overhaul:

> It should be based on genuine dialogue between the people and the policy-makers and lively political discussion among citizens themselves. People from all walks of life should have the right to fair and full information about the European Union, and be confident that the views and concerns they express are heard by the EU institutions.
>
> (Ibid.: 4)

The WPC indicates that by enhancing the European debate, it aims to attain 'the people's support for the European project' (ibid.: 4) and promoting 'a pan-European culture' (ibid.: 5) that would reinforce a European identity. The final goal of this project is to facilitate Europe's penetration into the political-ethical constitution of the self. The following long quote from the WPC explicates how the Commission diagnoses the problem, and the remedies it suggests, one of which it prescribes as central for civil society:

> In today's Europe, citizens exercise their political rights mainly at the national and local level. Political rights linked to the European dimension have been introduced, such as the right to participate in the elections of the European Parliament. However, people learn about politics and political issues largely through their national education systems and via their

national, regional and local media. They consider the manifestos of political parties dealing with national, regional and local issues, and they discuss these issues mostly in their own communities.

In short, the 'public sphere' within which political life takes place in Europe is largely a national sphere. To the extent that European issues appear on the agenda at all, they are seen by most citizens from a national perspective. The media remain largely national, partly due to language barriers; there are few meeting places where Europeans from different Member States can get to know each other and address issues of common interest.

Yet many of the policy decisions that affect daily life for people in the EU are taken at the European level. People feel remote from these decisions, the decision-making process and EU institutions. There is a sense of alienation from 'Brussels', which partly mirrors the disenchantment with politics in general. One reason for this is the inadequate development of a 'European public sphere' where the European debate can unfold. Despite exercising the right to elect members of the European Parliament, citizens often feel that they themselves have little opportunity to make their voices heard on European issues, and there is no obvious forum within which they can discuss these issues together. A pan-European political culture – with pan-European political groups and foundations – is still developing.

Europe also needs to find its place in the existing national, regional and local 'public spheres' and the public discussion across Member States must be deepened. This is first and foremost the responsibility of the public authorities in the Member States. It is the responsibility of government, at national, regional and local level, to consult and inform citizens about public policy – including European policies and their impact on people's daily lives – and to put in place the forums to give this debate life.

There is also a real interest in building the European dimension into the national debate. Citizens sense that there is something missing from a national debate which ignores aspects of public policy that are of direct relevance to them. Far from being in competition, a stronger recognition of the European dimension in national political exchange can only add to its credibility.

That is why national public authorities, civil society, and the European Union institutions need to work together to develop Europe's place in the public sphere.

(Ibid.: 4–5)

The Commission, as the above statements reveal, had the objective of increasing turnouts in the European Parliament elections as the concrete example of the realisation of democracy at the European level. Nevertheless, the Commission's proposals included strong political ambitions that went beyond increasing the amount of voters in European Parliament elections, such as requiring national authorities to integrate the EU dimension into school curricula and enlightening citizens about the impact of European policies in their daily lives. To enhance Europeans' engagement in EU governance, the Commission attempted to create a political-ethical space for EU governing within and beyond the nation-state. Therefore, although the WPC claims that listening to the citizens will be the basis of the Commission's communication policy, it rather concentrates on empowering citizens. This focus entails, first, the education of the citizen; second, citizens' relations with other citizens; and finally citizens' relations with the public and the public institutions.

The WPC evaluates the role of education in the communication policy in five aspects. First, it connects education to active citizenship, which will be elaborated on in the following section. Second, it suggests that political socialisation with respect to the EU 'should not [only] be confined to teaching school pupils about EU institutions and policies', but also 'should help people of all ages to use tools such as the internet to access information on public policy and to join in the debate' (ibid.: 7). Third, it emphasises that education policy should give attention to migrants and the disabled, who might otherwise 'find themselves excluded from the public sphere' (ibid.: 7). Fourth, it asserts that the 'EU programmes can be of direct support in fostering the European dimension. Programmes like Leonardo da Vinci, Socrates, Erasmus, Youth in Action, etc. provide educational and training opportunities for thousands of students and young people across Europe' (ibid.: 7). Fifth, it emphasises the benefits of the information technology programmes that tackle exclusion from the public spheres (ibid.: 7).

Hence, education becomes not merely a focus on describing the EU and changing people's minds about the virtues of involvement in the EU's consultations. It aims at enhancing the skills of the people, such as their ability to use the internet. In other words, EU governing requires not only enlightened citizens, but also capable citizens. In this sense, therefore, the EU intervention is a conduct of conduct of the individuals.

Furthermore, the WPC supports the creation of physical arenas for the discussion of European issues in order to connect citizens to each other. Houses of Europe, which were opened in Tallinn, Dublin and Madrid in 2007–8, were examples of this. The previous EU initiatives – Plan D, Youth in Action and Culture, and Citizens for Europe – also supported trans-European projects for civil society in this respect. The WPC also suggests using the 'existing and planned EU programmes to connect and mobilise European citizens', noting that an example of this, Erasmus, developed 'a network that connects 150,000 students from all Member States', so that 'their websites [could] serve as a hub for posting activities, organising face-to-face meetings and engaging in wide-ranging debates on European issues' (ibid.: 7). On the one hand, the Commission here refers to previous technologies; on the other, it creates new ones.

The WPC asserts that 'bridging the gap between Europe and citizens means creating and maintaining links between citizens and public authorities all the way from the local to the European level' (ibid.: 7). To illustrate this, it points to the transparency of EU decision-making and the consultation procedures with interest groups.

One of the points the WPC highlights is that the emergence of the European public sphere has been hindered by the poor coverage provided by the national media of EU-related news: 'Regular major events such as European Council meetings do attract coverage in national newspapers, but during the intervening periods there is no comprehensive coverage of EU affairs' (ibid.: 9). The WPC advances three action plans to close the information gap (ibid.: 9). The first one involves giving Europe a human face. Chapter 2 has mentioned that World Bank policies on economic development also uses the human face analogy within the scope of participation and social inclusion policies, arguing that this has aimed to embed neoliberalism in society. The EU, however, connected the human face analogy to its communication deficit, resulting from the diagnosis that people cannot clearly identify the impact of the EU in their lives:

> The European Union is often perceived as 'faceless': it has no clear public identity. Citizens need help to connect with Europe, and political information has greater impact when put in a 'human interest' frame that allows citizens to understand why it is relevant to them personally. EU institutions and all levels of government can do more to 'give a human face' to the information they provide.
>
> (Ibid.: 9)

The second target of the action plan aiming to close the information gap stresses the use of the national, regional and local dimension to disperse common information about EU issues. The third target, on the other hand, emphasises the internet as a new channel for communication on European issues. Nevertheless, the WPC reiterates the steering role of the political institutions: 'However, political leadership is needed if Europe is to fully exploit the Internet's potential and ensure that it does not create new divisions in society' (ibid.: 9).

As we can see, rather than focusing on the media as an independent actor, the WPC locates the origin of the problem and its cure in the political institutions, prescribing the need for a human face for the information they provide. This however is a problematic understanding of the publicisation of the political information and knowledge via media, since it entails an understanding that manipulation of political news is carried out by the political authority itself. The WPC's proposals to increase the EU's visibility in the media also show how the Commission uses similar symbols and styles of reasoning in different contexts. For instance, the Commission previously used the metaphor of giving Europe a human face in relation to the Commissioner's visits to member states. In fact, these two instances complement each other. While the visits imply giving a human face to European government through the agency of bodily representation of a European bureaucrat, the visibility of the EU in the media associates the human face analogy to a mental frame, human interest and needs. In other words, the Commission tries to de-mystify and em*body* the EU power bodily and discursively by relating it to the human. Further, the WPC repeats its language on different levels, nationally, regionally, and locally, when it refers to the 'spatial dimension'. In doing so, it discursively constitutes the spatial frames.

Europe for citizens and active European citizenship[7]

In relation to its previous initiatives for connecting with citizens, the Commission launched another programme in 2007: Europe for Citizens.[8] This policy initiative was a continuation of the Commission's diagnosis linking citizens' lack of interest in EU politics to European citizenship and European identity. In this respect, Europe for Citizens drew upon the key competences that every citizen should acquire within the scope of lifelong learning. These competences cover 'all forms of behaviour that equip individuals to participate in an effective and constructive way in social and working life, and particularly in increasingly diverse societies, and to resolve conflict where necessary' (Com 2006, *Key Competence for lifelong learning*: 9). Furthermore, it emphasised the need for empowering citizens to 'fully participate in civic life, based on knowledge of social and political concepts and structures and a commitment to active and democratic participation'.[9] Here, the Europe for Citizens programme locates the volunteering that was central to active European Citizenship. It explicated the reasons for promoting volunteering as follows:

> By giving one's time for the benefit of others, volunteers service their community and play an active role in society. They develop a sense of belonging to a community, thereby also gaining ownership. Volunteering is therefore a particularly powerful means to develop citizens' commitment to their society and to its political life. Civil society organisations, associations of a European general interest, town twinning associations and other participating organisations often rely on volunteer work to carry out and to develop their activities.[10]

The Europe for Citizens Programme includes four different categories of actions: Active Citizens for Europe; Active Civil Society in Europe; Together in Europe; and Active European Remembrance. The first entails town-twinning and support for citizen projects. The second concentrates on support for think tanks and civil society organisations, and the projects developed by these civil society organisations. Defining this as 'pondering Europe', the second action plan explains what it expects to achieve through the support of this strategy:

> This collaboration can take a variety of forms of actions, such as seminars, thematic workshops, training seminars, the production and dissemination of publications, information campaigns, artistic workshops, amateur sporting events, exhibitions, grassroots initiatives etc. Partners interested in organising debates should focus on stimulating discussions related to the priorities of the programme which involve a broad range of stakeholders from different countries, including other civil society organisations, citizens and policymakers. As their name suggests, reflection exercises should nourish and structure the collective consideration of such issues as European values, identity and democracy. These exercises should involve civil society organisations of all kinds, experts, decision-makers and ordinary citizens. Special

84   *European governance and civil society*

attention should be given to reflecting the cultural and spiritual diversity of Europe. Networking activities should seek to establish the foundation for, or encourage the development of, long-lasting and enduring networks between civil society organisations from different countries which are active in a particular field.[11]

While the third action plan, Together in Europe, focuses on high-visibility events, studies, surveys and opinion tools, and information and dissemination tools, the fourth concentrates on building a common identity through remembrance (Delanty 2005):

Decades of peace, stability and prosperity separate Europe from the devastation of World War II. But to ensure that the mistakes of the past are not repeated, to appreciate the present and plot a course for the future, it is important to keep the memory of that period alive.[12]

Nevertheless, the stress on remembrance does not only cover memories of war, but also includes a condemnation of Nazism and Stalinism as the dark side of European history:

The legacy of Nazism and Stalinism underscore just how important and valuable our current democratic values are. By commemorating the victims, as well as preserving the sites and archives associated with deportations and myriad other actions, Europeans, particularly younger generations, can draw lessons for the present and the future from these dark chapters in history.[13]

Having devised a fourfold strategy for developing a European citizenship, the Europe for Citizens programme places great emphasis on European values, history, culture and cultural diversity as the basis of European identity. Despite the fact that the programme defines active European citizenship as the involvement of the citizens and civil society organisations in the process of European integration, it does not elaborate an understanding of citizenship and identity as phenomena that would emerge from within the very act of involvement or participation of strangers in solving society's common problems, as suggested for instance by Putnam (1995), Barber (1984) and Habermas (1996). Though at the outset it indicates its stance that active European citizenship should be the full participation in social political life, Europe for Citizens do not elaborate this view. Rather, it approaches a rather communitarian understanding of identity, stressing the importance of values and history. Ultimately, instead of treating participation as a normative value in itself, a medium of political integration, it delineates participation as a means, a catalyst, for discovering the already-existing values, culture and history of the Europeans.

In other words, Europe for Citizens opted to define European identity as a social reality, as if it were already there, so that through the activities initiated by the active European citizenship programme, Europeans would discover the identity they had been unaware of. In other words, the Commission proposed Europe for Citizens as a method for discovering a European identity that was already there. Posed in such way, this approach defines Europeans as the people who do not know who they are, so that through the very act of cross-country mingling and 'intercultural dialogue', they access, or recall, the knowledge of their common identity based on a shared culture, history and values. In this way, it characterises active citizenship and participation, as epistemological means of finding out the ontology of the self (i.e. the European citizen). The following statement from the Europe for Citizens website illustrates the way this programmatic act portrays the core of European identity, and its ultimate goal of promoting it: 'For citizens to give their full support to European integration and to develop their sense of belonging to the European Union, it is important to bring common European values, history and culture to the fore'.[14] Nevertheless, in stressing the importance of a shared culture and history as the basis of community building, this idea excludes those who do not share the same culture, history and values.

In sum, the Commission's discourse on connecting with the citizens started with a goal of *explaining itself*, and then was revised as *listening to the people*, before ultimately being linked to active European citizenship and culturally-oriented European identity. In this process, the roles of NGOs were portrayed as the interlocutors of EU governing that explained the EU and its governing powers to its members by reinforcing active European citizenship, while linking public demands to the decision-making in the consultations. The governance theory neglected the fact that the discourse on the involvement of civil society also embodied elements of creating a European identity on the basis of participation. Some scholars suggest that EU governance cannot evolve into a democratic system, since there is no European *demos* (Cederman 2001; Schore 2006; Weiler 1999; Habermas 2001). The proponents of the normative school in European studies (Eriksen *et al.* 2005), on the other hand, argue that strangers can develop a sense of commonness in their common activities that aim to govern their lives. Regarding European integration, it has not been possible to follow the path of nation-building, for instance in building a common language, common culture and even common history. Therefore, the idea of building identity – and reinforcing legitimacy – on the grounds of participation, in line with the writings of Tocqueville, Putnam and Habermas, might have become very attractive for the Commission. For it tried to integrate the participation discourse into its legitimacy crisis diagnosis, which suggested that the legitimacy crisis of EU governance stemmed from the alienation of the citizens from EU politics. Consequently, during the 2000s, the Commission focused on closing this gap with Plan D for Democracy, Debate Europe, the Communication Policy, Active Citizenship and Europe for Citizens. These all referred to the NGOs as partners in the Commission's project of creating a European public, European public sphere and European *demos*. In other words, the EU supported NGOs as the interlocutors of the art of government, which could carry the political rationalities to the margins. Tables 3.2 and 3.3 depict a summary of the evolvement of participation and civil society discourses in EU policies.

86 European governance and civil society

Table 3.2 The shifting characteristics and roles of social organisations in Commission's civil society discourse

Com (1997, 241 final)	Politics, economy and society: social groups.
Com (2000, 11 final)	Legitimacy, governance: all groups as NGOs.
Com (2001, 428 final)	Governance, legitimacy; creating a public sphere.
Plan D, Com (2005, 292 final)	Linking citizens through the public sphere.
Communication Policy (2006, 35 final)	Linking citizens through the public sphere.

Transferring the (European) civil society discourse to Eastern Europe

The previous sections elaborated the Commission's attempts at promoting a European civil society. It revealed that the discourse of civil society appeared first in the EC's interest regulation policy and governance turn, where all non-state actors are involved in the EU decision-making consultation process, and second, in the Commission's initiatives for 'connecting with the people', i.e. Plan D, communication policy, Debate Europe and the Europe for Citizens Programme. While the Commission envisioned a pan-European civil society, i.e. networks of NGOs in the first case, in the second, it concentrated on mingling and mobilising the trans-European society, namely the horizontal actions among the national civil societies with the aim of establishing a European public sphere, which would lead the emergence of a European identity. Hence, in both cases the Commission conceptualised European civil society as a phenomenon that was explained by cross-border or border-transcending actions. Nonetheless, evaluated in this way, the European civil society conception excludes the state-society relations at the national level. For instance, the liberal inter-governmentalism of Moravsick (1995) and the social movements perspective of Della Porta (2007) and Imig and Tarrow (2001) show some similarities; in both, social groups address the national governments in order to influence European policies.

Moreover, there is a further option through which the civil society in Europe is Europeanised: it is the emergence of the hegemony of an understanding of a certain format of state-society relations in the European space, as an ideal type. Particularly in the enlargement policy, the Commission promotes the development of civil society as a part of the preparation for membership, i.e. a part of the implementation of accession reforms. It also aims to attain the consent of the people for membership and the implementation of these reforms. Nevertheless, it is quite interesting that the Commission avoids focusing on this policy of developing civil society in the latest members and the candidate countries in its general conceptualisation of the ECS. This could have been one of the crucial components of the EU's civil society discourse, so it could transcend the limited European Civil Society (ECS) definition, for instance, which is restricted to Brussels-based NGOs and cross-border interaction between the national civil societies. Nonetheless, it neglected the fact that its strategy of supporting the

Table 3.3 Development of civil society discourse in the EC

	The discourse	Conceptualisation	Regulation	Approach
Com (1992)	No discourse yet.	Early attempt at stressing the social groups' involvement in society; Elaborates the SOs as an interest group, but defines them as non-profit.	It introduces its willingness to regulate interest politics; hence it presents examples of interest regulation in some states, and in the UN. It adopts an open and non-accreditation approach for regulation.	It develops a pragmatic definition as non-profit organisations, and focuses on transnational organisations.
Com (1997, 241 final)	It uses social organisations in legitimising EU policies in the social economy. It adopts the third sector and governance approach to define the roles of social organisations.	It identifies the roles, characteristics, and functions of the social groups.	Involving social actors in the governance of the society.	It limits the groups that are active in social politics.
Com (2001, 428 final)	It links the CSOs to discourse on the legitimacy of EU governance at large.	It draws common features and the rationales for integrating NGOs (the term the document uses) to EU politics.	It relates to interest regulation policy.	It does not limit its focus on CSOs active in the social field, and it embraces the comprehensive approach.
Com (2002, 704 final)	It tries to develop a regulated interest politics, where each interest group is treated in equal terms.	The use of the CSO disappears, so that consultation and interest representation prevail as the concepts the EC uses to explain the EC's relationship with SOs.	It launches 'standards and principles of conduct' for interest regulation.	NGOs are interpreted as mere interest representatives.
Com (2006, 194 final)	It repeats its position of 2002.	It repeats its position of 2002.	It initiates a common database of registry for the interest groups.	It repeats its position of 2002.

NGOs at the national level aims to shape state-society relations in the new member states. Hence, it can be argued that the EU tries to foster a common understanding of state and society relations within Europe.

Civil society discourse holds an important place in the enlargement strategy. For instance, regarding Croatia, Turkey, the former Yugoslav Republic of Macedonia, Albania, Bosnia and Herzegovina, Montenegro, Serbia, as well as in Kosovo, the role of NGOs in the enlargement policy are defined as 'crucial in determining the pace and quality of the accession process, as well as generating public support for accession'.[15] Though the Commission stressed that the task of 'strengthening the role and influence of civil society in the enlargement countries ... primarily lies with the countries themselves', it set out a strategy of support for civil society development in these countries. In this respect, first, it has assisted the civil society projects under the Instrument for Pre-accession Assistance (IPA). This entailed 'improving consultations with civil society representatives and continuing work towards other measures to bolster civil society, for example by improving donor coordination and continuing work towards visa-free travel for citizens of the candidates and potential candidates'.[16] Second, the Commission decided to establish a 'permanent dialogue' between NGOs and the new and possible member countries. This conclusion was taken at the conference *Civil Society Development in Southeast Europe: Building Europe Together* in Brussels on 17–18 April 2008, which gathered representatives from the candidate and potential candidate countries. The other conclusion from this conference was to 'establish a virtual platform for CSOs from the candidates and potential candidates and the EU, to enhance dialogue, exchange good practices, search for partners and eventually develop specific projects'.[17] In what follows, this chapter will concentrate on the ways in which participation has been rendered and how it has been defined in the context of policymaking.

The stage and norms of civil society participation in EU governance: civil dialogue and consultations

In order to develop systematic relations with NGOs, the Commission started civil dialogue following the European Social Policy Forum in March 1996, which was organised by the Social Platform, including 100 participants mostly from the NGOs.[18] At the outset, the Commission indicated two goals for the civil dialogue:

> [1] to ensure that the views and grassroots experience of the voluntary sector can be systematically taken into account by policy makers at European level so that policies can be tailored more to real needs, and [2] to disseminate information from the European level down to the local level so that citizens are aware of developments, can feel part of the construction of Europe and can see the relevance of it to their own situation, thus increasing transparency and promoting citizenship.
>
> (Com 97, 241 final: 7)

Here the scope and form of civil dialogue has changed, in parallel with the shifts in civil society conceptualisation and interest regulation policy of the EC. In the 2000s, the Commission began defining civil dialogue as a consultation practice in policy – and lawmaking. *The EU at a glance: Eurojargon*[19], an online glossary of the terminology used in EU politics, reveals the paradigm shift in the EC in the definition of civil dialogue: '[Civil dialogue] means consulting civil society when the European Commission is drawing up its policies and proposals for legislation.' It should be noted that civil society in this definition does not necessarily connote NGOs, since the Commission broadened the definition of civil society in such a way as to include all non-state actors, including trade unions and business groups with the launch of the White Paper on European Governance (2001).

The NGOs, the actors of the civil dialogue, on the other hand, developed their own definition of civil dialogue (Fazi and Smith 2006).[20] This definition is a reaction to the Commission's definition, which portrays 'civil dialogue as a consultation practice covering a wide range of interactions between civil society organisations and institutions' (ibid.: 22). It illustrates these with bullet points:

- Civil dialogue covers various degrees of formalisation, ranging from informal to legally recognised structures, from ad hoc to continuous exchange;
- Civil dialogue also covers different degrees of involvement from the civil society organisations, ranging from information to consultation and active participation;
- Civil dialogue takes place alongside the whole policymaking process which includes the following phases: Agenda setting, Policy definition/decision-making, Implementation, Evaluation, [and] Feedback;
- It involves civil society organisations acting in the public interest (ibid.: 22).

(Fazi and Smith 2006: 22)

Here, civil society organisations connote the NGOs, in contrast with the Commission's usage of the term. This definition could disappoint those who perceive – or would prefer to conceptualise – civil dialogue as a form of participation designated for the social interests. Nevertheless, its definition on the EU at a Glance site and the EC's official website for civil society mentions neither civil dialogue nor participation. The Commission's civil society page,[21] instead of elaborating on the Commission's relationship with the social groups, rather explicates its relations with all 'external parties' as consultation practices, which include non-state actors, along with the two Committees within the EU institutional set-up: the European Economic and Social Committee, which represents various socio-economic organisations in member states, and the Committee of the Regions, which is made up of representatives of local and regional authorities. Moreover, on its official website, the Commission refers to the Amsterdam Treaty, instead of the Lisbon Treaty's Article 11 on participatory democracy, as the legal basis of the consultation practices with civil society. Protocol no. 7 on the application of subsidiarity and proportionality, annexed to the Amsterdam treaty, stipulates that 'the Commission should consult widely before proposing legislation, and, wherever appropriate, publish consultation documents'.[22]

The Commission outlines in the web page for civil society the objective of consultation with stakeholders to improve the policy outcome at an early stage of policy shaping.[23] For this objective, the Commission faces no normative quandary over whether the decision-making process becomes more democratic though involvement of non-state actors in the policy-making process, as the proponents of normative democracy in EU studies argue (Eriksen et al. 2005; Joerges and Neyer 1997). Rather, it emphasises the role of non-state actors in the policy-making process as improving the policy outcome. Hence, it is more compatible with the argument that evaluates the involvement of the civil society as participatory governance, and the output legitimacy orientation (Finke 2007).

NGOs, the agents of this process, on the other hand, refute the Commission's position with respect to its relations with non-state actors. While the Commission insists on its approach to NGOs being consultation, lobbying, and interest representation, NGOs identify its presence in EU politics strictly as participatory democracy. For instance, the members of NGOs stress the structural differences between other interest groups, especially economic lobbying groups, and they refuse to be treated under the same conceptual frame (as interest groups) and to be subject to the same standards the EU institutions employ with other lobbying groups.[24] The Commission's attempt to leave no distinction between the interest groups and the NGOs creates a tension, which can be observed in the recent reaction of the NGO sector to the European transparency initiative (ALTER-EU and CSCG 2008).

The regulation of interest intermediation

The Commission's powers and responsibilities influence the lobbying practices to the Commission (Bouwen 2009), as the Commission is responsible for the drafting of legislative proposals. As Bouwen underlines, this requires a substantial amount of technical and political information. Thus the commission depends on external resources. In return for access by interest groups to the Commission's policy formulation, the Commission demands resources that are crucial for its own functioning, such as expert knowledge and legitimacy. According to Bouwen, the Commission's executive and the guardian of the legal framework roles also have an effect on the lobbying, since the Commission's administration has largely been shaped by the responsibilities it has to achieve. With respect to this, he argues, the Commission employs various instruments to actively shape the system of EU interest representation, including money, rule-making power and governance style.

To regulate its relations with interest groups, the Commission showed its willingness to prepare a code of conduct in the early 1990s, due to the misuse of lobbying activities by some groups, such as using the Commission's symbols while presenting themselves to the public and distributing the official documents of the EU (Com 1992). In this respect, the Commission examined the situation of lobbying regulations in other countries, as well as the UN. The conclusion was that many states and organisations had no formal rules for lobbying, except Germany, the US, Canada and the United Nations. Their procedures for regulating interest politics included rules on accreditation, registration and codes of conduct. The Commission avoided an accreditation system, but launched a registration system and a code of conduct.

In 2002, the Commission set its minimum principles and standards in accordance with its aims of regulating the consultation with external groups (Com 2002, 704 final). The five principles of the consultation process were participation, openness, accountability, effectiveness and coherence. The five minimum standards were as follows: first, formulating clear contents for the consultations; second, ensuring that the relevant parties had an opportunity to express their opinions; third, publishing the results of the consultations for the general public on the Commission's web portal, *Your Voice in Europe*; fourth, allowing sufficient time for responses to the consultations; and finally, providing acknowledgement and feedback to those engaging in the consultations.

In the same document, the Commission also expressed the aim of establishing a registration system for civil society actors that would lay out the interests they represented, along with the extent of their inclusiveness and representativeness (ibid.: 17). Indeed, CONNECCS (Consultation, the European Commission and Civil Society) was put into practice as a database for civil organisations that involved, or aimed to involve, consultation between the Commission and two European committees (the European Economic and Social Committee [EESC] and the Committee of the Regions [CoR]). Registration in the database was voluntary, and the Commission stressed that CONNECCS was not an attempt to create an accreditation system of interest representation. For this reason, registration was not a prerequisite for an NGO to be involved in consultation. Furthermore, the Commission stressed that there were no negative consequences, in terms of their relations with the EU institutions, for civil society organisations that did not register. Rather, it specified the role of CONECCS as an 'information source for Commission departments and the general public' (Com 2006, 194 final: 7). CONNECS has become inactive since the launch of the registration system for all interest groups in 2008.

The Commission consulted the *Minimum Standards and Principles* with the Brussels-based NGO networks, and its aim to establish a registration system. Despite the fact that the Commission declared openness and non-accreditation as the tenets of its interest regulation policy, some European organisations indicated that only those registered in the database should be involved in consultation (Com 2002, 704 final: 11). Nevertheless, the Commission rejected the claims of these groups and made clear that it would continue to have an inclusive approach that would enable each individual and association to provide input. Doing this, EC tried to escape from a situation in which 'Brussels only talks to Brussels' (ibid.: 12). In sum, it was the NGO networks that proposed a restricted consultation mechanism in which their privileges were preserved, while the Commission insisted on an open consultation mechanism. In other words, the European NGO community was pressing for a neo-corporatist arrangement through formalised mechanisms, while the Commission insisted on keeping the NGO community in a neo-pluralist arrangement of the free competition of various interests.

Extending the registration system to all interest groups: the transparency initiative

In the second half of the 2000s, the Commission did not change its position on either the accreditation or the idea of a compulsory registration system (Com 2006, 194 final: 7). The Commission's interest regulation policy continued to be based on two aspects: a common e-database for all interest groups and a code of conduct. The European Transparency Initiative instituted the 'voluntary register of interest representatives' for all interest groups. This was put into practice in 2007, and the interest groups were required to provide information about their organisational objectives, their sources of funding and the interests they represented. In turn, the Commission would automatically send alerts about the consultations for those groups that registered the necessary information in the database. According to the figures of March 2010, there were 2,179 interest representatives registered in the Commission's voluntary database system.[25] Table 3.4 shows those interest groups.

Table 3.4 Interest representatives in the voluntary database: according to types of interest groups

Professional consultants/law firms involved in lobbying EU institutions	**135**
Law firm	11
Public affairs consultant	71
Independent public affairs consultant	35
Other (similar) organisation	18
'In-house' lobbyists and trade associations active in lobbying	**1,201**
Company	293
Professional association	700
Trade union	60
Other (similar) organisation	148
NGO/think-tank	**610**
Non-governmental organisation/association of NGOs	472
Think-tank	59
Other (similar) organisation	79
Other organisations	**233**
Academic organisation/association of academic organisations	52
Representative of religions, churches and communities of conviction	10
Association of public authorities	37
Other (similar) organisation	134

Source: https://webgate.ec.europa.eu/transparency/regrin/welcome.do?locale=en#en. (accessed 14 July 2011).

It was not only the Commission that employed a register system to regulate interest politics. The European Parliament also devised an e-database for interest groups, and according to the figures accessed at the beginning of March 2010, there were 1,778 registered organisations and 2,859 accredited lobbyers on the list.[26] However, it was not possible to track the amount of lobbying organisations registered as a certain type in the Parliament's database, since it did not follow the same structure as the Commission. Nonetheless, the Parliament and the Commission decided to abandon these differences by establishing a common register of interest representatives in the EU institutions.[27] While the preparations were continuing, they launched the pragmatic solution of a website to enable access to the register system of the two institutions.[28]

Along with the database for the interest groups, *the Code of Conduct*[29] constituted an important component of the Commission's interest regulation. The Commission first formulated a code of conduct in 1992, which was further improved in the *Minimum Principles* (Com 2002, 704 final) and the European Transparency Initiative (ETI) (Com 2006, 194 final). In 2008, the Commission and the Parliament agreed upon a common code of conduct for the regulation of interest politics.[30]

Green Paper on the European Transparency Initiative

The Commission launched the European Transparency Initiative in relation to the reform of the decision-making structure of the EU. As the ETI puts it: 'The commitment to widen opportunities for stakeholders to participate actively in EU policy-shaping is one of the Strategic Objectives 2005–2009 with which the European Commission launched a 'Partnership for European Renewal' [Com 2005, 12 final]' (Com 2006, 194 final: 2). Apart from bringing the e-database for the interest groups to the fore of the interest regulation policy, most importantly, the ETI introduces lobbying as a new concept, claiming that it is a legitimate activity in a democracy:

> Lobbying is a legitimate part of the democratic system, regardless of whether it is carried out by individual citizens or companies, civil society organisations and other interest groups or firms working on behalf of third parties (public affairs professionals, think tanks and lawyers).
>
> (Ibid.: 5)

While the Commission defines lobbying as 'all activities carried out with the objective of influencing the policy formulation and decision-making processes of the European-institutions', it describes lobbyists 'as persons carrying out such activities, working in a variety of organisations such as public affairs consultancies, law firms, NGOs, think tanks, corporate lobby units ('in house representatives') or trade associations' (ibid.: 5). Moreover, it reiterates the Commission's traditional approach of putting all groups under the same category.

However, lobbying, the ETI continues, is not free from shortfalls that could damage the legitimate representation of interests, such as 'unlawful lobbying practices – fraud and corruption – abusing the openness policy, and misleading the decision-making process'. The quality of the information is also a concern, since insufficient information provided by the lobbyists could have negative consequences. Furthermore, the ETI refers to the debates on legitimacy of NGOs' lobbying, since some NGOs are funded by the Commission, and questions their representativeness and transparency. Nevertheless, NGOs have been critical towards the current system of representation, since little room to manoeuvre is left in lobbying because of the financial dominance of the corporate sector with which they have to compete.

Moreover, the presentation the lobbying, 'regardless of whether it is carried out by individual citizens or companies, civil society organisations and other interest groups or firms working on behalf of third parties (public affairs professionals, think tanks and lawyers)' (Com 2006: 5) reveals the change in the EC's policy on legitimacy. Traditionally, the consensus among the EU institutions asserted that the legitimacy of the EU rested on territorial representation, as European Parliament stresses: 'The decision-making process in the EU is legitimised by the elected representatives of the European peoples.'[31] When the indirect legitimacy of EU governance began to be criticised, society's participation in EU decision-making and EU governance was presented as a remedy. The Commission posits three ways of interaction between the EU institutions and society: participation in European parliament elections, the institutionalised advisory bodies of the EESC and Committee of the Regions, and less formalised direct contacts of the social organisations (Com 2002, 704: 4–5). Consequently, the scholars explore the question of whether the will of the people is reflected in EU decision-making through the aforementioned channels. With the ETI, the Commission proposes a new understanding of legitimacy that abandons the normative necessity of the people's participation in politics. It inaugurates a new debate over whether the lobbying activities, regardless of the actors carrying it out, legitimise EU politics.

Clarifying the boundaries of interest representation and interest representativeness

The Commission opened up the transparency initiative and the system of registration for interest representation to the discussion of the stakeholders. The feedback proved that there was a need to clarify the activities that did not fall under the category of *interest representation* (Com 2008: 323). Accordingly, the Commission emphasised that the following would not be considered to be interest representation:

> legal and other professional advice which was related to the right to a fair trial of a client; the activities of the social partners within the scope of social dialogue; and the Commission's direct request for factual information, data or expertise, and participation in the consultative committees by the request of the Commission to provide expert knowledge.
>
> (Com 2008: 323)

Furthermore, individuals and public authorities could not claim to be interest representatives, and social partners could only fall into the category of interest representation when they wanted to promote an interest outside the scope of the social dialogue. In the end, the Commission also tried to solve the confusion it created by introducing the concept of lobbying: 'All interest representatives should register, including such entities that do not consider themselves 'lobbyists'. Registration shows that an organisation represents interests. It does not mean that those registering can be labelled 'lobbyists' '.[32] The Commission then described the lobbying activities as

> contacting members or officials of the EU institutions, preparing, circulating and communicating letters, information material or argumentation and position papers, organising events, meetings or promotional activities (in the offices or in other venues) in support of an objective of interest representation.
> (Ibid.: note 32; see also Com 2007, 127 final and Com 2008, 323 final)

One of the aims of this book is to examine whether the practices of civil dialogue and participatory democracy discourse at the EU level correspond to the normative understanding of democracy, in such a way that civil society participation contributes to EU democracy. In this respect, the interest regulation policy has been elaborated, since non-state actors try to influence EU policymaking on this basis, and social actors are no exception. Scholars of normative democracy who concentrate on the participation of civil society have neglected this dimension, focusing on such ad hoc deliberation mechanisms as the Convention on the Constitution of Europe. Instead, scholars of public policy and law (Obradovic 2005; Curtin 1999; Armstrong 2002; Greenwood 2007; and Smismans 2003) attempt to establish the link between interest regulation and democracy. Nevertheless, these scholars fall short of developing a critique of the Commission's interest regulation policies by, for instance, missing the crucial point that the Commission tried to conceptualise civil society in its broadest sense to entail all non-state actors, and moreover, lobbying as civil dialogue, if not participation. The more serious question is, then, the extent to which the Commission's approach entails an understanding of politics that excludes the politics, trying to constitute a system of decision-making open to experts and expert knowledge.

Competing discourses on defining civil society in EU institutions

The neglected role of the EESC in European Civil Society Discourse

The European Economic and Social Committee (EESC) is a consultative body in the EU institutional setup, along with the Committee of the Regions (CoR). It was established in 1957 as a corporatist arrangement, with the idea that the representatives of capital and labour could take part in the European integration process (Jeffery 2002). Currently, the EESC comprises three groups: the representatives of employers (group I), employees (group II) and the various other interests (group III, which includes farmers, professional associations and consumer groups). The EESC members are nominated by national governments, and the number of members is shaped by the population of the states.

Although the EESC was established as a consultative body, which would enable channelling capital and labour interests in decision-making, it has recently redefined its institutional identity as the bridge between Europe and organised civil society (EESC 2009). Smismans (2003) explains this as the EESC's strategy to avoid being marginalised in the EU institutional setup. It is debateable, though, whether the EESC could manage to strengthen its position with this move. Acknowledgement of this new identity has not come from the EU institutions, civil society organisations or academia. Nevertheless, it could be argued that it has had an impact on the civil society discourse of the Commission in two respects. First, it brings to the fore the argument that civil society can contribute to the legitimacy of EU governance at large, and this argument has indeed been adopted by the Commission. Second, the EC fulfils the content of this discourse in borrowing the civil society (organisation) definition and the criteria for the legitimate CSO from the EESC's work.

The EESC suggests that 'ensuring the participation of grassroots-level players, through their representative organisations, in policy-shaping and decision-making processes is therefore a key instrument to reinforce the democratic legitimacy of public institutions and their work and activities'.[33] Nevertheless, instead of elaborating this through the deliberative approach, it moves to a more instrumental approach, concentrating on the functional roles of the NGOs, namely, advertising EU governance and creating a European identity. It argues that these will enhance the people's acceptance of the EU project. First, in this respect, the EESC posits that NGOs play an important role as the agents of democracy and in mobilising the public for European integration (EESC 1999). Second, it suggests that a pan-European identity, in addition to and beyond national identity, could emerge through participation:

> ...additional identity criteria are required to create a European identity. If European citizenship is defined simply as the sum of all national citizenships, then a 'European' must be the sum (or synthesis) of several national identity criteria, which all derive from a common tradition and the values of democracy and human rights.... This means, however, that the democratic process at European level – even more so than at national level – must provide a range of participatory structures in which all citizens, with their different identities and in accordance with their different identity criteria, can be represented and which reflect the heterogeneous nature of European identity.... The European Parliament is elected by Europe's citizens in their capacity as national citizens (residing in a particular Member State), i.e. exercising their democratic rights as part of their national (territorial)

identity.... But people's identity is also defined by membership of interest groups in the diverse shape of civil society organisations. These identity criteria, relating to people's role in civil society organisations, are not covered by representation in the EP. It is precisely these identity criteria, however, which are taken into account by the Committee as the representative of civil society organisations; this enables the Committee to promote democratisation at the European level, and to show Parliament that it provides genuine added value in the democratic European decision-making process. The Committee cannot compete with European Parliament, in power terms alone, but it complements Parliament's legitimacy in a way that makes sense.

(EESC 1999: 6)

Instead, the EESC suggested a negative definition of civil society, resting on the explanation of what civil society is *not* instead of what it is: 'Civil society is a collective term for all types of social action, by individuals or groups that do not emanate from the state and are not run by it.' (EESC 1999: 6) In other words, the EESC suggests that ontologically, civil society covers the space in which the state is absent. Moreover, it depicts the CSOs in abstract terms as the sum of 'all organisational structures whose members have objectives and responsibilities that are of general interest and who also act as mediators between the public authorities and citizens' (EESC 1999: 7). What merits attention in these definitions is that even though CSOs are illustrated as all forms of non-state organisations, they are assigned a mediator role between society and the public authorities, considering that they operate on the basis of general interest. In other words, despite the fact that the EESC defines civil society in Lockean terms, as a social ontology able to organise and function external to and (more importantly) without the existence of the state, it distances itself from this liberal approach in its CSO definition in favour of a Hegelian definition, associating organisations of civil society with the state. In it, civil society takes the role of mediating between public institutions and citizens, and acts on the basis of the public interest.

Although the Commission has provided a definition of civil dialogue that entails the consultation practices in terms of the interest regulation policy of the Commission, the EESC tried to elaborate a more detailed definition of civil dialogue, emphasising the difference between participation and consultation. The Commission has had a tendency to equate civil dialogue with consultation practices, for which it uses participation, consultation and interest mediation interchangeably, and in some cases as synonyms. For instance, the Commission website for civil society does not include any references or explanations for participation and participatory democracy, but it illustrates the history of interest representation in EU politics as the form of interactions with civil society. On the other hand, while the EESC defines consultation as 'open to all the organisations having expertise' in their field, it describes 'participation' as an 'opportunity for an organisation to intervene formally and actively in the collective decision-making process, in the general interest of the Union and its citizens' (EESC, SC/02, 32006: 5). To the EESC, both the consultation and the participation practice can 'enable civil society organisations to be part and parcel of policy framing and preparing decisions on the development and future of the Union and its policies' (ibid.: 5).

The conclusion is that while the Commission adopted the civil society and civil society organisation definition developed by the EESC, it was hesitant to adopt its civil dialogue definition. The reason for this can be that the Commission was against the NGOs' formal involvement in the EU decision-making process. The EESC was suggesting a structured mechanism for functional representation, a neo-corporatist interest representation regime, which would also require accreditation for some of the groups. Nevertheless, this contradicted the Commission's traditional policy on interest regulation, which is based on the principles of openness and non-accreditation, a neo-pluralist interest representation regime.

Nonetheless, the involvement of NGOs in decision-making was not free from any problems. Within the EU institutions and academic milieu, two main challenges to the legitimacy of NGOs' involvement in EU politics were addressed (Smismans 2003; EESC 1999). The first questioned the transparency and internal governance of the CSOs, and the second problematised the representativeness of any NGO claiming the title of European civil society organisation. Having noticed the problems in civil dialogue, the EESC formulated another strategy to strengthen its institutional position, since the Commission did not have a clear criterion of representativeness, a tool and an authorised institution that would determine whether any organisations met the criterion. The EESC authorised itself as the institution for this task, so that it could 'give the dialogue with OCS [organised civil society] greater credibility by enhancing the legitimacy of these organisations and networks' (EESC, SC/023, 2006: 7). Nevertheless, the question remained what the legitimacy of the EESC would have to be to have discretion in determining the legitimacy of the organisations, even though the EESC presented its new institutional identity as the bridge between Europe and the citizens, referring to the Nice Treaty.

To the EESC, only those cases where the civil society organisations engaged formally in the decision-making representativeness became a condition. On the other hand, consultation practices did not require representativeness criteria since the consultation focused on 'hearing the points of view and collecting the expertise of civil society players' (ibid.: 5). Argued in this way, therefore, there should be no representativeness problem for the NGOs in civil dialogue, since civil society participation, as the EESC suggested, still does not exist in the EU decision-making structure.

The EESC emphasised that the representativeness of civil society organisations was problematised in three ways: whether they represented the individual interests of their members instead of the general interest; whether they had transparent internal governance; and whether they could exert a real influence on the process of formulating policies and decisions (ibid.: 4).

In its 2002 *Opinion on the White Paper on Governance*, the EESC identified nine criteria for a European organisation. According to this paper, a European organisation

> should exist permanently at Community level; provide direct access to expertise; represent general interests that tally with the interests of European society; comprise bodies that are recognised at Member State level as representative of particular interests; have member organisations in most of the EU member states; provide for accountability of its members; have authority to represent and act at European level; be independent, not bound by instructions from outside bodies; be transparent, especially financially and in its decision-making structures.
>
> (EESC, SC/028, 2006: 5)

In 2006, the EESC reconsidered the criteria of representativeness it formulated in the *Opinion on the White Paper on Governance*, proposing three main criteria: the provisions in the organisation's statute and their implementation; the organisation's support base in the member states; and qualitative criteria.

(a) The statute and its implementation: Although the EESC introduced having a statute as one of the criteria for the representativeness of the NGOs[34], it did not justify the argument that European civil society should have a statute in order to prove its representativeness. This related to a normative variant of the conceptualisation of European civil society that imagined a certain form of civil society. This has exclusionary aspects, because not all the European NGO networks had statutes. While the Social Platform and Concord (the network of development NGOs) had statutes, Green 10 and the Human Rights and Democracy Network did not attempt to initiate a statute until 2010. Moreover, in addition to the exclusionary potential, the statute requirement also entailed a threat to the polymorphic character of civil society, harmonising the organisational frames through unification of their bureaucratic structures.

(b) The organisations' support base in the member states: The EESC's second main criterion for a European civil society organisation was the scope of the organisation's membership. According to the EESC, a European organisation must have had 'member organisations in the vast majority of Member States', and 'it must be represented in more than half of EU Member States' (EESC, SC/023, 2006: 12). This was further elaborated in the following problematic way:

> The guiding principle should be that, whether it be national or transnational, an organisation's membership in a European organisation should not only meet the membership criteria provided for in that European organisation's statute, but should also meet the criteria stipulated in the member organisation's statute.
>
> (Ibid.: 12)

Therefore, the EESC did not only aim to harmonise a European associational structure, it also aimed to create a similar structure in the national organisations.

> A national member organisation should adopt the same practice as the European organisation to which it belongs, making public its statute and activity report, which mirrors the organisation's structure and operating methods. It would be desirable, as required by the Council of Europe, to know the number of individual members who are directly and indirectly connected with the organisation.
>
> (Ibid.: 12)

(c) Qualitative Criteria: The qualitative criteria were the most problematic in that they excluded new-comers to the system, and aimed to create a Europeanised civil society in which groups that did not follow the rules of the game could never be integrated. The qualitative criteria, as the EESC elaborated, 'referred to an organisation's experience and ability to represent citizens' interest in its dealings with the European institutions, and the confidence and reputation it enjoys with these institutions on the one hand, and with other sections of European organised civil society on the other' (ibid.: 12). Hence, to the EESC, a European NGO should prove capable of providing input to the system, and furthermore, this should not be questioned within the NGO community.

In sum, the EESC tried to legitimise the NGOs' involvement in EU decision-making, which in turn could empower itself as the bridge between Europe and the citizens. The representativeness of European Parliament was not questioned since the MPs were elected, and were thus held to represent the people and the general will. Corporate representation was not a problem, since it was clear which companies were represented, even if that meant representing the interests of their shareholders. But civil society organisations were not elected bodies, and not all the people that the sector claimed to represent could be shown to be members. For instance, an organisation that claimed to stand for the rights of the elderly could not present evidence that all elderly people supported its activities. This, then, became the question posed by the political authority: why should the political system take CSOs or NGOs seriously?

The EESC's ambition of becoming a gateway to the legitimacy of civil society organisations and civil dialogue has not found support from academic circles, EU institutions and European civil society organisations. Smismans (2003) argued that the EESC had the objective of not marginalising the institutional setup, due to the fact that interest groups were abandoning the EESC, attempting to instead directly influence the Commission and Parliament. On the other hand, the Parliament criticised the EESC's existence – for instance, some MEPs proposed its abolition, claiming that the EESC was functioning 'without a democratic mandate' and 'helps to strengthen corporatism at the at the expense of democracy'.[35] Some NGOs (e.g. human rights organisations) in the Human Rights and Democracy Network, along with environmental organisations in Green 10, decided not to participate in the Liaison Group, which the EESC established in 2004 to formalise the civil dialogue (CSCG, *Making your voice heard*, 2006: 9). The NGO networks that participated in the Liaison Group tried to gain 'political and symbolic' benefit from the situation of engaging formal relations with a EU institution (ibid.: 9), especially the NGO families that prioritised the sectoral dialogue.

European Parliament and civil society

Smismans (2003) argues that since civil society discourse comprises elements that could challenge territorial representation, the European Parliament and the European Committee of the Regions were critical of it. Nonetheless, the Parliament could not remain silent with respect to the discourse of connecting with citizens. Instead of adopting the EC and the EESC's approach, since it posed a threat to its institutional power, it reproduced its own discourse on civil society, based on the premises of representative democracy:

> Because it is directly elected, Parliament is the European Union institution best qualified to take up the challenge of keeping open the channels of communication with European Union citizens. Members of the European Parliament (MEPs) are in regular contact with citizens and are directly accountable to voters.... All European Union institutions of course understand the importance of dialogue with citizens as part of the European Union project. Nevertheless, their responses were essentially to do with the debate on Europe's institutional architecture. Although this issue is vital, it is also important to focus on the day-to-day concerns of ordinary people.... The European Parliament therefore now proposes involving citizens in a permanent dialogue on the European Union's future.[36]

The Parliament developed its challenge to the Commission on the civil dialogue and civil society discourse in two ways. The first concerned the different approaches of the respective institutions on interest regulation policy. The Parliament and the Commission have different approaches on the structured and formalised dialogue with civil society. The Commission prefers to regulate relations with civil society on the basis of the principles of openness and transparency, and rejects having an accredited mechanism with the interest groups. Nonetheless, it should also be noted that the Commission's attempts (e.g. preparing an internet-based registration system and a code of conduct) have been regarded as de facto accreditation (Balme and Chabanet 2008) or a system that lies somewhere on the continuum between structured and open (personal communication, Conny Reuter, May 2009). In contrast to the Commission's strong rejection of the accreditation of interest intermediation, the Parliament uses an accreditation system that includes access to Parliament buildings (five or more days per year). Moreover, the Parliament publishes the names of accredited lobbyists on its website. However, this list only includes the names of badge holders and their institutions. Like the Commission's interest representation system, it too does not include any information about the lobbyists' interests, or the organisational features the lobbyist represents.

Second, the Parliament advocates a different ontology of civil society, criticising the neo-pluralist arrangement of the EC, and the neo-corporatist suggestions of the EESC. The Parliament claims that it also favours an open dialogue. However, it interprets openness as something other than interest intermediation. It challenges the conceptualisation of the sector-based civil society approach: 'Furthermore, Parliament aims to transcend the traditional sector-specific structures of civil society (social affairs, the environment, development, education, and so on), so as to enable different points of view to be heard and a broad range of options to emerge'.[37] Instead, the Parliament launched two AGORAs, as an alternative way of 'combining the voices of European citizens with their elected representatives',[38] which aimed to present an alternative to the sector-wise civil dialogue implemented by the Commission. The first AGORA was held on the Future of Europe (8–9 November 2007), and the second on climate change (12–13 June 2008), both of them in Brussels with the participation of about 500 NGOs.

In conclusion, it can be argued that the institutional power struggle over civil society discourse led to the emergence of different and competing conceptualisations of European civil society. The Commission's discourse has been to some extent influenced by the marginal institution in the EU setup, the EESC. The Parliament, however, has transformed the discourse in terms of its institutional interests. For instance, the AGORAs introduced a different definition of European civil society, transcending the sector-specific Brussels based pan-European civil society focus. The irony is that, on one hand, the EP emphasises representative democracy as the unique source of EU legitimacy, and therefore presents AGORAs with respect to representative democracy, in which elected representatives *listen* to the citizens without necessarily giving them a vote. On the other, the Parliament borrows a spatial term – AGORA – from ancient Greece, where it was used to denote direct democracy. With the AGORA initiative, the Parliament proved that it was not indifferent to civil society's discourse of involvement in EP politics. The question is the extent to which the strengthened role of the EP, in the Lisbon treaty, can affect the ontological evolution of civil society and the discourse of connecting with citizens.

Concluding remarks

I have noted in Chapter 2 that the general trend is to celebrate NGOs as democratising agents of European governance, either as institutionalised public spheres beyond the nation-state (Magnette 2001; Armstrong 2002), or as civic partners of European governance (Kohler-Koch and Finke 2007). I have also noted that the European Commission's European civil society discourse and the NGOs have not been substantively criticised. These critiques often (Warleigh 2001; Smismans 2007; Armstrong 2002) advocate a gradual enhancement of the obstacles for the emergence of a democratising civil society. Both the

Table 3.5 EU institutions' different approaches to European civil society

The Commission and civil dialogue	The EESC and civil dialogue	The EP and civil dialogue
• Open, no accreditation, interest representation. • CONNECS, Principles and Standards, ETI. • The database for registration. • Interest representation, lobbying, consultation, social and civil dialogue (ref. to treaty of Amsterdam). • The use of the discourse first in social policy then in general EU governance to legitimise its actions. • The ambiguities in the conceptualisation: interest intermediation vs. participation, social groups as lobbyists, and business groups as civil society. • Emphasis on interest intermediation, equating all groups as interest groups. • On the website, the whole story is consultation and interest intermediation. • It did not change the principles, such as openness, and no accreditation. • It has initiated policies to regulate interest politics: CONNECS, Minimum Standards, and ETI. • It has related the discourse on CS to contextual EU politics, such as the administrative reform and governance (see *White Paper on Governance*), legitimacy problem (WPEG and then Plan D, and Communication Policy). • It continued discussions on the conceptualisation of civil society, mapping out the legal status of CSOs in each member state, the role and functions of CSOs in politics, economy and society, and it has provided normative claims about the characteristics of civil society organisations in its discussion papers such as 1997, 2001.	• Influence on the conceptualisation of civil society and the CSO. • Claims to be the intermediary of CSOs (ref. to Nice). • Detailed work on the conceptualisation of the civil society and CSOs. • Including social partners in the civil dialogue as CSOs. • Discussing critiques of CSOs such as representativeness and accountability. • Discusses CSOs in relation to the legitimacy problem. • Elaboration of participatory democracy. The differences between EESC and the EC: • Political *vs.* pragmatic approach. • Participation *vs.* consultation. • Preference for accreditation vs. openness.	• Accreditation in parliamentary buildings. • Critique of the formation of a European CS on the basis of the sectoral; in other words objecting to neo-plural and corporatist arrangements between the EC and the interest groups since it declares the only legitimate source of EU governance is territorial representation. • CSOs could participate in the expert groups of EP committees. Nevertheless, parliamentarians question the legitimacy of CSOs; they conceive them as advisory groups. • Arranged two AGORAs, bringing around 500 CSOs from different sectors to discuss first the future of Europe, and second climate change. The differences of the EP's approach: • The EP's approach stands as a critique of the EC and EESC, not merely as a matter of the practice of CSO involvement; the EP is critical about this administrative arrangement itself.

governance and the normative approach have been limited in problematising the Commission's attempts to build a European civil society. They have been in a way civil society reductionist, in that they consider civil society to be an inherently autonomous agent. The governance takes for granted that there is *a* European civil society waiting to be integrated into the governance mechanism, sharing the responsibility of EU institutions. The normative approach, on the other hand, has proposed a rights-based identity that can be reinforced through participation, and has defended the intermediary function of civil society. Similarly, it has derived from the ontological assumption that civil society has always been there, waiting to democratise decision-making and linking the authentic public reason to the decision-making processes. The normative approach also has taken for granted the normative claim that civil society is good, and whatever comes from civil society is good per se. Both approaches share an a priori normative stance: that the involvement of civil society in governance mechanisms unquestionably legitimises EU governance. The governmentality approach, by contrast, denaturalises this a priori normative position, considering it as one style of reasoning among others. It also questions the civil society ontology of the governance and normative approaches.

The fact is that the Commission has engaged proactively in a strategy of constituting an ECS and EPS, as well as integrating the social organisations to the consultation processes of decision-making. Considering this, an NGO is not an essentially non-state phenomenon, and whatever it performs does not necessarily democratise and legitimise a political system. Therefore, the more provocative question should be why the EU engages in defining civil society, and what the consequences of this politically driven process are.

The normative approach could regard the Commission's efforts to empower EU NGOs, such as financial support and incorporating them into the consultation mechanism, as democratising participatory procedures (Huller 2010). The governance approach, on the other hand, considers the Commission's civil society initiatives necessary attempts for the governance turn. The governmentality approach conceives of these as political technologies. It asserts that the art of government has extended beyond the territories of the nation-states. Defined as advanced liberalism (Barry *et al.* 1996) or neoliberal governmentality (Lemke 2002, 2007), this art of government includes the empowerment of the self and society for their own auto-government (Cruikshank 1999; Rose 1992, 1996). The Commission's civil society discourse first elaborates the NGOs in terms of the governance debate. However, such art of government also generates the subjects of government, i.e. the population and the citizen. The governance approach ignores this (Lemke 2007), while the normative approach defines an autonomous, a rights-based European identity. Rather, the identity and consent-building role of the NGOs are incorporated into the Commission's civil society discourse, and merged with the technologies of European citizenship. This merges the European art of government, the expert solution to social problems (e.g. Majone 1996; Jachtenfuchs 2001; Kohler-Koch 2006) with the government of the self, government of society, and government of society through society.

European governance and civil society 105

This chapter elaborated on the EU's discourse on European civil society and connecting with the citizens on this basis.

It endeavoured to discuss these two subjects in relation to each other. In this respect, it examined the Commission's following initiatives: White Paper on Governance, Plan D, Europe for Citizens, Communication Policy, civil dialogue with non-state actors, and the Commission's interest intermediation policy. It elaborated the historical background of integration of social organisations in EU politics, as well as EU institutions' attempts to establish (European) civil society (organisations). In particular, it drew attention to those concepts used by the EU institutions in their approach to ECS, such as participatory democracy and active citizenship. Three conclusions can be drawn from the analysis of the Commission's civil society discourse: (1) the definition, role and constituents of the ECS is contextual and contingent on the EU institutions' use; (2) while developing policies about incorporating the social actors to EU decision-making processes, the Commission has been under the influence of its interest intermediation and neo-corporatist policies (social dialogue); and (3) the discourse transformed and adapted to different contexts, along with the technologies and strategies it developed and carried from other contexts.

Although the Commission held a normative ambition to promote participatory democracy as an additional source of legitimacy to representative democracy, it has not developed a solid definition of civil society and has never explained why the involvement of civil society would enhance the legitimacy of EU governance. Two different understandings of the conceptualisation of civil society have been outlined above, namely the socialising impacts of civil society, civil society as a domain of different rationality. The Commission has not referred to any of these understandings in order to justify its discourse on civil society. It has instead, first, defined civil society on the basis of the nature and composition of the actors: 'This is the collective name for all kinds of organisations and associations that are not part of government but that represent professions, interest groups or sections of society. It includes (for example) trade unions, employers' associations, environmental lobbies and groups representing women, farmers, people with disabilities and so on' (Com 2000). In the early 1990s, when civil society as a category did not even appear in EU jargon, these organisations were described as non-profit making organisations. In the second half of the 1990s, they were called voluntary organisations due to the Commission's interest in organisations operating in social policy. The term NGO appeared in Commission terminology in 2000. However, by this time the Commission had a broader perspective and tended to cover all sectors of civic organisations. It was in 2001, with the *White Paper on Governance*, that the Commission started to use the concept of civil society. The *White Paper* tried to cover all non-state actors under the pragmatic category of civil society organisation, a category it borrowed from the 1999 EESC document. However, it introduced several ambiguities. For instance, on one hand, the NGOs were regarded as a synonym for European civil society; on the other, the trade unions and employer's associations, and even churches and communities, were identified as civil society organisations. Furthermore, in 1992, the Commission continued to collect these groups under the overarching category of interest groups, when it came to regulation of interest politics.

Second, the Commission's civil society discourse rests on a negative definition of civil society, in that it describes civil society in terms of what it is not: it is the non-state space. Third, defining civil society in accordance with the mentality of its constituents, i.e. the institutions, it excludes the non-organisational and un-institutionalised space of civil society, such as social movements and media. Despite the fact that non-institutionalised social movements are not considered constituent of European civil society, they fit into the Commission's negative definition of civil society as non-state space. Though they could also be institutionalised, they use different strategies of collective action and social mobilisation, such as protest and contention (Della Porta and Diani 1999; Imig and Tarrow 2001). Fourth, this definition avoids defining civil society as a space where a different form of rationality could evolve (Cohen and Arato 1992; Habermas 1996). Fifth, the Commission's civil society discourse leads to confusion, in that it equates civic organisations with business-oriented organisations. Although some conceptions of civil society draw a clear demarcation between the state and non-state actors (Jensen 2006; Cohen and Arato 1992; Habermas 1996), the Commission mingles social groups and economic interest groups.

In sum, European civil society is a politically constructed discourse; and the context and process through which it has evolved is also integral to its constitution. In other words, the Commission's approach to civil society, its shifting terminology for the civil society actors, its shifting strategy for the actors to be included within civil society, and its attempts to fit the discourse into the changing context, are all intrinsic to the evolution of its discourse on European civil society.

The second conclusion is that while developing policies about incorporating the social actors to EU decision-making processes, the Commission has been under the impact of its interest intermediation and neo-corporatist policies (social dialogue). In other words, the Commission has tried to adapt prior knowledge into the newly-emerged context; however, this has caused some problems. Initially, the implications of this can be seen in the Commission's inconsistent and shifting terminology in naming this process. Though the Commission termed the interactions with the social groups as *civil dialogue*, the same procedures have been also considered *interest representation* and *lobbying*. Consequently, NGOs' contact with EU institutions has gone under different names, such as *consultation*, *participation* and *interest articulation*.

The involvement of extra-political and/or non-political entities in the EU's political mechanism is not new. For instance, trade unions and employers take part in the decision and law-making processes in social policy as social partners under social dialogue. On the other hand, representatives of businesses, law firms and consultation firms have a lobbying presence in EU politics. Furthermore, they join the expert advisory committees by participating in policy- and law-making. Nevertheless, these existing practices of involving extra-political and/or non-political entities as social partners and interest groups hinge upon the development of civil dialogue as an independent practice of civil society's participation in EU politics. Civil dialogue is not developing as an independent initiative with its own dynamics. It has, however, started under the influence of the interest intermediation policies with the trade unions and employers' associations, and with the lobbying activities of the business groups.

There are significant differences with the civil society organisations and the social partners and corporate interest groups. For instance, social dialogue has a quasi-legal base, and the representativeness of trade unions and business associations are not questioned by the Commission. Nevertheless, one of the central critiques of the NGOs is that it is not obvious whom they represent. Though the Lisbon Treaty provided a constitutional basis for civil dialogue under the participatory democracy clause (Article 11), it does not guarantee the right of a social organisation to participate in EU politics with no qualifications. To prove their legitimacy as a civil society entrepreneur, each organisation should prove its representativeness and transparency. On one hand, the Commission is under the irresistible temptation to use the discourse of civil dialogue and civil society as a cure for the democratic legitimacy problem, while expecting that participation through the NGOs would create a sort of European identity. On the other, it questions the legitimacy of organisations that aim to influence EU politics.

Furthermore, it would be problematic to define the relations between the EU institutions and NGOs as a lobbying activity. The initial implication of this view is that NGOs are considered mere lobbyists. Recent research has shown that Brussels-based lobbying activities have been carried out mostly by the corporate sector until very recently, and the corporate sector still has an unarguable asymmetrical influence in lobbying activity (Greenwood 2007). Lobbying entails all kinds of activities that aim to influence policy-making processes, and this is the motivation of both NGOs and the corporate sector. Nevertheless, the problem starts when all activities of extra-political political actors are reduced to the categorical definition of interest articulation (the partners of social dialogue are not considered interest groups by EU institutions, since social dialogue has a quasi-legal basis). Furthermore, this approach considers both the corporate sector and NGOs as categorically equivalent entities, treating them as interest articulators. The question is whether the corporate sector and NGOs defend the same kind of interest (i.e. profit maximisation vs. welfare maximisation), so that they can compete in the same league of interest competition. When it comes to the comparison of NGOs with trade unions, they share similar views and it is largely possible to draw parallels between them. However, compared with trade unions, NGOs represent a greater diversity of groups and claims, and several NGOs engage in issues beyond the scope of social policy and labour rights. For this reason, they too cannot be defined as social partners.

Third, drawing a historical inquiry into the development of the Commission's ECS discourse, this chapter shows how the discourse transformed and adapted to different contexts, along with the technologies and strategies it developed and carried from other contexts (given the intense motivation of EU institutions to transfer the discourse to new, prospective, and neighbour states of the EU). The incorporation of the NGOs was first considered in the context of the interest intermediation in the early 1990s; then, it was related to the Commission's ambition to advance its power in social policies (in this case the Commission's interest in the voluntary sector). At the beginning of the 2000s, the Commission integrated the discourse of two parallel issues: the governance turn and connecting with the citizens. Developed by the World Bank, the governance turn presented a new style of governing, a more plural and inclusive system, in that it was open to the contribution of multi-level actors and stakeholders in the decision-making (Shore 2009: 3). This discourse was translated to EU governing while the EU was experiencing a legitimacy problem: the problem of attaining consent for EU governing. The Commission not only translated the discourse on governance from the World Bank, but also implemented the discourse of participation as a strategy of winning the consent of the people.

Moreover, the Commission's discourse has been shaped, developed and transformed in terms of the conflicting strategies of the EU institutions. Whereas the EESC has been successful at influencing the Commission's discourse, the European Parliament preferred to be indifferent – if not hostile – at the beginning, later challenging the content and procedures of the discourse. As a result, first, the institutional power game between the Commission and Parliament was extended to the ECS discourse. Second, challenging the Commission's Brussels-oriented and sector-based conception, the Parliament brought in an alternative perspective. For instance, the EESC has played an active role in inscribing the norms and procedures that would be applied to CSOs, which would include involvement in the Commission-level consultations. It formulated the representative criteria for NGOs, their mode of conduct. Furthermore, the civil society definition of the Commission is borrowed from the EESC's communication to the Commission. Since both the EESC and the Commission do not derive legitimacy from territorial representation, it can be argued that the two institutions were aligned. Nonetheless, this alignment contradicted the interests of the European Parliament and Committee of the Regions. These two institutions did not support the Commission's civil society discourse at the outset. However, they also developed their own approach to civil society, refuting a sectoral approach. For instance, the Parliament initiated two citizens' AGORAs: the AGORAs were designed as meetings of collective deliberation, though one that did not orient decision-making.

Before continuing with the analysis of the Social Platform, we should evaluate whether the Commission's discourse aims at entrenching the procedures of democracy, or reproducing the technologies of European governing.

Drawing inspiration from the literature on governmentality, I try to contribute to governmentality research by depicting how ECS discourse tries to render Europe governable; which technologies the Commission has implemented for the ECS discourse; how this discourse has been translated into different locales (for instance Eastern Europe); the extent to which the discourse is contingent on the institutional power struggle (i.e. EU institutions' power game); how the

Commission uses funding for civil society organisations as a disciplining instrument; how the ECS discourse subjectivises and governs the self and the organisations; the extent to which the discourse is embedded in the imperatives of neoliberal government; and how the NGOs are prescribed to a role to translate this to local NGOs, through, for example, technologies of capacity-building, participatory governance and active citizenship.

In this analysis, moreover, the discourse is not external to the social relations; it is embedded within them. It includes such disciplining elements as Commission funding for the survival of NGOs and their various projects. NGOs have to follow certain procedures in order to receive this funding. However, they are incorporated into the governance mechanisms and become a subject of government with their free choices. Further, the discourse is open to revision and change, and is articulated by several actors. As shown, whereas the European Economic and Social Committee (EESC) plays an important role in shaping the discourse, the European Parliament challenges it, rendering its own definition of European civil society, and entrenching new procedures of connecting with the citizens. Furthermore, the discourse is not a mere apparatus of social control that is designed to mask hidden dynamics of rule. Rather, it is the imperatives of the discourse itself that render the society governable. With respect to the EU, what is being rendered knowable and thus governable is the European Union itself (Shore 2006, 2009; Haahr 2004; Williams and Haahr 2005a, b; Merlingen 2006).

Notes

1 However, the document does not mention which states do this.
2 See http://ec.europa.eu/commission_barroso/wallstrom/communicating/conference/dialogue/index_en.htm (accessed 13 July 2010).
3 See http://europa.eu/debateeurope/index_en.htm (accessed 12 June 2010).
4 See www.springday2009.net/ww/en/pub/spring2009/homepage.htm (accessed 17 June 2010).
5 Ibid.
6 Defining the political actors and civil society as the partners in a meta-institutional set-up, the WPC defined the EU polity in a Gramscian way, in which the state was the combination of the political society and the civil society.
7 See http://ec.europa.eu/citizenship/annexes-citizenship/doc135_en.htm#2. (accessed 17 July 2010).
8 It has a budget of €215 million.
9 See http://ec.europa.eu/citizenship/annexes-citizenship/doc135_en.htm#2 (accessed 19 June 2010).
10 See http://eacea.ec.europa.eu/citizenship/programme/objectives_en.php (accessed 18 June 2010).
11 See http://ec.europa.eu/citizenship/programme-actions/doc46_en.htm (accessed 21 July 2010).
12 Ibid.
13 See http://ec.europa.eu/citizenship/programme-actions/doc48_en.htm. (accessed 21 July 2010).
14 See http://eacea.ec.europa.eu/static/en/Copy%20of%20citizenship/guide/features_en.htm. (accessed 26 July 2010).

15 See http://ec.europa.eu/enlargement/civil-society-development/index_en.htm (accessed 28 July 2010).
16 Ibid.
17 Ibid.
18 As a note, this should not be confused with the European Social Forum, which started in 2002 as a consequence of the anti-neoliberalism movement.
19 See http://europa.eu/abc/eurojargon/index_en.htm (accessed 29 July 2010).
20 For details, see Chapter 4.
21 See http://ec.europa.eu/civil_society/index_fr.htm (accessed 23 April 2010).
22 See http://ec.europa.eu/civil_society/apgen_en.htm (accessed 23 April 2010).
23 Ibid.
24 The President of the Social Platform, C. Reuter, personal communication, May 2009; and Beger (2004). Beger elaborates on participatory democracy and civil dialogue. In this paper, he does not refer to concepts such as interest representation and the Amsterdam Treaty, or to the recent European Transparency Initiative, in which the EC develops its relations with the interest groups and also outlines its relations with civil society organisations within this frame. Nevertheless, European CSOs refer to the Lisbon Treaty in order to depict their presence in the EU politics in terms of participatory democracy. They do not refer to other EC initiatives that develop civil dialogue in terms of interest representation, such as the Minimum Principles and ETI. However, this does not mean they ignore or resent it. CSOs register in the registration database. However, they have some critiques of this, which are raised by the Civil Society Contact Group and ALTER-EU.
25 The address for the 'voluntary register of interest representatives' is https://webgate.ec.europa.eu/transparency/regrin/welcome.do?locale=en#en (accessed 14 July 2011).
26 The list of lobbyists accredited by the Parliament can be accessed at: www.europarl.europa.eu/parliament/expert/lobbyAlphaOrderByOrg.do?language=EN (accessed 14 July 2011).
27 See http://ec.europa.eu/commission_barroso/kallas/doc/joint_statement_register.pdf (accessed 15 July 2011).
28 See http://europa.eu/lobbyists/interest_representative_registers/index_en.html (accessed 15 July 2011).
29 See *Code of Conduct* (High-Level Working Group on a common register and code of conduct for lobbyists) https://webgate.ec.europa.eu/transparency/regrin/welcome.do?locale=en#en (accessed 14 July 2011).
30 *The Code of Conduct* established that interest representatives should comply with the following principles: always identifying themselves by name and the entity or entities they work for or represent; declaring their interests and, where applicable, the clients or members they represent; never obtaining or trying to obtain information, or any decision, dishonestly; never claiming any formal relationship with the Parliament or the Commission in their dealings with third parties, nor misrepresenting themselves as to the effect of registration to mislead third parties and/or EU staff; ensuring that, to the best of their knowledge, information which they provide is complete, up-to-date and not misleading; not selling to third parties copies of documents obtained from the Parliament or Commission; not inducing the EU staff, or Members' assistants or trainees, to contravene rules and standards of behaviour applicable to them; if employing former EU staff or Members' assistants or trainees, respecting their obligation to abide by the rules and confidentiality requirements which apply to them; observing any rules laid down on the rights and responsibilities of former Members of the European Parliament and the European Commission; and informing their clients of their obligations as lobbyists towards the Commission and the Parliament.
31 A5–0399/2001: [original reference].
32 See European Transparency Initiative (ETI). Frequently Asked Questions (FAQ) on

the Commission's Register for interest representatives. Available at: http://ec.europa. eu/transparency/docs/reg/FAQ_en.pdf (accessed 17 July 2011).
33 See www.eesc.europa.eu/sco/intro/index_en.asp (accessed 18 May 2010).
34 According to EESC, the statute for a European Organisation should contain the following: 'the association's areas of activity and purpose; membership criteria; the operating procedures, which must be democratic, transparent, and include the accountability of the Board vis-à-vis its member organisations; the financial obligations of the member organisations; that an economic audit and an activity report must be submitted annually and be available to the public' (EESC, SC/023. 2006: 10).
35 *European Voice*, 11.10.2007: www.europeanvoice.com/article/imported/eesc-abolition-/58460.aspx (accessed 15 March 2010).
36 See www.europarl.europa.eu/parliament/archive/staticDisplay.do?language=EN&id=189&pageRank=1 (accessed 12 June 2011).
37 See www.europarl.europa.eu/parliament/archive/staticDisplay.do?id=189&pageRank=3&language=EN (accessed 12 June 2011).
38 See www.europarl.europa.eu/parliament/archive/staticDisplay.do?language=EN&id=189&pageRank=2 (accessed 12 June 2011)

4 A case study on the Social Platform

A performing agent of European civil society

This book has started from the argument that governance, when it is considered as a new form of governmentality, has implications on subject (and subjectivity) formations, with the latter having the capacity and willingness to participate in new governance settings. According to this reading, governance is not necessarily an improvement in our understanding of democracy, but a reconfiguration of power relations. The previous debate suggested that the idea of empowering civil society actors in order to legitimise governance (Weiss 2000; Schmitter 2003b; De Schutter 2002; Smismans 2007; see also Bohman 2005) does not necessarily promote democracy and create public spheres. I have, instead, proposed studying the constitutive impacts of this political project –constitutive in the sense of how power creates certain type of subjects and makes them amenable to governance.

The first chapter illustrates conceptually how the discourse on NGOs might relate to the consolidation of political power, as well as how power constitutes subjects. The second chapter critiques the discourse of participation, one that has been developed within the context of economic development by the World Bank and United Nations. With a particular focus on the Foucault-inspired interpretation of Europeanisation, Chapter 2 endeavours to deconstruct the symbiotic relationship between the NGOs and democracy that is far too often taken for granted. Chapter 3 investigates how the European Commission has engaged in developing the participation and European Civil society (ECS) discourse in the context of EU-level decision-making and European democracy at large, in a similar vein to which it has been developed by the World Bank. Chapter 3 thus traces the role and the influence of the Commission in flourishing of social actors, as well as in establishing the norms (including a code of conduct, transparency initiative and enshrinement of an article in the Lisbon Treaty) under which these actors would be involved in the Commission's consultation regime. Chapter 3 shows that the EU's relevant policy programmes, which aim to cultivate legitimacy through the ECS discourse, have been developed in accordance with the motto of connecting with the citizens, and within the context of the Commission's motivation to enhance its power in social policy, and the perceived legitimacy crisis of EU integration due to citizens' apathy.

This chapter discusses the implications of the theoretical and analytical debate, elaborated in Chapter 1 and 2, and the implications of the Commission's initiatives by examining the Social Platform of European NGOs. It comprises four main sections. First, I describe the administrative structure of the Social Platform; I examine its reflection in major developments with respect to European integration during 2000, such as the introduction of new modes of governance, attempts to prepare a constitution for EU enlargement, and the motto of bridging the gap with the citizens; I elaborate upon the Platform's position on the social policy of the EU; and I describe its relations with EU institutions. Second, this chapter inquires into the Platform's administrative structure, working strategies and communication instruments. As governmentality implies shaping the conduct of conduct and acts upon action, the survey finds it necessary to examine the implication of the rationalities of government on the Platform's daily practices. By analysing the Platform's administrative structure and working methods, therefore, we will trace the instruments and knowledge that it implements in its daily functioning. In addition, how the Platform represents its objectives and inscribes its performances could uncover the extent to which it receives the rationalities of government.

Third, this chapter depicts the Platform's training initiatives, which are also referred to as capacity-building to the NGO community, both at EU and national level. Capacity-building programmes have been seen as empowerment programmes that intent to involve actors in new forms of governance (Phillips and Ilcan 2004). This survey suggests that conscious and unconscious normalisation of political rule can also be detected on administrative culture and working strategies, which implies harmonisation of the *way of doing* and *perception of things* in accordance with the tenets of political rationalities. A similar argument has been develop by Laura Cram (2006b), who argues *banal Europeanism*, with reference to Billig's (1995) banal nationalism concept, an implicit and unconscious normalisation of the EU can be observed in such instances of daily practices, including carrying EU flags in national passports and identity cards, conforming with EU legislation, and walking past EU flags (such as at customs) (see also Walters and Haahr 2005b). Fourth, this chapter discusses the Platform's position on participation discourse.

In turn, this chapter tracks the implications of (good) governance (i.e. the idea of opening the governance structures to social actors in order to foster legitimacy as well as the administrative reform known as New Public Management) and the Commission's ECS discourse on the Social Platform. The empirical material entails the Social Platform's annual reports; working strategies; its reflection papers on social policy, participatory democracy and governance; interviews with the president and communication officer of Platform, the coordinator of the Civil Society Contact Group (CSCG), and three persons from European Network Against Racism (ENAR); and the observations on the Platform's conference about the 'civil dialogue', one that social NGOs operating both at European and national level participated in.

Fazi and Smith (2006) suggest five different ways through which the NGOs are institutionalised at the EU level: (1) the national organisations representations' in Brussels (e.g. the Italian environmental organisation Legambiente, which has had a branch in Brussels since 1999; (2) the permanent offices of the international organisations in Brussels, such as Greenpeace, Amnesty International and Oxfam; (3) the Brussels-based European NGO umbrella networks or platforms that appeared during the 1990s with the financial support of the EU, such as the European Network Against Racism and the European Women's Lobby; (4) the second-level umbrella organisations of the networks of European NGOs, (e.g. the Social Platform, Green 8, Human Rights Development Network, development NGOs' CONCORD alliance, consumer groups' BEUC platform, and the cultural groups' EFAH platform)[1]; and (5) the Civil Society Contact Group (CSCG), which represents the European NGO community with the participation of the second-level supranational networks, particularly in promoting participatory democracy at the EU level (ibid.). The EU NGO as a concept, therefore, excludes the Brussels representations of national NGOs (first model) and the branches of international NGOs (second model).

This book's object of inquiry, the Social Platform of NGOs, is the alliance of European federations and networks of 40 non-governmental organisations active in the social sector (i.e. the networks are the third organisational type). It is also a member of the CSCG coalition (the fifth organisational type). The members of the Platform claim to represent thousands of organisations, associations and voluntary groups at the local, regional, and national levels, including organisations of women, older people, people with disabilities, the unemployed, people affected by poverty, gays and lesbians, young people, and children and families, along with those organisations devoted to issues such as social justice, homelessness, health and reproductive rights and racism. Stated in this way, the Platform represents people who are not represented, and whose voice is not heard in Brussels. In other words, the Platform and its member associations claim to represent the excluded in EU politics.

As Chapter 3 outlined, starting from the early governance-beyond-the-state in the 1990s the Commission has played a direct role in establishment of the European NGOs through financial support, mostly in the social field, including the European Women Lobby (EWL), European Youth Forum (EYF) and the Liaison Committee of Development NGOs to the EU (CLONG), European Anti Poverty Network (EAPN), the European Disability Forum (Tarasenko 2010; Cram 2006a). These organisations, in turn, became members of the Social Platform when it was established in 1995 by the encouragement and financial support of the European Commission. Following to the Maastricht Treaty (1992), the Commission issued a *Green Paper on Social Policy* (1993, 551 final), which entailed developing mechanisms for co-operation with the Commission and NGOs. In order to put this claim into practice, the Commission's Directorate-General for Employment, Social Affairs and Inclusion, decided to launch the European Social Forums, the first of which would be convened in 1996. Cram (2006a) states that in 1995, the Commission created and funded the Social Platform to act as its interlocutor for the social actors with the Commission at the Social Forum. Starting from the first European Social Policy Forum, the Commission's interactions with NGOs have been labelled as civil dialogue (see also Cullen 2005; Sánchez-Salgado 2007; Cram 2006a; Greenwood 2007b).

Next, the Platform became a formal legal entity under Belgian law, and this change was prompted by critiques concerning representativeness and accountability of the NGOs. In the late 1990s, as shown in the previous chapter, the European Economic and Social Committee (EESC) asserted that EU NGOs should adopt a statute in order to prove their legitimacy (EESC 1999). The Commission accepted the EESC's proposal (Com 2002, 704 final; Com 2006, 194 final). In turn, the leaders of the Platform started to debate whether EU support would be suspended if the Platform did not adopt a legal statute. Since the Social Platform depended on EU funding, it adapted a statute in 2001 and became an independent legal entity under Belgian law.

In its internal governance statute, which was adopted in 2006, the Social Platform introduces itself as the *Platform of European Social NGOs (Social Platform)*, the alliance of representative European federations and networks of non-governmental organisations active in the social sector.[2] Cullen says 'the platform marked the first attempt to gather a group of NGOs characterised by diverse organisational cultures, sectoral interests and ideological orientations within such a collaborative context' (Cullen 2005: 72). Forty-seven European NGOs in social policy (in July 2013) make up the Platform, and they can be organised as a federation or a network at EU level. They claim to represent thousands of organisations, associations and voluntary groups at local, regional, and national levels, including organisations of women, older people, the disabled, the unemployed, people affected by poverty, homosexuals, young people, children and families, and organisations addressing such issues as social justice, homelessness, health and reproductive rights and racism (see note).[3]

The goals of the Platform are twofold, although perhaps contradictory. The Platform asserts its aims in the internal statute as follows:

> the eradication of poverty and the elimination of social exclusion; the elimination of discrimination in all its forms and the promotion of equality for all; equality between women and men in all areas of life; the promotion of participatory democracy; the engagement of social NGOs in an enhanced, structured civil dialogue at the EU level; and the involvement of people experiencing or at risk of poverty, exclusion and discrimination in decision-making processes affecting them.
> (Social Platform, *Internal Statue*, 2004)[4]

The Platform, however, reports its objectives in EU governance to the Commission in different terms, for example, as instituting regular input on EU policy formulation, engaging network actions with multiple stakeholders (including EU institutions, other NGOs and trade unions), promoting exchange and practices for enabling mutual exchange of information, and creating more democratic, open and accountable systems (SP, AR 2001[5]). These aims presented by the Platform in its various communication tools can help us understand what the Platform is, the purposes it works to achieve and its ambitions, desires and motivations.

A case study on the Social Platform

The Social Platform is a NGO network that endeavours to solve social problems and maintain equality by engaging in EU decision-making settings. To attain its goals, it, in the broadest terms, deals with the following issues: corporate social responsibility; demographic and social change; employment; equality and anti-discrimination; fundamental rights; the future of Europe; the integration of migrants; the Lisbon Strategy for 'growth and jobs'; participatory democracy and good governance; public procurement; services of general interest and social and health services; social protection and social inclusion; and sustainable development (SP, WP 2005).

The Social Platform offers two types of membership, full membership and associate membership. It also allows some organisations to participate in the Platform's work as observers. Full membership is restricted to European NGOs; international NGOs can engage with the Platform only as associate members. National NGOs, on the other hand, are generally accredited as observers. As stated in the statute and internal rules[6] of the Social Platform, the criteria for being a full member of the Platform include being a network or federation that comprises organisations, not individuals. Further criteria include establishment as non-profit and non-governmental, an active role in the social sector, working to promote the general interest and social cohesion and having separate legal personality. Further, according to the Platform's internal rules, prospective members should prove they are structured and managed in a democratic way. The Platform officially states that democratic NGOs are run by an elected body whose decisions and membership are not subject to approval by any external entity. As shown in the previous chapter, these criteria show a strong parallel with the criteria for NGOs' representativeness, which were drawn up by the EESC. The Platform thus determines which organisations can be its members according to the moral imperatives of political rationality, i.e. a certain form of organisation, which suggests a good and appropriate way of organising. This implies that only those organisations that adapt to these requirements can take part in the Platform (and thus in the new forms of governance), consider the rationalities of governance and project new forms of subjects – subjects that are constituted, motivated, directed and guided in order to become an actor in European governance. This chapter will further elaborate on what the Platform understands by democratic management and how this is performed.

There are two main differences between full members and associates. First, although both have to pay membership fees, the Platform reimburses the expenses of full members when they attend meetings of the General Assembly and the Steering Group. The associate members are responsible for their own expenses when they take part in the Platform's meetings. Second, associate members have no right to vote or fill administrative positions. The voting rights of both can be suspended if membership fees are not paid. Observers can attend meetings of the General Assembly, but have no speaking or voting rights. They are kept informed of the Platform's activities and invited to its seminars and conferences.[7] With respect to members' perceptions of Platform membership, the secretariats of the European Network Against Racism and Solidar consider the

Platform to be a good example of the collaboration of civil society at the European level (C. Reuter and P. Charhon, personal communication, May 2009). Since the Platform is one of the main umbrellas for the NGO networks[8] and is entitled to participate in the Commission consultation regime, it can be further argued that Platform membership enhances credibility within the NGO community and the EU institutional milieu.[9]

The funding of the Platform is one of the most controversial issues that have hindered its positive reception. The Social Platform is funded under the Community Action Programme to Promote Active European Citizenship grant programme. Critics claim that this threatens the autonomy of the Platform. Some have defended EU funding by comparing it with state financial support for political parties (Fazi and Smith 2006; and see Sánchez-Salgado 2007). Commission support accounts for 70 per cent of the Platform's total budget. Funds for specific projects make up 13 per cent of its budget, and the remainder comes from membership fees and other contributions from members (SP, AR 2007). The Platform indicates that this fund is used for 'providing information to its members on relevant EU developments, organising forums for them to exchange experiences and share knowledge, and arranging meetings between representatives of the EU Institutions and social NGOs'[10]. However, the budget that is assessed in the annual report 2007 shows that administrative costs, including the salaries of the Secretariat, constitute 70 per cent of total costs.[11]

The Social Platform is primarily a lobbying organisation that aims to influence EU institutions. Table 4.1 shows which EU institutions and sub-departments the Platform has contact with. As this table shows, it can access most EU institutions, whereas it has more strained relations with the European Commission. The Social Platform is financed by the Commission, meeting with it twice a year, and is, together with its members, registered as an interest group in the Commission's online database for taking part in online consultations. The Platform is also in contact with several DGs that are relevant to the Platform's policy focus. It has, however, recently developed relations with the European Parliament, particularly following NGOs being recognised by the Parliament (e.g. in the Gabrowska report (European Parliament 2008) and two citizen AGORAs [NGO meetings in the Parliament]). The Platform (and some other NGOs) and now try to reach the European Council (P. Charhon, C. Reuter, L. Sedou and G. Siklossy, personal communication, May 2009).

The Parliament did not support the Commission's project of incorporating non-elected entities into EU decision-making processes, and it thus ignored the NGOs for some time – up until the time it organised the first AGORA in 2007 (see the previous chapter). As has been shown, by launching the AGORAs as an alternative to the Commission's online consultations, the Parliament challenged the Commission's functional and Brussels-based approach to civil society. Although this approach could have had negative impacts on the privileged position of the Social Platform in the Commission's approach, the Platform approached the Parliament's challenge positively, arguably due to two aspects (C. Reuter, P. Charhon and G. Siklossy, personal communication, May 2009).[12]

Table 4.1 The Social Platform's contacts with European institutions and other actors

European Commission Directorate Generals	European Parliament Committees	Council of the European Union and permanent representations of EU Member States	Other EU institutions and agencies	Other stakeholders
DG SANCO (Health and Consumer Protection) DG COM (Competition) DG ECFIN (Economic and Financial Affairs) DG EMP (Employment, Social Affairs and Equal Opportunities) DG EAC (Education and Culture) DG INT (Internal Market and Services) DG JLS (Justice, Freedom and Security) DG ELARG (Enlargement) DG Research DG Budget SG	LIBE (Citizens' Freedoms and Rights, Justice and Home Affairs) EMPL (Employment and Social Affairs) JURI (Legal Affairs and the Internal Market) ENVI (Environment, Public Health and Consumer Policy) AFCO (Constitutional Affairs) FEMM (Women's Rights and Equal Opportunities)	EPSCO Council (Employment, Social Policy, Health and Consumer Affairs) JLS Council (Justice and Home Affairs) European Council	EESC (European Economic and Social Committee) CoR (Committee of the Regions) FRA (European Union Agency for Fundamental Rights) Eurofound (European Foundation for the Improvement of Living and Working Conditions)	ETUC (European Trade Union Confederation) EEB (European Environmental Bureau) CSCG (Civil Society Contact Group) Think tanks

Source: SP, AR 2007: 6. Table created by author, drawing on the information provided by the source.

First, with the AGORAs, civil society organisations were officially recognised by the Parliament. As this means that the Parliament has accepted NGOs as legitimate actors of governance, it was an important step for the NGOs in that the Parliament confirmed their relevance to EU politics. Second, in contrast to the Commission's approach that defined the NGOs as mere lobbyists and consultants, the Parliament officially recognised NGOs as actors of civil society (SP, *Reference Paper: Shaping civil dialogue*, 2008). In sum, it can be argued that in order to not leave the championship of the ECS discourse to the Commission, the Parliament strategically contacted the NGOs in the Brussels power game.

EU politics, governance turn and Platform

The roots for the idea of involving the NGOs to European decision-making stemmed from the Maastricht Treaty (1992), inscribed into the Green Paper on Social Policy and put into practice with the European Social Forums. This project can be considered as part of Delors' project to create European social and economic space; and, it continued under Santer Commission (1995–9). However, the Santer Commission had to resign in 1999 due a corruption scandal about the mismanagement of EU funding and nepotism in recruitment. The Prodi Commission (1999–2004) started working under such conditions, under which the prestige of the Commission was significantly damaged. The Prodi Commission, on the one hand, engaged in a decisive administrative reform of the Commission, based on the Kinnock Report, which suggested an activity-based management strategy, as well as including a proposal for a new staff policy (Kassim 2008).[13] On the other hand, the Commission proposed a new administrative-mentality for the EU institutions with the *White Paper on European Governance* (WPEG) (Com 2001, 428 final), including opening the decision-making processes to civil society. The *White Paper* was received critically by academic community (see Joerges *et al.* 2001), who considering it a political intervention into EU structure.

In the early 2000s, the Commission placed special emphasis on creating a European civil society (ECS) discourse: it incorporated ECS into European governance by granting stakeholder status (see Chapter 3). The Commission's ex-president, Romano Prodi, explained the role of ECS in (the new) Europe as follows: 'It is time to realise that Europe is not just run by European institutions but by national, regional and local authorities too – and by civil society' (SP, AR 2004: 5). As Prodi declared, the representatives of ECS, the EU NGOs, started engaging in EU politics during the 2000s. For instance, the Platform took part in three important incidents: governance reform, drafting a Constitution for Europe (2002–4) and enlargement (2002–4).

The WPEG was a key Commission initiative for an administrative reform of EU governance (see the previous chapter for details). Despite the Parliament's critical stance toward civil society's engagement in the decision-making process due to their accountability and representation problems, the WPEG defined civil society as the constituents and stakeholders of governance. The WPEG was the continuation of a governance turn fostered by the Commission with the introduction of new modes of governance, such as the Open Method of Coordination (OMC) (Mosher and Trubek 2003; Eberlein and Kerwer 2004; and Haahr 2005). The Platform's annual report shows that the Platform participated in preparations of the WPEG. In this respect,

> it has widely circulated its *Democracy, Governance and European NGOs Position Paper* [published in 2001], was an active participant in the hearings held by the Commission ahead of the release of the Paper, organised meetings with various members of the Governance team, spoke at numerous conferences, and wrote many articles on this issue. In addition, members of the Governance team spoke at various events held by the Platform.
>
> (SP, AR 2001: 14)

Following the WPEG, the Platform concentrated on putting the promises of the WPEG into practice:

> The Platform will make proposals to the Commission regarding the implementation of the recommendations of the Commission's 2001 *White Paper on Governance*, which proposes more structured and consistent forms of consultation with society, including the establishment of 'partnership agreements' with NGOs in certain sectoral areas.
>
> (SP, WP 2003: 12)

Furthermore, it tried to secure a legal basis for consultations: 'a legal basis for civil dialogue between decision-makers and NGOs is crucial in building a socially just Europe that is able and willing to take the needs of all into account' (SP, AR 2001: 14). This position has not been altered during the 2000s. In others words, the Platform declared its willingness to participate in new power configurations, emphasising that it was capable of fulfilling its roles.

However, the Commission has not been willing to formalise its relations with the Platform. These relations have rather been set up in a somewhat nebulous way (i.e. biannual meetings and internet consultations, especially during pre-policy formulation processes), so that the Platform's engagement in formal decision-making processes has been kept at a minimum level (Fazi and Smith 2006). In the meantime, multi-stakeholder forums, which were presented in the WPEG as an indicator of partnership governance, were not commonly implemented. The Platform participated in only one forum in which it formally enjoyed stakeholder status: the 'Multi-stakeholder Forum' between 2002 and 2004, which dealt with Corporate Social Responsibility, a policy initiative published by the Commission in 2002. Other stakeholders in this initiative were business representatives, such as UNICE and the European Roundtable of Industrialists, and the ETUC (SP, AR 2002, 2003 and 2004).

Convention on the future of Europe, constitution turn and the Platform

Against this backdrop, the Convention on the Future on Europe was set in 2001 by the European Council, which prepared the *Draft Treaty establishing a Constitution for Europe* in 2003. The Convention concerned EU NGOs in the sense that they were included in the discussions. Yet, one of the vice-presidents of the Convention, Guliano Amato, emphasised the importance of the 'support of civil society in legitimising the final outcome of the Convention's work' (*Economist* 2004). In turn, some scholars also considered this as a democratising promise (De Schutter 2002; Magnette 2003). During the Convention period the Social Platform played an important role. It mobilised the largest NGO networks working in the fields of human rights, environment, and development in order to take part in the debate. With respect to this, during the early 2000s, the Platform initiated several campaigns about the *Future of Europe*. These campaigns, such as the Future of Europe, Citizens' Assembly and act4Europe, aimed at mobilising the NGO community for EU issues.

The Platform launched the Future of Europe initiative in 2001. The Platform's 2001 annual report states that this initiative 'in a way marked the broadening of the Governance debate'. The Platform once again in this report emphasised that 'it plays a leading role in bringing together the various European NGO sectors' (SP, AR 2001: 14). For instance, the Citizens' Assembly project was introduced within the context of the Future of Europe initiative. It was held in Brussels in December 2001 and continued until 2004. The Platform claimed that Citizens' Assembly mobilised more than 700 NGO delegates, government representatives and members of civil society from all over Europe (SP, AR 2001: 14). It focused on different topics related to the future of Europe, including globalisation, migration, the eradication of poverty, the EU Charter of Fundamental Rights, and the European Constitution (ibid.). In 2001, many of the participating NGOs joined in drafting the declaration, 'Europe is our Future'. This declaration suggested extending EU authority in several areas:

> We call for the extension of authority of the European Union in the fields of employment, poverty, social exclusion, equality between men and women, sustainable development, services of general interest, food safety, cultural diversity and the fight against discrimination in order to guarantee an upward convergence of policies and national legislation, notably from the point of view of fundamental rights.
>
> (SP, AR 2001:15)

By the leadership of the Social Platform, a group of NGO network coalitions formed the Civil Society Contact Group (CSCG), which initiated a campaign about the *Future of Europe* (act4europe) – i.e. the Convention's work – aimed at mobilising the national level NGOs.[14] The CSCG started as a loose network, with its organisational work and management initially handled by the Platform. For instance, the Platform hosted and co-funded its coordinator person. The

Platform declared the objectives of the *act4europe* project as follows: 'Citizens have grown dangerously disillusioned with the European project. The Convention on the Future of Europe is thus a vital opportunity to reverse this trend' (SP, AR 2002:9). With respect to this, act4europe published a toolkit for NGOs in order to inform them about the ongoing debate on the *Future of Europe* and activate them in participating in it.[15] The Campaign's second toolkit about the work of the Convention was distributed at the *Social Policy Forum* in 2002. At the end, the Draft Treaty establishing a Constitution for Europe contained an article about participatory democracy: Article I-46. This article, then, took place with a minor change replacing the use of constitution with the treaties in the ratified Lisbon Treaty, and appearing this time as the Article-11 (see participatory democracy section for a discussion about this article and the Platform's reaction to the notion participatory democracy and governance). Participatory democracy, the norm of which was enshrined in the Lisbon treaty, involves not only the involvement of civil society in EU decision-making processes, but also allow the citizens submitting any legal proposal, with no less than one million signature.

The Platform also took an active role in the Constitution ratification process. It was invited to the Convention on drafting a European Constitution with other stakeholders and played a role in mobilising NGOs, trying to orient their interests towards the EU. It tried 'to facilitate the engagement of social NGOs at national level to engage with the debates around the ratification of the Treaty' (SP, WP 2005: 17). In this respect, it provided legal expertise and analysis about the Constitution and prepared a toolkit for NGOs together with the Civil Society Contact Group (CSCG), a coalition of European NGO networks. Furthermore, it organised a conference on the Constitution with the Contact Group and a seminar for Platform members on activating NGOs in ratification debates.

The Platform's own perceptions about the Future of Europe initiative and the Citizens' Assembly project as shown in quote below can help us draw an initial conclusion:

> [This] was the first time such a broad coalition of organisations had united to organise an event of this nature, showing that civil society is ready to talk with leaders in a peaceful and constructive manner.
>
> (SP, *AR* 2001: 14)

> The organisation of the Citizens' Assembly in Brussels (December 2001) demonstrated the Platform's ability to mobilise European civil society organisations, and to provide an effective, peaceful, and high-profile civil society presence at EU Summits.
>
> (SP, WP 2001:1)

First, The Platform revealed that it was, itself, along with the other EU NGOs, the right agent and partner in the process of European political restructuring. NGOs presented their consent and willingness to be agents in this process; thus, they declared that they were ready for formalised deliberations with the political power. In the meantime, they carefully drew a line between themselves and the protesting and deliberating actors of civil society, and thus, in a way, confirmed that they would not challenge the new constellation. The Platform, then, perpetuated the idea of engagement of social actors in deliberative settings, while discarding from collective action the protest as a modus operandi. In other words, the Platform and the EU NGO networks seemed to have had high hopes about the practice of being involved in the deliberative settings. As Young (2001) points out, however, empirical studies on deliberative arrangements showed that those settings are prone to be dominated by the white male power elites and by hegemonic discourse. Given this, Young (ibid.) continues, stating that protest is preferred by social actors as a more effective way of political communication in raising the awareness of the public and the political authorities.

The second conclusion of the Citizen's Assembly is that the Platform and some other European NGOs alike were willing to further the European political project, revealing zeal for the idea of deepening European integration. The interviews conducted within the scope of this research also confirmed continuation of these thoughts. In other words, the Platform and the NGO community alike have acted like pan-European intellectuals who had shifted their interests to the EU, while striving for the European cause. The founding fathers of the European project have predicted transformation of the private or instrumental interests of the actors towards the EU. Yet, the Europeanisation of civil society extends beyond this anticipation by gaining the consent of social actors in striving for the European project. Practised in this way, Europeanisation of civil society has resulted in the usage of the sponsored NGOs as the interlocutors or brokers of the EU. This practice undermines the presumed role of the NGOs in creating alternative projects or in carrying the subaltern projects to European level.

Third, the kind of participation that the Platform advocates has an uneasy relationship with normative democracy. This functional interpretation of democracy has been found to be problematic, as it neglects the institutions of representative democracy and forming collective will processes. This view assumes that citizens are represented by the NGO networks just as the Platform per se. However, as a critique of this, some commentators argued that having participated in 'civil dialogue', the Platform helped in advancing the Commission's institutional power and its consultation regime (e.g. Smismans 2007; Cram 2006), as well as in legitimising the Commission's rule in the respective policy fields (Cram 2006). We will elaborate on the theme of participation in detail under the participatory democracy section. Now I would like to turn my attention to the Platform's influences on the NGO community.

Enlargement and network visits

The political rationalities of the governance turn imply governing society through the dynamics and resources of society (Kohler-Koch and Rittberger 2006; Jachtenfuchs 2001). Thus, it meant empowering citizens' associations, so that they would be capable of managing the complex requirements of bureaucracy. The Platform, with this regard, not only fulfilled a stakeholder role in joining the Brussels consultation regime, but also took on the role of conveying the knowledge of EU governance to the NGO community. It initiated several conferences and seminars to circulate the imperatives of new modes of governance among its members to inform them about the existence of these policies and train them for the new era. During the 2000s, the Platform had a special focus on NGOs in Central and Eastern Europe, organising the following network visits to new member states: Poland (2002), Czech Republic (2003), Cyprus (2004), Hungary (2004) and Latvia (2004). It organised conferences and seminars to train these NGOs in political advocacy, fundraising, communication techniques and skills, and NGO management. It published toolkits about state-NGO relations, such as 'Civil dialogue in the candidate countries: Building bridges across a wider Europe' (SP, AR 2002: 19). The Platform's training activities can be considered, on the one hand, as intrinsic to political socialisation of the EU (i.e. representing the EU as a legitimate ruling entity); and, on the other, as an endeavour to constitute a certain NGO type, a collective action style.

The Platform and the discourse on bridging the gap with citizens

The Turin IGC summit in 1996 diagnosed the legitimacy crisis of EU governance in a lack of citizens' interest; since then the motto of bridging the gap with the citizens has been recognised as norm by the EU institutions (Kohler-Koch and Finke 2007). Accordingly, *White Paper on European Governance* (Com 2001, 428 final; see also previous chapter) suggested overcoming this by relating its proposals about governance reforms to re-conceptualisation of democracy. This new type of democracy would integrate social groups into decision-making processes and implementation of policies, linking citizens' interests to governance. The Platform, on behalf of its member NGOs, volunteered for this task:

> NGOs stimulate democratic renewal by providing a channel for citizens to engage in dialogue with policy-makers.... We believe that creating this kind of ongoing dialogue with politicians and policy-makers will help bring about a European Union which is more in touch with its citizens, and is more focused on improving their lives.
>
> (SP, AR 2005:3)

During the early 2000s, the Platform insisted that it was 'an important way of helping bridge the gap between citizens and the EU institutions and therefore reflecting the views of citizens' (SP, WP 2005: 7). Conny Reuter (personal communication, May 2009), the president of the Platform, explains the role of the Platform in this process:

> We must defend the interests of all our member organisations; on the other hand, we must connect to citizens. The most important challenge is to understand, this kind of lobby, what we are doing, is not only for one or two

topics. We have connected with the citizens and given them the idea that through us they are involved in EU politics, so that they participate.

Nonetheless, participation in the way the president of the Platform describes – and has been advocated by the Platform since its emergence (see below a detailed discussion of the Platform's position) – is a theoretically and practically contested issue (Kohler-Koch 2010). This functional interpretation to democracy neglects the institutions of representative democracy and collective will formation processes, and assumes that citizens are represented by the NGO networks like the Platform per se (Smismans 2006).

The Platform's participation in EU governance on the other hand can be seen as insignificant. Based on the Commission's definition, the roles of the Platform in EU governance can be defined, first, with its epistemic contribution, particularly to the Commission in its proposal preparation process; second, coordination of policies, such as of Open Method of Coordination, in the EU (see also Obradovic 2005). The previous research, however, shows that the Platform and other NGOs alike are not well integrated into the implementation and coordination of EU policies, if not totally excluded; though a few successful practices have been observed, such as in Finland (Smismans 2006). Further, the Commission's consultation regime with the Platform, which is also named as civil dialogue since 1996, has several shortcomings, encumbering the significance of the Platform's participation. Namely, the consultations does not go beyond 'right to be heard' (since there is no legal ground for this practice); the Platform does not receive appropriate feedback, and it is not informed about whether and how its opinions had an impact on policy proposals (Obradovic 2005). In sum, considering also the findings of the earlier research, it can be argued that the Commission's discourse on participatory governance, involving civil society actors into EU governance, does not necessarily result in effective and actual contribution of the Platform, at least for now. Moreover, the most important function of civil dialogue is considered to be in legitimising the decision-making processes within the EU institutional set-up (Kohler-Koch and Finke 2007). As a critique of this, having participated in civil dialogue, the Platform does not necessarily legitimise EU at large, but helped in advancing the Commission's institutional power and its consultation regime (Smismans 2007; Cram 2006a), as well as helping to normalise the Commission's ruling in the respective policy fields (Cram, ibid.).

Social Platform and social Europe

The Social Platform is primarily a network of NGO networks working on social policy. As indicated, it emerged as a consequence of the *Green Paper on Social Policy* published in 1993. This paper marked the Commission's early attempts at expanding its room to manoeuvre with respect to social policies, a policy domain for which the Community method did not apply. The Commission, then, chose a strategy of mobilising NGOs, in 1997 detailing the roles of voluntary organisations in social policy (see previous chapter). Following the Lisbon Treaty in

2000, NGOs were not only related to social policy, but also to the new modes of governance (e.g. Open Method of Coordination) and the democratic deficit of EU governance. Therefore, we examine both the Social Platform's position on social policies and the democratic deficit. The following focuses on social policies; we will detail the Platform's views towards the Commission's policies for legitimising EU governance at the end of the chapter.

I will be interrogating what the Platform thinks and does in terms of EU social policies. I will try to show how a Foucault-inspired interpretation of Europeanisation enables us to understand their thoughts and actions. To be clear, the central question that motivates this analysis is how EU social policies and the Platform's perception of these policies may relate to the creation of a new form of subjectivity and a new form of governmentality – defined as an ethics and ethos (Larner 2000). Posed in this way, this inquiry makes it necessary to think about social policies developed at the EU level from the perspective of governmentality. Nonetheless, this attempt has significant limitations, as governmentality approach to EU social policy is still rudimentary (see below) and its improvement is far beyond the confines of this book, as this book particularly focuses on the Commission's civil society discourse and its implications on the Platform. Within these considerations, when applied, this elaboration considers the EU's interests (particularly those of the Commission) in social policies with respect to the following questions: Which aspects does the European social policy entail? On which aspects of human life and through which instruments does it plan to intervene – in other words, what is the *ethical substance* upon which it acts? And finally, what does it hope to achieve – what is its *telos*? The exploration of these questions can enable us to locate the Social Platform in this project.

Governmentality differs from other interpretations of European social policy. Two such options for studying social policy are the allocation of governing responsibilities between many different actors (Mosher and Trubek 2003, Eberlein and Kerwer 2004) and policy framework analysis (Ferrera *et al.* 2002; Begg and Berghman 2002). Daly (2006) states that, the former, favoured by the political scientists, is the most common approach to European social policies. This view suggests the social dimension of the EU is 'hollow and, over time, halting and limited' thus 'the EU is harshly for not having achieved systemic change in national social policy and convergence towards a supranational model of social policy' (Daly, ibid.: 463). The second view, suggested mostly by social policy specialists, argues 'the EU has an articulated social policy in number of key domains (for example, worker protection, health and safety in employment, equal opportunities between men and women)' (Daly, ibid.). As Daly outlines, a newly emerging sociological literature (e.g. Carmel 2003; Savio and Palola 2004) on the other suggests:

> to understand EU social policy, one must look beyond it, to the EU's engagement with, if not European society, then a European social realm. In this, the smallest and generally newest literature, the EU is represented as

carving out a social space for itself which allows it to fashion key aspects of social identity, institutions and social relations in the Member States, as well as a social sphere that transcends national boundaries. Social policy, then, is not an end itself.

(Daly 2006: 463)

Pertinent with the latter, the governmentality approach, then, tries to grasp the underlying ethics and morality of these policies: it implies an ontology, ascetics, deontology and telos of government (see chapter one for the elaboration of this conceptual discussion). It concerns the relations between power and subjectivity. For instance, it examines what has been promoted by the European Employment Strategy (EES) (1997) and Lisbon Strategy (2000) as an appropriate and good way of handling social protection, health care, employment, and social integration in that political programming target the individual as an object of manipulation, and an area of intervention.

Yet, the discussion on the EU social policy is beyond the limits of this book: it relates work to social protection and it entails an understanding that can be summarised as making work pay for welfare provisions. The tenets of these policies were depicted in the EES (1997) as activation, adaptability, flexibility and the entrepreneurial spirit. The Lisbon Strategy integrated lifelong learning, skills development and constant mobilisation into the very heart of the new social security paradigm. In other words, European social policies relate social policies to employment and concentrate on nourishing individuals' skills so that they can take part in the labour market. Begg and Berghman (2002: 186) assess this turn as 'redirecting attention from employment to employability and from job security to lifelong learning'. However, I argue that this redirection is not a mere policy change, but can also be studied as intrinsic to an ethos of constituting a new subjectivity – a subjectivity that takes on the responsibility of its own risk and self-development (e.g. Barry *et al.* 1996; Simons 1995; Rose 1996; Lemke 2002; Cruikshank 1999).

EU social policies that address social exclusion, with this regard, show certain parallels with the doctrines of Third Way, and we have already debated this issue and the connection between Third Way and participation discourses in Chapter 2. Dean (2006: 5) elaborates the shift with respect to the conceptualisation of equality and inclusion: 'Third Way has redefined "equality as *inclusion* and inequality as *exclusion*". Objectives of equality and social justice are no longer concerned with material outcomes, but with opportunity structures'. Dean, then, concludes that 'the primary role of social policies is not the distribution of resources to provide for people's needs, but to mitigate risk and to *enable* people individually to manage risk' (ibid.: 5). In a similar vein, the EES and Lisbon strategy concentrated on developing (activating) the skills of the individual as the major policy of the new social policy paradigm. In our work, it is argued that this paradigm has further consequences for subject, market and state relations.

The EU social policy, thus, can be thought of pertaining to the following aspects of our survey. First, the proposed method of social policy governance,

Open Method of Coordination ascribes NGOs the task of monitoring the *National Action Plans* (NAP) – though, as mentioned, this has not been put into practice well (Obradovic 2005). With respect to this, the Platform, then, organised training seminars for the national organisations about their (latent) role in the OMC and concentrated on mobilising them to force their governments to be included in the NAPs. The OMC is also pertinent with the conceptual concerns of this book in terms of its relationship with the advanced forms of liberal art of government. According to Haahr (2005), the OMC on the one hand recognises the autonomy of the states; but, on the other restrains them as they are subjected to a certain calculative and disciplinary regime. This implies it gives liberty to the member states to comply with a pre-set of indicators (e.g. in the fields of social inclusion and employment) and benchmarks, However, it also entails mechanisms of surveillance through peer reviews and non-binding monitoring of the implementation of these policies. The evaluation of the success of the OMC is not within the scope of this study. However, it can be pointed out that the peer reviews of the country reports, which are discussed at the Council meetings, proved to be inefficient in disciplining the poor performers – and replacing the public pressure; since diplomatic courtesy, mostly, prevented their public embarrassments (Wyplosz 2010).

Second, the EU social policy can be studied in relation to the governmentality approach, the theoretical focus of this study. Foucault suggests that neoliberalism (referring to German *ordo* liberalism and Chicago School) differs from classical liberalism (e.g. of Smith and Ferguson), as it abandons the very premise of the latter: the distinction between the politics and economy.[16] Therefore, neoliberalism – as Foucault defines – is based on an anti-naturalist claim that suggests markets can be constituted and kept alive and capitalist rationality can be re-defined, considering particularly the failure of liberalism during Nazism (Lemke 2001). This allows different forms of state intervention to bolster market competition, such as through legal measures. Moreover, this new form of liberalism, as Chicago school maintained, 'embraces the entirety of human action to the extent that this is characterised by the allocation of scant resources for competing goals (ibid.: 197)'. With respect to this reading, social domain is defined as an extension of the economic domain, which implies market rationalities, such as cost-benefit calculations, can be applied to decision-making processes in social life (ibid.: 200). In articulating the Foucault's lecture on neoliberal governmentality, Lemke (ibid.: 200) posits how rationalities of neoliberalism differ from the one that classical liberalism envisaged:

> Now, neo-liberalism admittedly ties the rationality of the government to the rational action of individuals; however, its point of reference is no longer some pre-given human nature, but an artificially created form of behaviour. Neo-liberalism no longer locates the rational principle for regulating and limiting the action of government in a natural freedom that we should all respect, but instead it posits an artificially arranged liberty: in the entrepreneurial and competitive behaviour of economic-rational individuals.

Whereas in the classic liberal conception, homo economicus forms an external limit and the inviolable core of governmental action, in the neo-liberal thought of the Chicago School he becomes a behaviouristically manipulable being and the correlative of a governmentality which systematically changes the variables of the 'environment' and can count on the 'rational choice' of the individuals.

Having interpreted liberalism in this way, Foucault was associated with the French regulation school of political economy (Power 2011), because social policy, then, according to this frame is 'not limited to transferring and redistributing monies but stands out for its active creation of the historical and social conditions of the market' (Lemke 2001: 195). The norms of the EU social policy strategy that aims to upgrade the skills of individuals, such as the activation, adaptability, entrepreneurial spirit, then can be assessed from this perspective. Then, they may well be conceived as attempts of intervention into the conduct of humans.[17] Third, the EU social policy can be studied in terms of the transformation from welfare to workfare (Jessop 2002a, 2004, 2007) and from employment to employability. This does not necessarily contradict the arguments of Foucault, with its stress on the recommodification policies and targeting the abilities of humans as objects of political intervention for an economic purpose. When it comes to the Platform, the central questions are where it stands regarding this process and how it receives and perceives the EU social policy discourse.

Social protection and empowering of citizen's associations

In 1998, the Platform presented its position on Europeanising social policies in a policy paper, *Adapting to Social Changes*. In this document the Platform set out the principles of social protection, the responsibilities of EU institutions and member states in new governance methods, and the role of NGOs, while making suggestions of its own. The Platform defended two principles of social protection: the recognition of social protection as a fundamental right and recognition of social protection within the scope of a general interest at the European level. The latter underpins the social democratic sources of the Platform's position. Accordingly, the document emphasised the values of social protection as solidarity, redistribution and social responsibility. These values, in fact, are different from what neoliberal forms of governmentality (or advanced liberalism) suggest. Contrary to advanced liberalism's notion of empowering the individual to take responsibility for his or her own risks, the Platform defends the notion of collective risk-taking. The Platform's redistribution proposal aims to correct market inequalities. Furthermore, the Platform recommends empowering citizens' associations in terms of sharing responsibility collectively. The conclusion to be drawn from these principles is that the Platform tries to generate a notion of universal from within a discourse that puts a great emphasis on particularisation. The reflection of this particularistic discourse can be observed within the contemporary ethos of the art of government – advanced liberalism (an ethics of individualism). The Platform's suggestion, in that sense, grasps both the shortcomings of neoliberal discourse and European governance in formulating a link between particular and universal. Neo-Foucauldian scholars have emphasised that the tenets of current forms of power stress technologies of agency (e.g. the notion that there is no society as such, only the individual). For instance, governmentality as a form of power defined by Foucault involves both individualising and totalising aspects (Foucault 1991). The Platform's stance on social policy, as suggested in *Adapting to Social Changes,* is a suggestion for ethically entrenching this link by conceptualising a European general will by reallocating risk and any repercussions of market failures. However, one crucial point addressed, in this respect, by the Platform requires special attention: the empowerment of citizens' associations. Associations, according to the proposal, carry the burden of risk while involving a process of general will formation. In other words, the Platform suggests a kind of associational democracy that would embody the ethical burden of general interest formation (through a republican interpretation) and the functional encumbrances of problem solving (e.g. the associational democracy of Cohen and Rogers 1997). The document explains, 'identifying new roles needs bringing out new forms of solidarity, participating in dialogue on national and European social policies, organising and managing services, and undertaking any social protection assignments given to them by public authorities'. The Platform's assessments here can be interpreted as a new form of state, society and market relations. They denote a project of not leaving the space to market dynamics that are left beyond the control of the state. On the one hand, it specifies strengthening supranational governance institutions (and rescaling governance), while on the other, it requires strengthening extra-governmental associations of citizens:

> [T]he place of the non-profit sector, whose organisation is more flexible and responsive than the state, must be maintained and recognised. Close to citizens and their needs, non-profit organisations manage social services in accordance with the values that they hold as their own: taking the person into consideration as a whole, and not just as a consumer or a user, the provision of specific guidance and mediation for people in difficulty, and the availability of voluntary work. When delegating services to the non-profit sector, the state should provide adequate resources for it to fulfil its role: clear conditions of co-operation, and sufficient and sustainable finances.
> (SP, *Adapting to Social Changes* 1998: 12)

Sharing responsibilities through subsidiarity

Concerning the distribution of responsibilities in social policies, the Platform supports the subsidiarity principle. *Adapting to Social Changes* (SP 1998: 7) asserts on which levels the EU should take on responsibility: it 'should assert and guarantee social principles and standards', such as by 'including core obligatory rights in the treaties', conducting 'systematic impact studies on the social effects of legislation' and 'adapting structural funds'. The states, according to this formulation, 'should remain the guarantors of compulsory social protection systems'. This suggestion is, in fact, in line with the principles of the OMC; nevertheless, it suggests some different dimensions to the administration of social policies at the EU level. The first concerns the inclusion of a core of obligatory rights in the treaties. Having defined the EU level as a sort of constitutional guarantee for social rights, the Platform next suggests the implementation of social standards. Furthermore, the Platform suggests examining the effects of EU level legislation; it therefore defines the EU as an authorised auditor, whereas it perceives the national social policy regimes as amenable to EU surveillance. The last recommendation of the Platform, on the other hand, entails the adoption of European Structural Funds to be used particularly in the field of social policy.

Protection beyond employment and protection of employability

The Platform further argues in *Adapting to Social Changes* that the social protection policies should not be limited to employment, but should also extend to housing, education and the environment. It defends cash benefits and service provisions for dependent persons, including children and older people. Furthermore, it argues that flexibility measures should not hinder the stability and security of workers, particularly those who work under temporary and part-time contracts. In this document, the Platform recognises the neoliberal discourse on transformation from employment to employability by suggesting the conversion of unemployment insurance into employability insurance. The following quotation refers to this situation while relating to collective risk sharing:

> Workers, and even the unemployed, cannot be asked to pay for their careers and employability on their own; it must be an overall, collective responsibility shared between workers, companies, social partners, initial and lifelong training organisations and the education system, while providing compensation for career breaks and interruptions, both financially and in terms of social protection.
> (Social Platform, *Adapting to Social Changes* 1998: 14)

The critique of workfare

In 2000, the Platform asserted its five key priorities in social policy in a position paper, *Social Platform: Meeting the Challenges of the Century:* social inclusion, employment, universal standards on health care, equality between men and women and adequate pension systems. Although the Platform had presented its reservations on the EU's workfare-oriented social policy measures during the early 2000s, it concretised this critique in its response to the Commission's communication in *Making Work Pay* (2004). The position paper stressed that the Commission's approach was 'determined by the funding of social protection regimes rather than social inclusion objectives'. It was furthermore 'leading to cuts in benefits, or compulsory work, creating further poverty and social exclusion and undermining the very of essence European Social Model'. Activation discourse was the second point the Platform critiqued:

> The language of 'activation' and 'incentives' is indicative of the underlying assumption that the key reason for unemployment is that most of those who don't work are unwilling to do so, and therefore that employment can be stimulated by encouraging, even forcing, people to work.
> (SP, *Making Work Pay* 2004)

The Platform hence criticised the *re-commodification* of social policies, a process in which individuals would be left to their own devices in struggling with market forces. The Platform's proposal, therefore, was to (re)strengthen public services – just like in the golden days of the Keynesian welfare system. Accordingly, it suggested investing in public services to create more jobs, and it particularly recommended investing in the public sector. On the other hand, the Platform was content with the Commission's 'non-financial measures to help people work', including childcare facilities, training opportunities and lifelong learning.

The distribution of wealth

One of the aspects that might show the Platform's attitude towards European social policy is its position on the redistributive policies. Here, a comparison of the Platform's views with another umbrella network might be helpful to see conflicting views on this issue. The representatives of NGOs – the Platform and the Civil Society Contact Group (CSCG) – developed two different interpretations of how European funding should be allocated within Europe. In these papers they expressed the relevance of civil society's participation in the decision-making behind the EU budget.[18] According to the Platform and other representatives of NGOs, solidarity should not only be depicted as a matter for the member states, but it should also entail the relations between European citizens. This entailed the argument that 'redistribution should be considered as an inherent component of the project of European integration', which would 'preserve an element of solidarity essential to ensure that the EU project goes beyond the mere construction of a European economic area' (SP, *The EU Budget* 2007: 5). Asserting that 'the wealth which was created within Europe must be shared and redistributed', the Platform proposed that public policies should address poverty and social exclusion on the basis of the needs of the people, with 78 million people in EU member states living in poverty or at risk of poverty. In this respect, the Platform pointed out that European social funds play an important role in which NGOs could participate in the budget process, and hence in the allocation of resources, which the Platform calls a system of participatory budgeting.

Moreover, the Platform pointed out that the EU budget paid little attention to social challenges, such as 'social and demographic change, growing inequalities, rising poverty, deterioration of working conditions in certain sectors, downgrading of social protection systems, and lack of care infrastructures' (ibid.). In this respect, the Platform urged that, as opposed to growth and competiveness, EU governance should prioritise the principles of a 'social and sustainable Europe', a commitment that was adopted by EU leaders in 2006 (European Council 2006). If these were not applied, the Platform warned, people could be left marginalised, which could become 'a recipe for resentment, conflict and exclusion' (SP, *The EU Budget* 2007: 3).

The CSCG took a different position than the Platform to the EU budget. It argued that the EU had no right to intervene in the national politics of member states in the allocation of resources and redistributive measures. Therefore, the CSCG suggested, EU money should be spent on the basis of a value and rights-based budget (CSCG, *A Value and Rights-based Budget* 2008). To the CSCG, the tenets of rights in Europe comprise the rule of law, environmentalism, respect for diversity and gender equality. Whereas the Social Platform advocated a more proactive role for the EU in redistributive regimes, the CSCG suggested a limited role for the EU in setting up the framework for a high standard of living for all. Related to the value and rights approach it favoured, the CCSG defined a high standard of living as a 'healthy environment, access to decent work and lifelong learning opportunities, participation in culture, work-life balance, access to services of general interest, possibilities to take part in public debates, and legally binding social and political rights' (ibid.: 3).

In sum, a remarkable difference is observable between the discourses of the Platform and the CSCG. The latter claimed that the political rationalities, in this case the empowerment of individuals, should be determined by EU governing. In other words, the CSCG's proposal ascribed more intense governing roles for the EU. Addressing the EU as the appropriate institution for determining the parameters of a high standard of living, the CSCG's proposal rendered the very aspects of the constitution of the self (i.e. self-realisation, empowerment by political rationalities) as the object of EU government. In sum, the different approaches of NGO representatives towards the EU budget reveal no consensus about the limits and technologies of EU governing.

Postmodern paternalism

The European social policy tradition, particularly throughout continental Europe, has been identified with embedded liberalism, where the state became actively involved in the governance of the economy. In the current economic restructuring (defined as the workfare era), the state's role as an entrepreneur providing full employment for all is being de-emphasised (Jessop 2007). However, its paternalistic features – to take care of the population – have been redefined (Dean 2010). The postmodern paternalistic role of political power has now been defined as determining guidelines, frameworks and manuals for doing things and empowering the self as the master of its own care. The discourse of activation and lifelong learning are a reflection of this process. When it comes to EU governance, it can be argued that EU social policy has been developed as an art of government – guiding the actions of actors. One of the main reasons for this can be the EU's lack of control over the national labour market, industrial relations, social protection regimes and taxing. Hence, conducting the conduct of others (e.g. the member states, and also European citizens) seemed to be a viable option of EU social policy. Having sketched this trend, I argue that while the Platform is relatively critical of the workfare elements of this project, it recognises the idea of intervention into human realm through European instruments. In other words, the Platform has provided criticism of the transition from welfare to workfare, while supporting measures taken in the name of the employment to employability. Furthermore, with respect to a critique of workfare elements, it has limited this critique to persons that cannot participate in the labour market (both temporarily and permanently). It has, thus, provided a limited criticism for the *re-commodification* and *individualisation* processes, orienting to market-correcting instruments. Further, we should add that the Platform's criticism does not necessarily point out a contradiction within the rationalities of capitalism, but suggest solutions within its confines.

A rights-based approach to European social policy

Throughout the 2000s, the Social Platform has advocated a rights-based approach for the governance of social policies in the fields of social inclusion, pensions and health. In other words, it has debated these social policies from the vantage point of fundamental rights. An illustration of this can be seen in its contribution to the *Evaluation of the Open Method of Coordination on Social Protection and Inclusion* (2005: 4):

> At the core of the OMC must be a fundamental-rights approach to the policy areas covered, in line with the Charter of Fundamental Rights.... Fundamental rights are violated not only when people do not have access to basic means for survival, but when they are unable to live in dignity due to poverty and social exclusion.

The question then becomes: what kind of rights does this approach correspond to, i.e. positive or negative rights? It is difficult answer this only by looking at these lines; yet, it can be deduced that the Platform would affirm the state regulations fighting against the aspects that threaten the dignity of the humans, considering that The Platform conceives of the states as the guarantors of compulsory protection (SP, *Adoption to Social Change* 1998). When its emphasis on the state's role in empowering the individual through techniques of training and ensuring an adequate minimum income also taken into account, it can be argued that the Platform advocates a positive-rights approach. Thus, it addresses rights as an instrument for improving living conditions vis-à-vis the classical liberal notion of rights that aim to protect the individual from external intervention. Defined in this way, this approach differs from the traditional liberal interpretation that ascribes a minimal role to the state, strictly restricting the state intervention to economic and social realm. In other words, the Social Platform interprets these policies from the positive rights tradition. Nonetheless, a certain right in *itself* does not of necessity bring equality and wellbeing, but needs to be translated into policies and backed by enforcement measures. The competencies of the EU with this regard are, however, still limited.

Upgrading skills and lifelong learning

At this point, we should further focus on the Platform's ideas about lifelong learning and activation. In a position paper, *Social Investment: more quality jobs and solidarity* (2009), the Platform proposes some ideas for upgrading skills according to the needs of the new labour market. At the EU level, it suggested

> establish[ing] a European system of early identification of skill needs..., ensur[ing] that the European social fund targets initiatives for the most vulnerable and groups at risk, [the] establish[ment of] a per cent on the unemployment in training.
>
> (Ibid.: 5)

The Platform's proposals for upgrading skills at the national level, on the other hand, concern 'develop[ing] employability strategies for the most excluded, combin[ing] vocational training with basic skills training (especially for lower-skilled people), and invest[ing] in social and health services' (ibid.: 5). The Platform suggests further training strategies for the most excluded: 'In order to address early school leavers, non-formal education, vocational education and voluntary activities should be promoted as they often are more useful than formal education in developing social/interpersonal skills and self-esteem among vulnerable groups of children/youth' (ibid.: 6).

The Platform has affirmed lifelong learning (LLL) as a central tenet of social policies. However, it has proposed a wider definition that is not restricted to labour market integration. According to the Platform, lifelong learning and basic education can play a key role in combating social exclusion and promoting social cohesion. For example, 'active aging can mean that older adults remain engaged with their community and contribute in a voluntary capacity to their neighbourhood' (SP, *Contribution to Troika preceding the Informal Employment and Social Affairs Council* 2004). In this way, the Platform relates lifelong learning to civic education, and thus to the enhancement of social capital. The Platform, however, could have been more critical toward LLL discourse, just as it endeavoured to be with respect to flexibility discourse. Mitchell highlights how one can approach LLL discourse from a further critical point of view in her examination of EU education policies:

> [EU education] program priorities focus on individual pragmatism and on the skills and mobility needed for economic success rather than on the formation of a democratic person operating on within the framework of 'ethical

> liberalism' ... instead of a concept emphasising democratic tools, personal development and critical thinking, lifelong learning has transmogrified into a concept primarily affirming the constant formation of work skills.
>
> (Mitchell 2006: 391–2)

It can thus be concluded that the Platform's reactions to EU social policy reforms, on the one hand, recognise a new paradigm change due to a transformation entailed by economic restructuring; however, on the other, these reactions lead to several points of criticism. The Platform principally supports the Europeanisation of social policies, advocating the social inclusion discourse and the empowerment of the individual through techniques of lifelong learning and training. Suggested in this way, the Platform's suggestions can be seen pertinent with the tenets of Third Way, combining the social democratic spirit of state regulation with communitarian ideas of solidarity as well as policies of activation – which makes the human capacities amenable to political intervention and economic logic. One of the most pressing proposals of the Platform, in this respect, is the introduction of a minimum income within the EU. The Platform also supports policies of skill developing in order to adapt to changing economic conditions; this may well be regarded pertaining to the conduct of conduct via the political programme of forming a new subjectivity of an active citizenship who is empowered, but left with the responsibility of bearing the all risks.

Up to this point, I have tried to evaluate the Platform's position of the EU social policies. However, this inquiry into the relationship between the Platform and European social policy *qua* social policy should move beyond the Platform's mere thoughts and also consider the context of its emergence, as previously elaborated. To recapitulate, this concerns the relative enhancement of the EU competencies with respect to social policies at Maastricht Treaty, acceptance of the employment as a common European problem with the Amsterdam and the introduction of the Lisbon Strategy. The Platform's establishment, in this context, has been explained with the Commission's aspirations of strengthening its institutional legitimacy via mobilising collective action with an explicit (and implicit) connotation that it represents the common European interests with respect to regulation of European social policy (e.g. Cram 2006). Yet, the Commission has tried to justify its sponsorship with its reliance on the external expertise for its task of proposal preparations, as recognised in EU treaties; it implies the Platform's position papers, which are elaborated above, would function to supply *epistemic* assistance. Nevertheless, as also shown, the Platform's contribution (and other social actors alike) is trivial with this regard, considering the findings of the earlier research. On the other hand, some has approached the Platform's work positively, as it allows the presence of some voices that would otherwise be absent (Cullen 2010). The latter view relates to the Platform's (and similar actors' alike) legitimating role (Kohler-Koch and Finke 2007), one that is vaguely defined and as previously discussed here based on an assumption. To sum up, the ideas of the Platform, which are assessed above, does not have any significant influence in Brussels in terms of policy-making.

Management of the Social Platform and influences of managerial formations

The organisational structure of the Social Platform and its working strategies can be explained in terms of managerialism. Managerialism is defined as a mentality and technology of managing anything independent from its content:

> [to manage] is a verb that can be applied to the processes of ordering and controlling people and things. It implies a separation between the actual doing of whatever is being managed (engineering or teaching) and the higher level of function of these processes. In other words, management is not about engineering or teaching, but the coordination of the doing of these things.
>
> (Parker 2002: 7)

It is based on the understanding that the performance (effectiveness and efficiency) of the organisations can be maximised by applying principles of management, and developing the skills of managers. The main features of management are associated with bureaucratic governance and professionalism, which may lead to autocratic leadership. Recently this coalesces with the New Public Management arrangements that suggest extending this administrative frame used by the private sector to public administration and organisations of civil society. In other words, if neoliberalism is understood as the spread of market and rationalities to wider corners of social life, then managerialism reinforces the circulation of those rationalities to public and civic spheres (i.e. NGOs). European civil discourse and its implications of the Social Platform can be studied against this social process with a particular focus on the examination of the administrative structure of the Platform.[19]

Decision-making processes

Focusing on the Platform's *administrative units*, *working methods* and *decision-making procedures* should make it possible to trace and observe the extent of bureaucratisation, managerialism and professionalism.

The Platform is administered by a coordinator and a President. Its organisational structure comprises the General Assembly (GA), the Steering Group (SG), the Management Group (MG), the Membership Accreditation Committee (MAC), and the Secretariat. The rights and obligations of each unit and the procedures of the decision-making process are defined in the statute and internal rules of the Platform. The GA is the highest level of authority in the Social Platform.[20]

Whereas the SG gives consent for the political positions developed by the working groups, the MC oversees the daily management of the Platform. The MC also controls the budget, represents the Platform at external meetings and events, and appoints and dismisses staff in the Secretariat. The Secretariat, located in Brussels, comprises eight persons, including a Director, who specialise in European politics and European-level citizens' interest representation. It is responsible for the Platform's day-to-day management,[21] and the institutional identity of the Social Platform is crystallised at the Secretariat. It is the Platform's permanent paid staff that occupies the Platform's office in Brussels; it prepares the Platform's communication tools, initiates the Platform's conferences, seminars, training courses, and study visits, and coordinates the Platform's administration.[22]

The former leaders of the Social Platform claim that its organisational structure and interactions with constituents resemble the way EU institutions function and operate:

> The Social Platform agreed internal rules in 1999 which prescribed that decisions ought to be reached by consensus, and discussions about the areas of competence of the Platform strangely resembled the disputes over subsidiarity between the member states. This balancing act between acting together and maintaining one's own specificity has been a constant feature of the process of increasing the coordination between NGOs. Although this did at times slow down progress, it created stronger sets of alliances.
> (Alhadeff and Wilson 2002)

Both ENAR and the Solidar confirmed this statement by stressing that they preserved their autonomy in their interactions with the Social Platform (P. Charhon and C. Reuter, personal communication, May 2009). Nonetheless, the relatively short history of the Platform shows that power has not been shared equally between the members – even though member's obligations and rights are enacted in the Social Platform's statute and the internal rules in order to provide procedural rights for the members to participate in the Platform's decision-making processes (i.e. general assembly and working groups). As Cullen's research (2005) reveals, some members, such as the gender- and left-oriented solidarity movements, youth and elderly groups, dominate the Platform's work at the expense of e.g. the elderly, antiracism, disability, public health and anti-poverty groups. For instance, the president of the Platform between 1998 and 2003, Giamperio Alhadeff, the current president, Conny Reuter, and the director of the Secretariat, Rochan Di Puppo, were all recruited from Solidar. Cullen (ibid.) explains this situation with the asymmetry of human and financial resources between the members.

The Platform's advocacy and communication instruments

The Platform produces different materials about its administration and advocacy work, such as position papers, resolutions, policy briefings and advocacy letters. Among the Platform's different communication tools are the monthly newsletter and weekly mailing, which are sent to all EU institutions and social partners. Subscription is free and open to the public. While the newsletter mainly includes information about the Platform's activities and EU policies, the weekly mailing also presents the activities of the Platform's members. Another communication tool is the Platform's website, which has been redesigned several times during the 2000s in order 'to improve the communication of the Social Platform' (recursively mentioned in the Annual Reports from 2001 to 2007). The Platform's websites include a short description of all its members, along with the Platform's publications, press releases and monthly newsletter. The members-only section contains internal and draft documents.

Communication (i.e. the tools for conveying the message) has been a central issue for the Platform's work. The Platform claims that its communication tools raise its profile and command a high level of recognition within EU institutions, social partners and the NGO sector. It has therefore been trying to develop its tools for communication, explaining its communication strategy as follows: 'to restructure and simplify the Social Platform website; publish several issues of ENGAGE; keep a consistent visual identity and a tone for all external communication; respond to media requests and proactively seek coverage where appropriate; and investigate 'new media' opportunities' (SP, WP 2009: 9). To these ends, it recruited a Communication Officer, a professional in the techniques of public relations. It redesigned (and redesigned) its newsletter, website, brochure, posters, and leaflets during the 2000s. Furthermore, as part of its techniques of communication, the Platform endeavoured to develop its writing style and formats in its reports for a better and more transparent mode of communication (SP, WP 2001). It soon became a model for the NGO community because of its success in implementing professional communication techniques. For instance, the graphic design used by the Platform in its reports was lauded as good ways of communicating in the lobbying toolkit prepared by the Civil Society Contact Group (CSCG, *Making Your Voice Heard in the EU* 2006: 18). The Platform, moreover, organised training seminars on communication skills for its members, in which journalists and communication consultants gave lectures.

Having emphasised which advocacy and communication tools the Platform uses and how they are developed, one can pose two interesting questions: What happens when the advocacy work of NGOs is bureaucratised, and what happens when NGOs' communication becomes an object of management (i.e. management by the Platform)? Since the Platform declares its objective as developing its communication skills, through e.g. techniques of clear writing and quality graphic design, one can argue that this approach has significant repercussions: communication is defined as a mentality of conveying a message independent from its content – thus is associated with the *knowing how rather knowing what*. This can lead to a mechanical articulation of information that abandons a sense of the human. One can argue also this can lead to *reification* of 'communication' – treating abstract concepts as if they were quantifiable things – when the techniques take over the substance (Chari 2010). Communication defined in this way takes on a different meaning, for example, than used by Habermas, as he elucidates the role of the organised civic action with its promise of communicative power: that is, civil society detects the issues of public concern; fosters public deliberation about these issues and in turn plays a catalytic role in articulation of them into decision making publics. The Platform, rather, manages *communication in itself* as a profession and *communication for itself* akin to PR techniques. This may be thought of in relation to a managerial type of NGO: it implies skills of managing an organisation independent of its area of work. This argument becomes more lucid when we also focus on how the Platform describes its goals and objectives under results-based management organisational frames. That is, this argument suggests communicating in accordance with a pre-defined systemised knowledge that is informed by economic rationalities, such as goal-orientation, efficiency, and cost-benefit analysis.

A split NGO persona: between a contentious alter-ego and peaceful stakeholder

Communication and advocacy instruments of the Platform also reveal its binary organisational identity, one that is divided between a contentious alter-ego and the structural restrictions of EU governance. A further question is how the Platform defines and perceives itself: an elite lobby organisation or a protest-oriented social movement. The Social Platform has not aimed to institutionalise protests, but influence policymakers through advocacy. Hence, it has kept a distance from practices of contention. It has protested EU decision-makers on one unique occasion, the suspension of the Commission's financial support for NGOs. The European Court of Justice annulled a Commission decision to fund 86 European projects on 12 May 1998, which were coordinated by European Social NGOs (Geyer 2001). Accordingly, the Commission temporarily suspended funding for several other projects for which there was no legal basis. The decisions of the ECJ and the Commission could have been a serious hindrance to EU NGOs, since their survival depended on the European funding. The Social Platform mobilised a campaign, the Red Card Campaign, to unify the NGO sector in protest of the suspension of their funding. The protest was successful and the funding resumed at the end of that year. This experience showed that survival of the European NGOs was not secure. Therefore, the Social Platform proposed a formal structure for the civil dialogue, claiming that this legal basis would provide security for their survival.

In the late 2000s, however, the Platform changed its stance from being a 'peaceful actor', and joined protests against the austerity measures implemented by several EU countries (Greece, Ireland, England) as a remedy to the economic crisis. These protests targeted cuts in social policy budgets and public sector salaries at the EU level. Pushing these economic policies in Brussels, for the first time the Platform participated in street protests in 2009. In particular, Social Platform President Conny Reuter gave statements against the austerity measures on the BBC. Otherwise, the Platform could before only appear in EU-oriented media, e.g. Euroactive and Stakeholder's Corner.

The Platform's own publications, on the other hand, show different self-images, i.e. images that shift between contentious activism and lobbying. The

Platform's magazine, *ENGAGE*, its annual reports and Facebook page in this respect present different self-portrayals. *ENGAGE* presents images of social movements, such as demonstrators carrying placards and marching. Furthermore, in the interview section with European NGO leaders, *ENGAGE* in each issue includes the question: 'Where was your last battle?' However, the Platform's other visual materials present other Platform images and identities: pictures from conferences, seminars and training sessions (with some reports also including pictures of those who are presumed to need special care, i.e. children and the elderly). Therefore, we observe two different images of the Platform: one of the indoor conference participant, peaceful and deliberative, and the other outdoors, protesting, and ready to challenge (though symbolically). When we observe the working reports and annual reports, the Platform presents its achievements on the basis of the conferences, seminars, training sessions, and study visits it organised or participated in. In other words, the Platform does not present the street protests it organised as proof of its accomplishments within the scope of its results-based management (see below), even though contentious actions are also activities. In sum, the presentation of what the Platform does and what it thinks it differs according to the target audience. Although the Platform defines itself as a European consultative organisation, it symbolically uses protest images; therefore, a symbolic contentious identity shapes the alter-ego of the Platform, keeping it connected with the social movement discourse and thus separating it from the mere lobby association.

Results-based management and political surveillance

The ethos of the new modes of governance suggests effective and efficient problem solving (Jachtenfuchs 2001; Mosher and Trubek 2003; Haahr 2005). This approach entails a moral connection between the performance of the agents and the outcomes they produce. The concept of outcome legitimacy developed by the governance approach is related to this view in that it establishes a link between the accountability and quality of governance structures. The governmentality approach argues that this view presents technologies of performance as techniques of restoring trust (i.e. accountability, transparency and democratic control) (Dean 1999: 169). Technologies of performance have constitutive effects when they are considered to be embedded within power relations, i.e. empowering or colonising the agency. Defined in this way, *performance machine*-like subjects are subject to the governmental rationalities and technologies. Technologies of performance transform professionals into 'calculating individuals' within 'calculable spaces', subject to 'calculative regimes' (Miller 1992).

For our study, the observation of the Platform reveals the emergence of calculating agents that are governed on the grounds of results-based management within civil society. The Platform has appeared to an example of a performance machine-like subject: it has to perform a set of goals that are planned, carefully calculated, and set out in reports. First and foremost, its establishment and activities at large are based on a mentality of achieving outcomes and reporting to sources of funding. Each year it determines some objectives and details how to achieve them. At the end of the year, it documents its achievements with a report to the Commission. These reports are used to measure the success of the Platform. The goals, indicators of success and the expected outcomes are set out in the Platform's reports and other communication tools according to special techniques. These techniques are not mere descriptions and presentations of the work, but should be considered from a broader perspective, i.e. the Platform's governing mentality – its knowledge and techniques of getting things done.

The Platform's working methods reveal its adherence to the principles of results-based management (RBM) and a logical framework approach (LFA). From the Platform's management documents, working programmes and annual reports between 2001 and 2010, it is clear that the Platform follows the working frame of LFA and RBM almost exactly. The OECD glossary of key terms in evaluation and result-based management defines RBM as follows:

> A management strategy by which an organisation ensures that its processes, products and services contribute to the achievement of desired results (outputs, outcomes and impacts), RBM rests on clearly defined account-ability for results, and requires monitoring and self-assessment of progress towards results, and reporting on performance.
>
> (OECD 2002)

The relevant concepts of RBM – benchmarking, inputs, outcome, outputs, performance, performance indicator, and performance monitoring – are also shown and defined in the OECD glossary. LFA was developed and implemented by several government and international agencies, including the United States Agency for International Development (USAID) and other national and international development donor organisations.[23] The Australian Agency for Development, AusAID (2005) and Swedish International Agency for Development, SIDA (2005) define LFA as an 'aid to thinking'. This approach 'establishes a logical hierarchy of means by which the objectives will be reached, and how outputs and outcomes might be best monitored and evaluated' (AusAID 2005: 1; see also World Bank 2000; Com, *Aid delivery methods*: *PCM* 2004). It also lays out an activity description (the components of the activity, roles and responsibilities of the units and management arrangements) and the activity rationale (the nature of the situation in which the activity is embedded, cause/effect logic in the activity, and expected results). Table 4.2 outlines the logical framework matrix.

This chart helps illuminate both a vertical and horizontal logic. The vertical logic (i.e. reading the columns up and down in the figure above) makes clear the causal relationships between different objectives. The horizontal logic, on the other hand, shows how the objectives will be measured and verified (ibid.). The vertical way of thinking is based on a linear temporal logic, a logic of which is explained by AusAID (ibid.: 16) as an *if-then* causality:

Table 4.2 General structure of a Logframe Matrix

General structure and content of a Logframe Matrix activity description	Indicators	Means of verification	Assumptions
Goal or Impact – the long term development impact (policy goal) that the activity contributes at a national or sectoral level	How the achievement will be measured – including appropriate targets (quantity, quality and time)	Sources of information on the Goal indicator(s) – including who will collect it and how often	
Purpose or Outcome – the medium term result(s) that the activity aims to achieve – in terms of benefits to target groups	How the achievement of the Purpose will be measured – including appropriate targets (quantity, quality and time)	Sources of information on the Purpose indicator(s) – including who will collect it and how often	Assumptions concerning the Purpose to Goal linkage
Component Objectives or Intermediate Results – this level in the objectives or results hierarchy can be used to provide a clear link between outputs and outcomes (particularly for larger multi-component activities)	How the achievement of the Component Objectives will be measured – including appropriate targets (quantity, quality and time)	Sources of information on the Component Objectives indicator(s) – including who will collect it and how often	Assumptions concerning the Component Objective to Output linkage
Outputs – the tangible products or services that the activity will deliver	How the achievement of the Outputs will be measured – including appropriate targets (quantity, quality and time)	Sources of information on the Output indicator(s) – including who will collect it and how often	Assumptions concerning the Output to Component Objective linkage

Source: Australian Agency for International Development (2005: 3), AusGuideline for Logical Framework Approach.

144   *A case study on the Social Platform*

- *if* inputs are provided, *then* the work program can be undertaken;
- *if* the work program is undertaken, *then* outputs will be produced;
- *if* outputs are produced, *then* component objectives will be achieved;
- *if* the activity purpose is supported, this should then contribute to the overall goal.

How does the Platform pertain to the RBM and LFA? These approaches provide initial information about the sorts of management and working strategies the Platform follows. It is therefore possible to observe the way the Platform thinks, i.e. relates itself to social phenomena and deals with social problems according to a set of pre-established ideas and a logical framework. This has been reflected in the Platform's yearly reports and communication tools.

Reports and communication tools as techniques of subjectification

Thus, the way the Platform disseminates its activities through its communication tools, and the way it presents its objectives in its reports, are aspects from which the implications of a professionally calculating and managerially thinking subject can be observed. Since these tools provide continuous information about what the Platform does (or what the EU does), they function as performance manifestations. They express specific objectives and break these objectives down into several components. They include the outcomes of these objectives, detail action plans and present means of measurement.

The beginning of this section mentioned the Platform's objectives up to 2006: campaigning, capacity building, civil dialogue and communication. These objectives were further divided into subcomponents. Table 4.3 demonstrates these objectives:

The Platform also categorises its activities according to its main goals, as shown in Table 4.4.

The Platform adopted a strategic plan in 2006, which brought about a revision of the objectives, but not the logical framework. The reason behind this change, as given by the Platform, was the adoption of a more efficient and effective management. Table 4.5 lays out these changes.

The Platform's annual reports have followed the same framework and explained the achievements of each pre-defined objective. They present the activities behind each objective as an indicator of success. Since annual reports have also had aimed to inform other stakeholders and the general public, these achievements were presented in a different format than the working programmes, i.e. explanatory text boxes, pictures and graphic designs.

The Platform has used different techniques in its communication. It has represented its result-based performances both qualitatively and quantitatively. Most often, it has verbally described its performance targets and end products. However, in some cases, it has employed numbers, pie charts and tables. Pie charts and graphs were first used in the 2007 annual report; below is an illustration of the Platform's end products in 2007 (see Figure 4.1). In the same report,

Table 4.3 The Platform's main objectives and sub-objectives

Main goal	Sub-objectives
Campaigning	• To influence EU policy formulation on a regular basis by promoting the combined views of member organisations. • To campaign on issues of common interest to its members, especially on social rights, EU social policies and programmes, and civil dialogue.
Capacity building	• To facilitate the exchange of experiences and practices of Social Platform members and enable the mutual exchange of information. • To help social NGOs improve their capacity to contribute to a better future for all, to influence EU policy, and to make meaningful contributions to the civil dialogue. • To build alliances with other relevant stakeholders, including other NGOs and social partners.
Civil Dialogue	• To facilitate relations with EU institutions and other international organisations when there is an appropriate link with EU policies, and to facilitate the process of dialogue and consultation while taking diversity into account.
Communication	• To promote awareness of relevant EU policy developments among Social Platform members. • To promote external awareness of the activities and role of the Social Platform and its members.

Source: SP (2005), WP. Note: The chart does not exist in the original document but is drawn here for illustrative purposes.

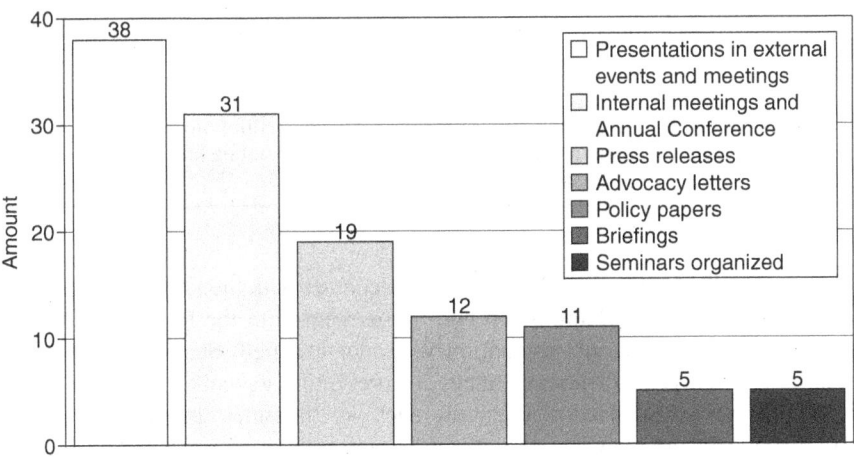

Figure 4.1 Quantification of Social Platform activities and publications in 2007 (source: Social Platform, *Annual Report* 2007: 7).

Table 4.4 The objectives of the Platform and its activities

Main goal	Activities
Campaigning	Lisbon Agenda
	Impact Assessment and Sustainable Development
	Public Procurement
	The Future of Cohesion Policies in Europe
	Corporate Social Responsibility
	Social Policy Agenda
	Open Method of Coordination
	Demographic change and the modernisation of social protection
	Employment and Social Protection
	Minimum Income (Wages)
	Services, Social Services, and Services of General Interest
	The Social Inclusion Strategy
	Anti-discrimination policies
	Gender equality
	Integration of Migrants
	Fundamental Rights
	The EU Constitutional Treaty
	Participatory democracy
	Funding of NGOs at local, national and EU level
Capacity building	Exchanges of experience between social NGOs
	Exchanges with other stakeholders
	Training
	Member support
	Study visits to new Member States and candidate countries
Civil dialogue	European Commission
	European Parliament
	Council of the European Union
	Other EU Institutions and International Bodies
Communication	Disseminating information to Social Platform members
	External communication activities: promoting knowledge of the Social Platform and social NGOs

Source: SP (2005), WP.

the Platform also quantified the intensity of contact with the EU institutions, e.g. 60 per cent with the Commission and 30 per cent with the Parliament, though the indicators behind this estimation were not clarified. Starting in 2007, the Platform employed a different strategy for presenting its work. Since then, it has used different visualisation methods, such as timelines, graphs and logical framework-inspired advanced charts.

The relevance of examining the Platform's reports and questioning the 'logic' behind such organisational structuring is twofold. First, we can trace the rationalities and the technologies of these mentalities, thus exposing how political power creates subjects and how subjects implement this logic in their practices. This analysis examines the episteme of governmental rationalities, i.e. their way of thinking and way of performing. It shows how political power shapes,

Table 4.5 Main goals of the Platform in the strategic plan adopted in 2006

Main goal	Sub-components, indicators
Strengthening the Sector: • to support the development of a strong, vibrant social NGO sector.	**Communicating the contribution of NGOs:** We will develop the collective identity of social NGOs, and communicate the contribution of social NGOs to social cohesion. **Leading on good governance:** We will establish the sector as a leader in good governance practices for NGOs by developing a Charter of Governance for European NGOs. **Capacity-building:** We will support members to achieve their objectives by developing mutual understanding and through skills training. **Supporting development:** We will support the development of links between European social NGOs and NGOs within the new Member States, Accession and Candidate Countries. **Securing funding:** We will seek to secure funding for the Social Platform to allow it to continue to function independently.
Reinforcing Participatory Democracy: • to strengthen participatory democracy by supporting a process of dialogue between NGOs and a more transparent European Union.	**Improving the dialogue:** We will develop a clearer vision of what kind of structured dialogue social NGOs want with the institutions of the EU, and seek agreement from the Institutions to implement this and to achieve a real stakeholders' approach. **Making the EU more democratic and transparent:** We will work to promote a more open, democratic European Union.
Shaping Social Europe: • to positively influence the development of the EU's social and economic model by focusing our policy work upon the relationship between economic and social policies, and by promoting our common vision for a social Europe.	**An Annual thematic focus:** Each year a significant part of our work will be structured around an annual theme chosen by our General Assembly. We will use the thematic work to improve understanding of key issues by NGOs, to access views from national and European social NGOs, and to provide a focus for our policy and campaigning work, hence improving our visibility and impact. **Pr Prioritising our campaigning work:** When establishing our policy priorities, we will evaluate how politically significant the policy is and to what extent we could influence it, as well as the level of shared interest amongst members, and the extent to which a collective input from the Social Platform could bring added value. **ma Making our advocacy work more efficient and transparent:** When implementing our advocacy work we will develop streamlined, transparent policy-making working methods to ensure that we are more responsive to emerging policy debates. **So Socio-economic research networking:** We will establish stronger links with researchers to support the development of our campaigning agenda, particularly around the links between economic and social policy.

Source: Social Platform, *Strategic Plan*, 2006; the texts here are reproduced from the original document.

manipulates and controls the conduct and the conduct of conduct. For instance, the rationalities do not directly act upon the subjects, but on their actions, mentalities and even logics. This corresponds to a form of power that does not constrain the actions of agencies and discipline by the threat or use of violence. This form of power, moreover, does not use the subject as a mere instrument for achieving political and social control. Rather, the kind of analysis conducted here, an analysis of the art of government, investigates how power creates subjects and makes them amenable to governing. Before political power incorporates agents into the governance of society, it constitutes them. For instance, the development agencies formulate frameworks, such as LFA and RBM, to shape the actions of the agents – it imposes a certain logic of management and constitutes a certain type of subjectivity that thinks in a linear mentality and is oriented towards results.

The second point of relevance of a critical approach to the Platform's management rationale and techniques concerns the relationship between the Platform's way of doing things and its redefinition of the political. How would the RBM and performance machine-like subjects influence normative concepts of political theory, such as legitimacy, democracy and civil society, for example? A performance-oriented approach to politics embodies a linear logic associated with things rather than people (Chambers and Petit 2004). This logic renders participatory democracy, social policies and the reshaping of NGOs as the objects of performance. It defines these goals as an end goal (*telos*), and the sub-component objectives and activities as the means of achieving these goals. What is wrong with this? The 2009 work programme presents what happens when participatory democracy and civil dialogue (i.e. a policy of incorporating NGOs into EU administration) has been conceptualised from the scope of RBM. Following LFA and RBM dictates, the Platform in this document presents achievements, objectives, expected results and proposed actions. It states that the Platform achieves 'a common position defining who we [NGO community] are, what we mean by civil dialogue and participatory democracy'. The objectives (indicators) of this achievement, which illustrate the way in which the Platform defines politics and particularly participation, are *then* listed as follows:

> (1) Structures and procedures are in place for a more effective civil dialogue at European level; (2) Platform members and their members are equipped to assess and improve civil dialogue mechanisms; (3) the various NGO sectors at EU level have common objectives on how to enhance civil dialogue and coordinate their advocacy work.
>
> (SP, WP 2009:3)

In terms of the expected results of its work in relation to participation, it refers to follow-up EU regulation on civil dialogue, the preparation of guides for its members and assisting NGOs to improve their own corporate structures. The achievements in strengthening the sector pillar of the Platform was illustrated in the work programme 2010 as follows:

A strong collective identity of social NGOs is established; the NGO sector is established as a leader at the European level in good governance practices; members are supported by developing mutual understanding and by sharing information and skills; [and] links are developed between European social NGOs within the new Member States.

(SP, WP 2010:11)

In sum, participation is reduced to mere association with accreditation in decision-making, and an indicator represented graphically. The working methods of the Platform (work plans, annual reports, strategic action plans) have been built in such way to achieve pre-planned aims. Since this structure has emerged as a result of the Commission's requirements, the question is the extent to which the working ethos based on constant reporting, being audited and being controlled colonises the Platform's actions and the staff's behaviours. In other words, how do the Platform and its staff receive and perceive the mechanisms imposed by the contractual agreements.

This question will be further elaborated in the next section, in which I will examine the Platform's documents on participation and participatory democracy. In other words, while the reports revealed how it represented its performance, its position papers will help us see how the Platform receives and perceives these concepts. The Platform's RBM and LFA-oriented working strategies revealed the extent to which it operates as a calculating performance-oriented subject. However, it should be noted that the style of reporting and documenting bureaucratic structures should not necessarily be interpreted as colonisation of the Platform by neoliberal governmental rationalities. The position papers will help us discuss whether the Platform thinks and acts differently in this respect. However, we should first mention the relationship between technologies of reporting and new mechanisms of social surveillance, before looking at the Platform's role in governing European civil society.

Reports as tools of surveillance

The techniques of reporting are embodied within power relations, in that political power develops a surveillance mechanism upon the agencies of governance. However, this surveillance is different than the Panopticon of penitentiaries. It is, instead, exerted on free agencies, and is in fact based on the idea of empowering agencies to calculate their actions, present their goals in an appropriate way, and then document their achievements. According to RBM, the agencies should perform initially in order to be audited. Whereas political rationalities render subjects via several techniques into performing subjects, auditing plays a disciplining role on both the performer and the performed. Hence, not only the content of the Platform's reports is pertinent for our inquiry, but also the very mentality of reporting that embodies an ideology of short-term performance-oriented actions. In other words, I propose an examination of the Platform's activities as an object of performance. We have mentioned that the Platform defined its objectives as promoting European society, strengthening the EU NGO sector and promoting participatory democracy. The interesting question is how one could calculate, quantify and document the objectives and achievements of these issues. Furthermore, what happens when these aspects become targets of performance? We have illustrated above how the Platform presents its goals and achievements. This illustration shows how participation has been advanced as a calculable phenomenon. One of the consequences of this is that the LFA style enables monitoring and control of the performances.

Furthermore, the Platform has also developed mechanisms of self-auditing for finances and an evaluation mechanism of its organisational structure and its working methods (SP, WP 2010). It revised its strategic plan in 2011, at the end of its five-year plan. For this task, it has temporarily recruited an expert to evaluate its previous strategy and administrative culture.

The Platform's endeavour to shaping (and reshaping) the NGO community

This chapter has so far illustrated the Platform as an object of government. We now turn our attention to the ways in which the Platform endeavours to create an NGO community, a community that would think, act and conduct itself like the Platform. One of the Platform's main objectives *strengthening the sector* serves constituting new type of subjectivity and new subject. In this respect, it disseminates the knowledge and technologies of European governance and trains its members through techniques of capacity building. The Secretariat in Brussels enjoys significant power in governance and the organisation of the Platform's activities, instead of merely coordinating the activities of its members. The Secretariat, along with the Platform's network of administrators, shapes the conduct of its members in terms of the European art of government. This chapter will now explain how the secretariat disperses the rationalities of government through training its members on participatory democracy and active citizenship. It evaluates how the Platform incorporates the NGO community into European governance, empowers it, and disperses knowledge of the EU, thus rendering Europe knowable and governable.

Representing the EU and the techniques of government: benchmarking and exchange of best practices

The Platform was set up to add a European value to the NGO community (SP, WP 2001: 3). The Platform in this sense has been carrying the vocabulary and practices of European governance. Thus, it has been helping the EU knowable by explaining and carrying the norms of government, such as benchmarking, knowledge sharing and the exchange of practices.

The exchange of practices can be studied in two different ways: participatory democracy vs. a functionalist approach. The proponents of participatory democracy argue that dialogic interaction promotes civic virtues and trust (Barber

1984). The functionalist approach, on the other hand, argues that the exchange of best practices entails the exchange of best practices of effective and efficient governance (Mosher and Trubek 2003). As the latter entails, inter-subjective exchanges do not necessarily promote civic virtues and trust, but serve some pragmatic aims of governing society. When it comes to the definition of *exchange*, both approaches share some common points. Both presume that exchange happens in a power void between equal actors (socially, culturally, and economically), even though some experiences prevail over others. Observed in the example of the Platform, the Brussels headquarters though play a significant role in determining what is to be exchanged by imposing a set of problematisations. The pro-active and master-like role of the Platform is noticeable with this regard, because it sets the frame for the interactions. Here, I would like to remind the conceptual model elaborated in Chapter 1, which depicts how the mentality of an NGO activist might transform due to engagement with other discourses. One of the overarching goals of is the reinforcement of expertise among EU social NGOs (SP, AR 2003), which implies perseverance to circulating a managerial-professional type of NGO. It aims to achieve this objective by its training activities or drawing upon external expertise.

The Platform aims to disperse a bureaucratic managerial structure to its members and local NGOs (especially within Central and Eastern Europe). In this respect, it drafted a charter of governance for European social NGOs (SP, WP 2009). Thus, the Platform aims to shape the organisational structure of other organisations, mode of their appropriate conduct. Structuring the organisations in a bureaucratic way pertains to the moral dimension of the neoliberal art of government. Moral, in this case, corresponds to the 'best' way of organising, since it promotes transparency and accountability. Circulating the morals and knowledge of governance to other NGOs, the Platform normalises the moral idea that NGOs should orient their actions towards the EU, collaborate with other stakeholders, and manage their organisations professionally. For instance, the Platform dedicated its annual theme to *Civil Dialogue in Europe*; it has mobilised the national NGOs in order to promote a legal basis for NGOs in national scale consultations, i.e. a certain type of state-society relation. In this respect, it prepared a model letter and disseminated it to national NGOs in 2000.

In sum, the Platform employs certain tools and strategies to mobilise its members. It initiates campaigns, uses tools of communication, prepares certain toolkits and papers and organises conferences and study visits. The Platform, in fact, develops a set of practices that shapes a certain type of NGO, one that has an ideal administrative structure, uses professional techniques of communication, is willing to orient its actions towards the EU institutions, and moves physically across Europe. Warleigh (2001) argued that NGOs are not capable of handling the political socialisation of their members. Due to the limitations of this research, we cannot guess what the implications of the Platform for local NGOs will be. However, a further study on the Europeanisation of NGOs should not only be limited to political socialisation, but should also examine the harmonisation of the practices, motivations and modes of conduct. As we see in the example of the Platform, an NGO might well engage in transferring the complex concepts (e.g. anti-discrimination, fundamental rights) and practices for the NGO sector, helping to render European space manageable.

Social movement literature (Ruzza 2004, 2005; Cullen 2005) argues that it is the collective identity and power of each constituent that integrates the network of social action. In contrast to this argument, it is here shown how the Platform can have constitutive impacts on its members by shaping their management and ideological stance – while it is itself constituted. Thus, the morality and ethics of these networks can be shaped due to the influence of the coordinating centre, i.e. the influence of the influenced. This can undermine bottom-up processes of identity-formation, instead fostering a new type of subjectivity, which is formulated by the Commission and put into practice by the Platform.

Platform and participation discourses

> In an age where cynicism dominates the political landscape, social NGOs continue to invigorate society, providing outlets for frustrated voices, gathering-points for kindred spirits, and – through the key services which they provide – a sustaining light in the lives of millions across Europe. NGOs can also offer expert contributions to political decision-makers, as well as a means for engaging citizens directly into the political process – participative democracy in action.
>
> (Giampiero Alhadeff, President of Social Platform in SP, *AR* 2001: 3)

> The Social Platform believes that [...] a permanent renewal of democracy can only be achieved with a strong legal base to guarantee consultation of citizens' associations.
>
> (SP, AR 2003:12)

Below I will track how the Platform conceives of the ECS discourse and its role in the European art of government. In this respect, I will concentrate on the Platform's policy and position papers, listed by the Platform under 'participatory democracy and governance'. These entail the Platform's reflections on the *White Paper on European Governance* (the Commission's attempts to incorporate EU NGOs into European governance in the early 2000s), active citizenship, the Communication Strategy, the use of the Commission's funds, and the incorporation of non-political actors into EU decision-making through the European Transparency Initiative. The previous chapter explained the Commission's ECS discourse and its specific interest in NGOs. Focusing on these positions, I will try to examine how the Platform receives and perceives the Commission's civil society discourse, along with how it defines participatory democracy, civil society and NGOs' incorporation into European politics.

The Platform and the White Paper on European Governance

The Social Platform was content with the *White Paper on European Governance*'s mention of civil society as key to promoting more involvement in shaping and implementing EU policy, and in this regard suggested proposals to establish a more structured consultation of NGOs within the EU's decision-making processes. The Platform commented on the *White Paper on European Governance* (WPEG) with respect to the EU's democratic deficit, principles of good governance, and the role of civil society (SP, *Democracy, Governance and European NGOs*, 2002). The Platform supported the *White Paper*'s diagnosis on the 'widening gulf between the European Union and the people it serves', and principally accepted the role the WPEG assigned it, i.e. a mediating agent that connected people to the EU. Nonetheless, the Platform did not agree with the explanation given for the 'disenchantment' of the people. The WPEG had diagnosed citizens' lack of interest on the basis of *communication* or *comprehension*; in other words, citizens had not yet fully understood the benefits of EU governance. The Platform rather suggested that disappointment in EU governance might stem from the EU's failure to deliver services that could improve citizens' lives.

The Platform also supported the WPEG's principles of good governance, namely *openness, participation, accountability, effectiveness* and *coherence*, and accepted them uncritically. As Føllesdal (2003) argues in his critique of the WPEG the Platform could have been more critical in proposing alternative principles such as the rule of law, political equality or fairness. Had the Platform mentioned that these principles of good governance were based on the World Bank's definition and standards of good governance (Pierre 2000; Weiss 2000) it could have carried out a key component of its civic control, or critical gaze. Moreover, it could in this way have presented alternative values and norms about governing the public sphere. In this sense, the Platform failed to grasp the current global transformation in governance, changes in capitalism and propose a different value system or counter-conduct, i.e. one not colonised by market or administrative values.

While the Platform was content with the WPEG's recognition of the role of good civil society 'in giving voice to the concerns of citizens and delivering services that meet people's needs', it strictly rejected the Commission's claim on 'tightening up [NGOs'] internal structure' (SP, *Response to the WPEG* 2002: 3). It regarded the latter as an intervention to their independence: 'the Commission had no legitimacy to direct the ways which the citizens choose to create and organise their associations which will vary according to the specificity of each NGO' (ibid.: 5). Paradoxically, as it was shown earlier in this chapter, the very same year it accepted a 'statue' and in 2008 and also codified internal rules.

The conclusion to be drawn is that the Commission exercised its power on NGOs by intervening in their organisational structures. The imperatives of this intervention have subjectifying impacts, and complying with the technologies of subjectivisation exerted by the Commission, the Platform has become a professionalised legal subject. This shows one of the aspects in which the Platform has become a subject.

Active Citizenship Programme (ACP) and the communication strategy

The Platform elucidated its position on the Commission's discourse of bringing the EU back to citizens with respect to the ACP and the Commission's communication policy. It stated that 'NGOs should be at the heart of [the Active Citizenship Programme], as they play a key role in fostering active citizenship; in fact, this is their "raison d'etre"' (SP, *Active European citizenship* 2005: 1). To the Platform, the ACP could be a useful instrument in bringing the EU back to its citizens, in the context of EU governance suffering from a democratic deficit, growing Euroscepticism, and even Eurapathy. In this respect, the Platform contrasted two different types of Commission strategies that could bring the EU back to its citizens. The first concerned information campaigns, which aimed to explain the role of the EU in people's lives. The second strategy rested on the idea that citizens could be involved in the construction of the EU polity. According to the Platform, the first of these strategies was a top-down strategy, and it warned that if it was not carefully implemented it could be considered 'EU propaganda'. Hence, this strategy would be unlikely to bring the EU to the citizens. Nonetheless, the second strategy, a bottom-up approach, could 'help promoting a greater sense of ownership with the EU project among citizens by promoting their direct involvement in the construction of a strong and integrated European community' (ibid.: 1). The Platform argued that this would be 'best way to get [citizens'] support', concluding that it had already made the aims of active citizenship a reality (ibid.: 2). Therefore, the Platform found this initiative to be a legitimising instrument of its activities at the European level. In this respect, it pointed out that 'the EU support enables the Social Platform to play a crucial role in disseminating information about the EU and retrieving feedback from the citizens' groups in a coordinated way' (ibid.).

Related to the abovementioned strategy of rendering itself knowable by presenting itself, as we uncover in Chapter 3, the Commission launched the communication policy in 2006 with the objective of closing the gap between citizens and the EU. The communication policy emerged from the idea that this gap would be closed if citizens could only learn about the EU. In this respect, the Platform stated that it aimed not to communicate Europe, but the EU institutions: 'For Social NGOs the priority is not to communicate "Europe" in general but to focus on the European Union, as centres of power where important decisions are taken that affect all of us and for which decision-makers should be accountable' (SP, *Communication* 2006: 1). Furthermore, the Platform rejected any duty to advertise Europe, rather asserting that communication with European citizens was primarily the responsibility of political bodies such as the Commission, elected governments and political parties. According to the Platform, despite the fact the media and NGOs could play a role in informing people about the EU, it

A case study on the Social Platform 155

was not because they had a responsibility to do so, but because it was in the interest of their members. Emphasising that NGOs were not the mere instruments of EU institutions, the Platform targeted the political sphere as having main responsibility for this task. It pointed out that the communication strategy did not prioritise the role of political parties, although 'most of the communication money was spent during elections' (ibid.: 5). In this respect, the Platform argued that 'political parties [had] huge responsibility in articulating a clear European programme and raising the accountabilities of MEPs or national governments on what they had achieved or intended to achieve at the EU level (ibid.: 2).

Having emphasised explaining Europe as the responsibility of the political, the Platform pointed out three flaws in the communication policy. First, the Platform claimed that the communication strategy should have concentrated on the transparency of decision-making, along with informing the people about the EU's institutional structure and the benefits of the EU for them. According to the Platform, 'knowing who takes the decision and how was only a first step', the second step then is being 'able to react' (ibid.: 5). The Platform further argued that individual citizens could not follow EU politics due to the complexity of EU websites, or the outright lack of information. In this regard, the Platform stressed that European NGOs could scrutinise the decision-making processes and main actors in the debate, including the member states and political groups in the Parliament.

Second, the Platform strongly criticised the Commission's proposal for establishing online consultation tools for the individual citizen as a way of dealing with the democratic deficit. It highlighted that 'giving too much attention to these tools only contributed to reinforce the "illusion of democracy" and clearly did not help in bridging the gap between those who have lost faith in the democratic system' (ibid.: 6). This system, according to the Platform, did not secure an inclusive participation mechanism for all groups in society, as experienced in Debate Europe when it tried to mobilise an online public debate; 90 per cent of the participants were male, between the ages of 18–44, and mainly used two languages (English [56 per cent] and French [23 per cent]).

Third, the Platform criticised the rationale behind the Commission's strategies of empowering citizens to communicate Europe, which entailed the Commission-driven projects of connecting citizens with each other, and connecting the citizens with the public institutions. The Platform found this to be unacceptable since it rested on the idea of 'forcing people to integrate to an existing mould' (ibid.: 6). In line with its previous statements, it stressed that the 'civil society dynamics are bottom-up processes that could not be simply taught or forced on people' (ibid.: 6). Rather, it emphasised that 'NGOs are extremely important in facilitating the communication between the EU leaders and citizens by focusing on things that matter for people' (ibid.: 6). To the Platform, this role of the NGOs was not grasped fully by the Commission. Therefore, the Platform argued that a true communication policy should develop formal procedures, which would enable the involvement of civil society representatives in decision-making. The Platform here repeats its previous recommendation: EU politicians should focus not on individuals, but NGOs.

One could argue that the Platform's bottom-up proposal entailed the tenets of direct democracy, in which people govern themselves. Nevertheless, the Platform's suggestion of involving people in the construction of Europe was not actually based on the literal participation of the all in decision-making. Instead, this proposal could only be achieved through some organisations that would enjoy the right to participate on behalf of society. As mentioned, at the current stage of European decision-making, the Platform's bottom-up approach – social self-government – corresponds to lobbying practices. In other words, as opposed to the suggestions about participatory democracy at EU level (Magnette 2003; Armstrong 2002), the Platform's approach is based on the idea of a kind of self-authorised *representative civil society* that acts on behalf of society – even though the society is not aware of being represented.

Having elucidated the ACP and the Commission's communication policy in terms of the bringing the EU back to citizens' discourse, the Platform furthermore claimed that NGOs play a crucial role in connecting citizens with EU governance. In this respect, it pointed out that NGOs disseminate the knowledge of Europe and explain the benefits of European governance, while criticising the Commission's exact objective as propaganda (an interviewee from the ENAR secretariat also claimed that raison d'être of European NGOs is to relate European policies to people). The question becomes why this very act of disseminating knowledge of the EU through civic intermediaries would be more democratic, or more justifiable, than the EU institutions' own attempts. In sum, the Platform related both policies to the work of the European NGO networks, and their objective of gaining legal accreditation in EU decision-making processes. The ACP and Communication policies directly address citizens through several initiatives that have been mentioned. The use of NGOs as an intermediary is one of those policies. Although the Platform provides a critique of EU policies, this critique is formulated in way that serves the Platform in strengthening its institutional position in the EU setup. Another implication of this is that it suggests a functionalist interpretation of politics in which NGOs play an intermediary role.

The European Transparency Initiative and participation through online registration

We have mentioned how in November 2005 the European Commission launched the European Transparency Initiative (ETI). An online registry for interest groups was introduced in June 2008 as part of this initiative. The ETI addressed those groups, namely the companies, business associations, consultancies and civil society organisations, which wanted to influence EU decision-making processes. Although the ETI was one of the concrete examples through which NGOs could be incorporated into EU decision-making, the Platform preferred not to play a leading role in this issue, but to follow the guidance of the CSCG. The CSCG and ALTER-EU played primary roles in reflecting on the online consultation procedures. They prepared guidelines for the NGO registry process

(ALTER-EU and Civil Society Contact Group, 2008). These guidelines focused on procedural details, such as clarifying which costs of the organisations would be included as lobbying expenses, how these would be calculated, and how to indicate the specific lobbying issues.[24]

In short, the ETI delineated the limits of EU interest politics. Whereas the Social Platform opted for a formalised, neo-corporatist decision-making procedure, the ETI showed that the Commission would not put this suggestion into practice. Rather, the Commission treated NGOs as mere interest groups and lobbyists, as we see on Chapter 3. Another ETI conclusion is that the CSCG has become a prominent figure in the NGO community by taking a guiding role in the techniques of lobbying organisations. Since its emergence in 2002 in the context of the Future of Europe campaign, the Contact Group has concentrated particularly on the techniques of participatory governance.

Defining participatory democracy

Whereas the previous section has elaborated how the Platform reflected on the Commission's ECS discourse, this section investigates how the concepts of participation, participatory democracy and civil society are conceived of and defined by the Platform. It examines the Platform's publications and brings together observations from the interviews with the Platform's leaders and the *Civil Dialogue* conference organised by the Platform in 2008.

Since the late 1990s, the Social Platform defended the NGOs' incorporation into EU decision-making on the basis of two aspects: (1) a legal basis for the NGOs' involvement in the EU politics, and (2) the accreditation of NGOs which would be consulted on the development, implementation and evaluation of the actions and policies of the EU.[25] It achieved its first goal – in a relative manner – by influencing EU lawmakers to enact an article about participatory democracy in the Lisbon Treaty, signed in 2007 and entered into force in 2009. Article 11 of the Lisbon Treaty stipulates the elements of participatory democracy at the EU level as follows:

1   The Union Institutions shall, by appropriate means, give citizens and representative associations the opportunity to make known and publicly exchange their views in all areas of Union action.
2   The Union Institutions shall maintain an open, transparent and regular dialogue with representative associations and civil society.
3   The Commission shall carry out broad consultations with parties concerned in order to ensure that the Union's actions are coherent and transparent.
4   No less than one million citizens coming from a significant number of Member States may invite the Commission to submit any appropriate proposal on matters where citizens consider that a legal act of the Union is required for the purpose of implementing the Constitution. A European law shall determine the provisions for the specific procedures and conditions required for such a citizens' initiative.

Based on the draft version of this article in the non-ratified constitutional treaty, Beger (2004), from the Civil Society Contact Group, explained why this article could be considered at best a relative achievement. To him, it was primarily the introduction of an article about participatory democracy in the draft Constitution that he considered a milestone in the development of participatory democracy and civil dialogue. Nonetheless, as he pointed out, even though this article includes some radical elements, such as regarding the citizens' initiatives as an important tool for getting citizens involved, it could eventually turn out to be a mere consultation regime: 'Some of the formulations in this article also give scope to becoming a blast of hot air with little to no consequence for civil dialogue as a concept of participation rather than a mere consultation' (ibid.: 6). Having emphasised this danger, Beger argued that the article on participation could block any further options for participation, since it could provide a legal basis merely for internet consultation. Indeed, Beger's worries became a reality with the Commission's launch of online registration for interest groups in 2008.

To continue with Beger's assessments, the technologies of participatory democracy introduced by the Commission (i.e. online consultations, Plan D for Democracy, and the Europe for Citizens programme) have proven to be symbolically inclusive, but exclusive in practice. The Commission's boundaries of legitimate European civil society privilege those organisations that comply with European integration and the rationalities of European government. For instance, the Commission's discourse has aimed to exclude protest, confrontation and conflict from the repertoire of participatory action, as shown in the previous chapter. It has been further shown that the Commission's discourse is based on a moral conceptualisation of civil society (i.e. appropriate and capable civil society vs. unfitting and incapable civil society), which externalises anti-systemic movements and radical voices. As the above section has shown, the organisations had to adopt the principles of good governance to be regarded as good. However, NGOs have faced more important challenges in order to legitimise their incorporation into the EU decision-making processes – for which they do speak.

The central critique that EU institutions have advanced against NGOs (see the previous chapter for a detailed discussion) concerns whom the NGOs represent. The Social Platform endeavoured to tackle this issue, which threatens the legitimacy of its involvement in EU politics, in the early 2000s. Furthermore, it claimed to represent (a) particular groups, i.e. NGOs, namely the umbrella NGO networks, or citizens, such as the disabled, (b) the interests of those who are unable to represent their interests by themselves, such as victims of human rights abuses, and (c) public interests, ideas, issues and values, such as the environment (SP, *Building a Structured Civil Dialogue* 2001: 4). Second, it asserted that the legitimacy of NGOs should be based on the criterion of transparency instead of representation: 'The term representativeness, when applied to NGOs, seems ambiguous because their representativeness is primarily qualitative ... it is deep-rooted in the nature of the relationships established by NGOs on the ground' (SP, *The Commission and NGOs* 2000: 5). In this respect, it states that the Commission should take some measures for the transparency of the NGOs' involvement in the decision-making process, with the NGOs establishing their own criteria for their internal governance, including transparency, accountability and representativeness (SP, *Building a Structured Civil Dialogue* 2001: 6).

In 2008 the Platform issued a reference paper to define the notions of participatory democracy, civil society and civil dialogue for its members (SP, *Reference Paper: Shaping an Effective Civil Dialogue*, 2008). Although this paper indicates that the production of such a reference document was agreed upon by the Platform's members, the extent to which it represents the members' views is not certain. The paper was prepared by an ad hoc working group. There is no clarification of whether the members had reflected on this or whether it had ever been opened to debate among the members.

In the paper, whereas civil society constitutes the space between the state, market and individual, the notion of a *civil society organisation* (CSO) 'currently refers to the organisations that mediate between these three' (ibid.: 2). According to the paper these organisations comprise 'political parties, sports clubs, music associations, consumer organisations, trade unions, business associations, charitable bodies and cultural groups' (ibid.: 2).[26]

The paper goes on to identify five structural and operational features of CSOs, which distinguish them from other informal networks or firms. First, CSOs are *structured as organisations*; second, they are *private*, so that they are not part of the state; third, they are *non-profit*; fourth, they are *self-governing*; and finally, their *membership is not compulsory*. These features of CSOs were also in large part mentioned by the Platform before, such as in its reflections on the WPEG and Communication Strategy. In contrast with its earlier position, the reference paper neglects to mention that CSOs represent the interests of the general public, which it explains in its discussion about alternative ways of defining civil society organisations. The reference paper compares several options for defining civil society organisations, such as NGOs, public interest organisations and citizen's associations. It finds no reason to refer to civil society organisations as public interest organisations, since 'it is difficult to capture what the public interest incorporates' (ibid.: 3). Even though, the reference paper continues, the Platform is open to use *citizen's associations*, it prefers the notion of NGO as a concept that 'describes all organisations that are outside of the governmental field' (ibid.: 3). Therefore, the paper explains, the Social Platform has named itself the Platform of European Social NGOs. However, the president of the Platform does not identify NGOs as non-state actors, claiming that they work for the public interest along with the public administrative units (C. Reuter, personal communication, May 2009).

The reference paper stresses that the roles of European NGO networks are different than the traditional social NGOs that provide services at the grassroots level. It lists four interconnected roles for European NGOs. First, the European NGO networks *build solidarity across member states, and create social capital at European level*, for they 'ensure information flows from the EU down to the national/local level' (ibid.: 3). Second, they *create a European democratic public sphere* in four ways: (1) fostering mutual learning through their interaction, (2) creating spaces for public debate, (3) aggregating the voices of their members, and (4) facilitate capacity building for their members. The third distinguishing character of NGOs is that they *channel voices* in the society, while strengthening the influence of local and national NGOs. It states that the networks transfer the voice of those who are 'often excluded from decision-making processes, unheard and forgotten, such as very poor people, victims of discrimination, homeless people, etc' (ibid.: 4). However, it mirrors this role of voicing the public concerns when it claims that one of the roles of the networks is to 'make [the grassroots organisations] discuss European decision-making' (ibid.: 4). Fourth, networks of European NGOS *act as challengers/watchdogs* in that they 'offer a critical and protesting voice at European level' and '[provide balance to] the voice of corporations in European decision-making' (ibid.). As a consequence of all this, the paper concludes that EU NGOs 'help [reduce] the gap between politicians and citizens' (ibid.: 4).

In sum, the reference paper defines a double role for the NGOs working in Brussels: as agents of civil society (third and fourth features), and as translators of the rationalities of European government (first feature). On the one hand it symbolically creates a participatory inclusive discourse by defining NGOs as the voice of grassroots civil society. On the other hand, it stresses the role of NGOs as the EU's interlocutors, which disseminate knowledge about the EU and normalise the idea that civil society recognise the EU as a governing entity. To the extent that NGOs affect what and how things are discussed, thought and practised within civil society in terms of the political rationalities, their premise of generating an alternative reason and functioning as a critical gaze fails.

Moreover, the democratic public sphere characteristics of NGOs, presented by the NGOs themselves, do not necessarily have democratising effects. These characteristics have constitutive effects on civil society by generating a form of knowledge, set of practices and a morality, the frames of which are drawn by the political power. Furthermore, the exchange of practices and training could disperse the ethos of neoliberal governmentality, as discussed earlier in this section. This process also has repercussions on the normalisation and internalisation of a certain 'regime of truth'– in this case the one fostered by the EU. Chapter 1 has illustrated how the process of dialogic interaction can lead to mentality leap. This illustration suggests an asymmetrical explanation for interaction and the circulation of norms, i.e. the subjectifying role played by power relations. This does not necessarily have emancipating and civilising consequences, i.e. as Linklater (2005) and Habermas (1996a) argue. However, a certain set of truth exerts itself as normal; a certain set of practices invades the practices of the other.

The reference paper under discussion advances five principles of a participatory democratic system: a democratic infrastructure (freedom of speech and right to assembly); the openness to entertain different views and trust people and authorities; equality and inclusiveness, which requires community empowerment, especially for the disengaged and voiceless; creativity, concreteness and flexibility in participatory actions (such as demonstrations, campaigning, volunteering, unpaid carers, educating children in a sport or art club, sending online letters, participating in an NGO, or being part of a local council's NGO); and a legal framework for the recognition of the rights and the duties of NGOs (SP, *Reference Paper: Shaping Civil Dialogue* 2008: 6–7).

The reference paper continues on to claim that participatory democracy can promote social cohesion, solidarity, social justice and a better life for everyone by first, engaging all people in the constitution of the society, and second, facilitating quality services for people. Participatory democracy could be the remedy for the legitimacy crisis of EU governance since it 'creates public space for discussion and therefore gives people more ownership of decisions and a more active citizenship', thus making citizens more politically active in the associations, and incorporating the interests of the politically disengaged people (e.g. those who do not vote) into decision-making (ibid.: 5). In this way, the reference paper suggests that the concept of citizenship could extend beyond the conventional political sphere, to regard people as actors in all areas of life. In other words, it conceptualises citizenship in terms of technologies of agency, so that it proposes empowering the individual. Consequently, the reference paper's participatory democracy understanding shows parallels with the republican approach to participation, in that it clarifies the social and political integrative promise of participation. However, as a challenge to normative political theory, it conceives of participation as an apolitical phenomenon by arguing that participation transcends the claims of ideology and political divides:

> Almost none of the serious problems people and communities face conform to the remits of political ideologies: By involving people to intervene, participatory democracy can produce solutions that are effective and legitimate, and go beyond traditional political divides. In that sense, it strengthens the legitimacy of decision makers/services providers since their decisions will be based on the real views of people. Participatory democracy therefore aims to improve trust and accountability.
>
> (Ibid.: 5)

The views suggested in the reference paper to a great extent parallel this *problem-solving* approach to politics, in which moral norms and values constitute the mode of conduct between actors in a given political institutional system. The principal value of this system is illustrated by the proponents of deliberative democracy as trust, in which people do not act as mere interest-seeking agents. This cosmopolitan, post-political imaginary world of politics was criticised by Mouffe (2005) for entailing an ideology-free conceptualisation of politics, if not necessarily the end of politics. The reference paper's emphasis, interestingly, overlaps with the problem-solving conceptualisation of politics, arguing that the political ideologies fell short of providing a solution to the 'serious problems of the people'. Therefore, to the reference paper, the participation of the NGOs could promise the legitimacy of the newly emerging community, where ideological politics and representational democracy have been exhausted. The reference paper further argues that NGOs could achieve this task by promoting a new understanding of politics, since they channel the *real* views of the people.

Another problem arises in the reference paper's argument if it is taken to represent the lobbying activities of NGO networks as ideology-free. One the one hand, it appreciates a post-ideological position, claiming that none of the political ideologies provides solutions for social problems. On the other hand, its suggestions for social problems do in fact stem from a certain political ideology. For instance, it supports a kind of Third Way approach to redistributive politics based on the principle of 'needs' – a leftist approach to wealth redistribution. Furthermore, the Platform is ideologically partial per se, since one of its three main objectives is to advocate a social Europe. In sum, the reference paper's ambition to go beyond political divides and find solutions to the 'real' problems of the people is itself an ideological gesture, as Žižek would call it, since the language of the ideology produces a discourse as if the 'real problems' and the 'ideological chimeras' could be taken separate from one another (Žižek, 1997).

The reference paper recognises civil dialogue as 'a component and tool of participatory democracy', in which organised civil society and public decision-makers, as well as civil servants at local, national and European levels, are involved. The reference paper's principles of civil dialogue are accountability and responsiveness, the political will and openness to make a difference, transparency and clarity, equality and inclusiveness, formal arrangements, procedures and financial support for civil society, a proper role and recognition for NGOs, and the inclusion of civil society at all stages (agenda setting, policy definition, decision-making, implementation, evaluation, and reformulation). Table 4.6, which appears in the reference paper, presents a scale to measure the involvement of civil society organisations in politics. The 'exclusion' and 'indifference' levels are self-explanatory; however, the remaining levels in the scale require some comment. One-way dissemination denotes the situation in which only public authorities provide information. In consultation, on the other hand, public authorities provide information to NGOs and invite them to give feedback. While in dialogue, NGOs can set the agenda and the public authorities can implement the NGO's interests, participation implies that NGOs' proposals are incorporated into official documents and programs. Finally, partnership denotes the extent to which the NGOs play a cooperative role in decision, design, production and administration.

Table 4.6 Scale of civil society organisation involvement

−1	Exclusion
0	Indifference
1	One-way Dissemination
2	Consultation
3	Dialogue
4	Participation
5	Partnership

Source: (SP, *Reference paper: Shaping civil dialogue*, 2008).

Publications are not the unique tools which the Platform defines and disperses its views about participatory democracy. As mentioned above, the Platform has concentrating on a certain theme each year since 2006. In 2008–9, this was civil dialogue – the incorporation of NGOs into the EU decision-making. As a part of this, the Platform organised the conference, *How can we shape the Europe we want?*, in Brussels.[27] The conference aimed to gather different actors related to European politics, including the members of the Platform and their national members, EU officials, and academics. However, NGO members from Eastern European and Balkan countries constituted the vast majority of participants.

The conference opened with a panel that comprised EU officials from the European Parliament and the European Commission, along with one scholar.[28] The panel was followed by four workshops: (1) the future of the Open Method of Coordination for social inclusion, (2) the problem of the source of NGOs' funding, (3) the role of EU NGO networks in bridging the gap between European and national levels, and (4) strategies to influence decision-making processes across the EU. The panels, workshops and plenary sessions discussed the roles of NGO networks in linking national NGOs to European politics, identified the current problems in performing these roles and proposed some solutions.

Several participants, mostly national NGOs, argued that there was a problem in civil dialogue, claiming that the current approach was based on the mentality of civil society involvement in a pre-defined European agenda. Furthermore, while the current approach focused on policy changes in the EU policies, national NGOs wanted to exert pressure at the national level. Therefore, they resisted the rationality in which they direct their energy towards the EU institutions. Some of the national NGOs were, on the other hand, more willing to be incorporated into European-level politics. This latter group, however, listed several problems: creating an interest in what happens at the EU level in the national level, the lack of expertise within the NGO community about European issues, the lack of information about the EU political agenda, the complexity of European jargon, the language barrier as a general problem in communicating beyond territories, NGO funding problems, insufficient NGO capacity and resources, and cultural and economic differences between countries.[29]

National NGOs, furthermore, indicated that their European networks had some flaws in their function of bridging the communication gap between the national and European levels. To them, EU NGO networks should take a leading role in facilitating and mediating their interactions with European institutions, training the national NGOs about the EU and its policies, and providing arguments for the national NGOs in order to foster policy change in domestic politics. The workshop participants further suggested several solutions to enhance interactions between the national and European levels, as well as influence EU institutions. First, to influence European policies, national NGOs would primarily provide information to their European networks. Second, to achieve this, national NGOs should be empowered, such as through capacity building, training, exchanging best practices and peer-learning. The third solution, on the other hand, involved persuading EU political authorities that they could make use of the NGOs. In this respect, one of the ideas was to empower national NGOs to push their governments in order to implement European policies, such as adopting new modes of governance (i.e. the Open Method of Coordination at the national level). Another suggestion for the EU political authorities was to use national NGOs as a 'trampoline' in their relations with non-EU states. The representatives' views reveal the extent to which the NGO community internalised the idea of becoming the agents and carriers of Europeanised political socialisation and political change.

In addition to the document analyses and the conducted interviews, the conference provided the opportunity of observing how the NGO actors – both the European NGOs and the national NGOs – conceive of participation, the role of NGOs in EU politics, and the role of the NGOs in politics in general. The initial observation of the conference resulted in three reflections on the tenets of government by in the EU. First, the conference was open to the participation of all possible 'stakeholders' (as the discourse on European Governance requires the collaboration of multiple actors). Second, the structure of the conference resembled EU institutions' meetings (as a reminder, the Social Platform's ex-president had also associated the Social Platform's internal governance with the EU structure). For instance, after each workshop the results were presented in the plenary by a 'rapporteur'.[30] Third, addressing the NGOs mainly from the perspective of new and prospective member states, the conference complied with the Commission's ambition of empowering civil society in the respective states (see Chapter 3). One of the components of this ambition is to translate the political technologies of government, i.e. NGO involvement in politics and the delivery of services according to the principles of good governance. In this respect, for those countries, as mentioned, the Platform and CSCG organise network development and capacity-building trips. For instance, the Solidar, one of the members of the Social Platform, initiated a study about the capacity and legal status of civil society organisations with 50 NGOs from the Western Balkans in 2009. This study involved a survey which focused on whether the respective countries had any specific law regulating CSOS, and whether the NGOs had sufficient capacity with respect to leadership, staff support, the organisation of working plans, communication skills and citizen engagement (Solidar 2009).[31]

Concluding remarks

In Chapter 3, the analysis of the EU discourse on the civil society and participatory democracy was crucially important to reveal the contexts in which the respective concepts are used by EU institutions, particularly the Commission, and put into practice. This chapter has traced the influences and effects of the EU's discourse, and examined how the Platform receives and perceives this discourse. It would accordingly be possible to assess it acts as agents of political and societal control, and carriers of political rationalities and technologies.

These assessments differ from the previous literature that examined the NGO phenomenon at the EU level. The literature of social movements defines a transnational coalition of NGOs as a movement advocacy coalition (Ruzza 2004) or a transnational advocacy coalition (Keck and Sikkink 1998; Cullen 2005). The central argument of this perspective is that collective social action organises transnationally in order to exert pressure on transnational governance mechanisms, in this case the politics of the EU. Contrary to what the social movement literature argues, the Platform does not frame its raison d'être as a mobilisation of contention either at the margins or in Brussels. Governance literature, on the other hand, seeks the promise of the NGOs in their contribution of the results of European policymaking processes. In this case, the Platform's contribution like as any other NGO that has been engaged in EU governance is, however, debatable. This is not of necessity due to under-performance of the Platform or of its incapability, but by and large due to the consultation system of the Commission that privileges a neo-plural interest intermediation system. Formalising the contribution of the NGOs in governance is a contentious issue either, due to issues with their representativeness and accountability. While concentrating on the NGOs as the source of the problem, we might though expect that the norms and procedures through which NGOs involve in governance could take different forms in the future as a result of the institutional changes taking place at the European level.

From a different perspective than the aforementioned literature, the main argument of this book is to debate the ways in which in discourses of participation and civil society have been institutionally defined at the EU level and in turn how an NGO, which has been formed as an effect of these discourses, perform a prescribed identity of European civil society. In the example of the Platform, it is argued that this identity maybe best described as a split persona, between a contentious alter-ego and a peaceful performance-machine stakeholder. Beyond the arguments of other literatures mentioned above, the performance of an NGO in a governance milieu thus can be examined in terms of a governmentality approach. The next chapter expands these concluding remarks and the implications of the theoretical and practical arguments of this book.

Table 4.7 summarises the framework of our analysis, and it is self-explanatory.

Table 4.7 Analysis of the Social Platform: the modes, procedures, and constitutive elements of interaction in different levels

Levels of action	The modes, procedures and constitutive elements of interaction
Between the Social Platform and EU institutions	Advancing the interests of EU NGOs that are members of the Platform, advocacy of common positions
Between EU institutions and the Platform	• Connecting with the citizens discourse • European civil society discourse • EU's interest policy • EU's communication policy • EUs discourse on participatory democracy • EU's role in the structural organisation of the EU NGOs
Intra-Platform relations	The aspects of studying the Social Platform: • Organisational structure, e.g. the strong role of the secretariat • The history and evolution of the Platform • The criteria of membership (drawing the boundaries of legitimate EU NGOs and ECS) • Participation in decision-making • The values of the Platform (promotion of participatory democracy) • The decision-making structure of the Platform • The source and the distribution of finances • The Platform's strategies such as working on the basis of an annual theme, empowering the Secretariat, avoiding protest and contention, supporting the accreditation system in order to consolidate its power and exclude radical voices from the legitimate definition of civil society

Members' interactions with the Platform	• The right to participate in the Platform's decision-making processes (general assembly, working groups) • The right to disseminate their work through the Platform, i.e. through the Platform's website and newsletter • To enhance their credibility within the NGO community vis-à-vis EU institutions by being a member of the Platform
The Platform's interaction with the members	• Rendering the EU knowable by disseminating information and promoting an understanding of EU policies through regular internal meetings, electronic communication and weekly online bulletin (*Weekly Update*). • Enhancing the visibility of their members by publishing their work on the website, in its online bulletin *Weekly Update*, quarterly publication *ENGAGE*, annual activity report, media announcements and brochures. • Providing expert knowledge for constituents through the exchange of ideas and practices among the constituents of Platform, training the communicative and administrative skills of its members, and benefiting from external expertise, i.e. in defining the central concepts, such as participatory democracy and civil society, and setting strategies for better lobbying • Stressing its role as intermediary for EU NGOs in attending regular meetings with European institutions • Reimbursing the travel and accommodation costs of its members • Enabling participation in two study visits to EU member and candidate countries
Members' interactions within the Platform	• A forum for interaction and the exchange of knowledge and experience among social NGOs, as well as for the flow of discourse within an institutional setting
Intra-NGO community communication	• The Platform reproduces the art of European government in its interactions with the environment

Notes

1. It should be noted that there are organisational differences among these networks. For instance, while the Platform has eight permanent staff, the human rights network has one coordinator (L. Sedou, personal communication, May 2009).
2. (N.15844[75084]) article 3.
3. www.socialplatform.org.
4. Adopted by the Social Platform General Assembly, 23 April 2004.
5. Hereafter, in my citations, SP stands for Social Platform, *AR* for Annual Report and *WP* for work programme.
6. Internal Rules, article 5.1, 2006.
7. It might be argued that he Platform uses the membership fee as an instrument to consolidate its power vis-à-vis its members. It is a way of securing power in the network; the member can participate and vote as long it pays its fees. The power of the member can greatly be reduced if the fee is not paid. The membership fee is thus a key for the Platform in the sense that it is one of the Platform's integrative elements, elements that attach different constituents together and help the central authority maintain its power over the network.
8. Other EU NGO umbrella networks are: CONCORD, the European NGO confederation for Relief and Development; Culture Action Europe, the Forum for the Arts and Heritage; EPHA, the European Public Health Alliance; EUCIS-LLL, the European Civil Society Platform on Lifelong Learning; EWL, the European Women's Lobby; GREEN 10, a group of leading environmental NGOs active at the EU level, and HRDN, the Human Rights and Democracy Network.
9. It should be remembered that with respect to the representativeness issue of European Civil Society, the EESC asserted having a reputation as a criterion.
10. www.socialplatform.org (accessed 13 May 2010).
11. In detail, the costs of Platform in 2007 were distributed respectively: staff 50 per cent, travel and accommodation 10 per cent, services 12 per cent, administration 20 per cent and specific projects eight per cent.
12. With this regard, the Platform wrote an advocacy letter to the European Parliament (the letter to the head of Parliament, European Parliament Agora, *A first step towards a structured civil dialogue with the European Parliament*, Platform, 2008). Here, the Platform also praised the procedures of the AGORAs in that all participants could receive equal opportunity to co-chair workshops and plenary sessions, as well as report on the different workshops. However, according to the Platform, AGORAs had a major flaw: not making explicit how the conclusions of the AGORAs would be incorporated into decision-making processes, so that participants could not receive feedback about their recommendations and contributions. The Platform further proposed that the EP should consider the AGORAs 'as a form of consultation when working on a report' (ibid.), and continue this on a formal basis.
13. The Prodi Commission also launched a new post of Commissioner responsible from the public communications of the Communication; Margot Wallstrom appointed for this task.
14. See the Social Platform, *AR*, 2003: 22.
15. This toolkit was downloaded 5,000 times in 10 days after it was published.
16. It should be noted neoliberalism, as Foucault uses it, does not have aim to replace – if not complementing – the common use of the concept, which concerns the market-driven economy and social policies, relatively open markets, and strengthening the role of private sector in setting the priorities of the state. Central to Foucault's concern was to elaborate upon the shift in the philosophical (and practical) grounds of classical liberalism; therefore, he investigates the origins of this turn within German *ordo* liberalism and Chicago school. Yet, this leads to conceptual confusion Rose (1996) offers using advanced liberalism.

17 The Commission's education policies was also analysed from a similar perspective (Mitchell 2006).
18 The Social Platform presented this as a position paper on its webpage under the category of participatory democracy and governance.
19 See also Skocpol (2003) for an account of how American civil society has become managerial.
20 The first GA was convened in 2001, the same year the Platform adapted a statute.
21 One limitation for our work was that it was not possible to observe how the decision-making processes in each different unit differ.
22 The administrative units of the Platform can only comprise the members of the Platform. In other words, official affiliation with one of the Platform's member networks is a prerequisite for assuming responsibility in these bodies. My fieldwork experience proved that some members of the Management Committee do not associate themselves with the Social Platform. During the arrangement of interviews, I contacted five members of the MC; only one person responded to my request, and that person, moreover, turned it down. After the failure to access members of the MC, I had the opportunity to meeting one person who initially did not reply to my emails during my field work in Brussels in December 2008. Taking this opportunity, I tried once again to arrange an interview with that person. Surprisingly, however, he denied affiliation with the Platform, instead insisting that he was working for another organisation (the European Volunteer Centre). When reminded that his name was on the Management Committee list on the Platform's website, he stated that the Management Committee has a supervisory function, and addressed the Secretariat in order to get information about the Platform.
23 These include AECID (Agencia Española de Cooperación internacional para el Desarrollo), GTZ (Deutsche Gesellschaft für Technische Zusammenarbeit), SIDA (Swedish International Development Cooperation Agency), NORAD (Norwegian Agency for Development Cooperation), DFID (Department for International Development), UNDP and EC. The World Bank has used LFA since 1997.
24 The guidelines pointed out some crucial shortcomings in the registry rules. For instance, the register did not require any clarification on the individual lobbyists. Furthermore, financial information on lobbying expenditures in the register was inconsistent and not sufficient for making comparisons (ibid.). For instance, the registration system required that only activities should be registered as lobbying. Hence, while the lobbying companies could just show the dinners with the politicians and civil servants as a cost of lobbying, civil society organisations were required to register their entire budget. Furthermore, since there was no requirement to name the individuals engaged in the lobbying system, former decision-makers could be involved in the lobbying business by providing their clients insider knowledge and contacts.
25 This was first expressed by the Social Platform in 1999 (*Lisbon Declaration, Developing Civil Dialogue in Europe to Strengthen Social Cohesion*).
26 This definition was borrowed from the EESC's 1999 document. The Platform's internalisation of this definition demonstrates how a marginalised EU institution might formulate a hegemonic discourse.
27 The language of the conference was English and simultaneous translation was provided during presentations.
28 The academics' representative on the panel was Beate Kohler-Koch, a prominent scholar in multi-level governance. The relationship between the Platform and Kohler-Koch is not limited to Kohler-Koch's participation in this conference. Moreover, the Social Platform also has a link on its website to Kohler-Koch's EU-funded research project, CONNEX (www.connex-network.org), which studies European politics in terms of the governance approach. This proximity between the researcher and the Platform is worth elaborating in that it enables us to track the ideas influencing the Platform. Throughout the book, Kohler-Koch's ideas have been contrasted with

170 A case study on the Social Platform

the deliberative approach in the discussion of whether the Platform acts as an agent of European governing. However, our survey reveals that the influence of scientific knowledge is also vital to an understanding of the European art of government.

29 The report on this workshop was published on the Platform's website, which also provided some help.

30 Each workshop had appointed a 'rapporteur' before the sessions started. The rapporteurs of the conference resembled the functions of the rapporteur in the EU institutional setup. The European Parliament, for example, defines the key functions of the rapporteur as follows:

> The rapporteur 'reports' the findings of the European Parliamentary committee to the plenary. In that capacity their opinion carries a lot of weight. If you want to influence a proposal it is important to ensure that the rapporteur is aware of your concerns.
> Accessed at www.europeanlawmonitor.org/EU-Information/What-Is-Guide-to-Key-EU-Terms/EU-Parliament-What-Is-a-Rapporteur.html, 6 October 2010

31 Solidar, Questionnaire: Capacity and legal status of CSOs in the Western Balkans, 2009.

5 Conducting a European civil society agency

Embedding neoliberal governance through managerial subjects

Focusing on the participation and civil society discourses that have been promoted by the EU, this book has critically examined the idea of involvement of the supranational intermediaries of civil society, defined as European NGOs, in EU governance. In the scholarly literature, this proposal has also been supported and considered to be a remedy for the EU democratic deficit. Having examined the Commission's European civil society (ECS) discourse and its implications on the Social Platform of European NGOs – one of the prominent umbrella organisations – this book, however, has suggested an alternative narrative, one that proposes understanding the NGO and participation phenomena from the vantage point of governmentality.

The conditions of formation of such governmentality in the European context have been shaped in the post-Maastricht era, in which the markets have been liberalised and the restrictions on the financial flows have been reduced. This era also introduced the notion of a European social and economic space to comply with the changing nature of European economic and social policies (Jessop 2006), which connected social policies to economic ones. The governing role of the EU in terms of economic and social governance took the form of a centre of supervision and super-vision (Jessop 2006). The latter is of particular importance as it shows the characteristics of the European government, the power of the EU in governing European societies. Thus, population as a 'natural collectivity of living beings' (Rose *et al.* 2006: 84) has been re-defined in a European spatial context, transcending their national boundaries. This is in a way reshaping of a liberal government, because both the state and the society needs to be rethought in this post-national situation.

These new rationalities and technologies of government, in a way, contest with classical liberal art of government because they intervene in civil society by inducing some actors to join governance settings, and often by coercing them to organise according to pre-set institutional frames. Government in this case borrowed and created principles and knowledges in pertinence with governance theory, civil society theories, NGO management, professional communication, Third Way, and social capital. These principles and knowledges are carried out by managerial guidelines, funding criteria, arranging spaces for the incorporation of NGOs into policy settings. The power of the EU government here is to conduct and conduct of conduct, facilitate knowledges, act upon actions of actors by setting frames for their cognition and behaviour via the organisational management (LFA and Project cycle management), and codes of conduct for participation practices.

Objects of government here are the European governance, the supply side of policymaking (NGOs), which is governed to be efficient, controlled, be accountable, and in turn legitimate the EU. As Rose *et al.* (2006: 87) suggests 'to govern, therefore, whether to govern a household, a ship, or a population, it was necessary to know that which was to be governed, and to govern in the light of that knowledge'. Chapter 3 elaborated on a survey commissioned by the EU on voluntary sector in 1997. The EU also launched framework programmes in order to search for European civil society, European public sphere aftermath of White Paper on European Governance and in context when the debates over constitutional treaty began in Laeken in 2000. To govern abstract concepts such as ECS and EPS, however, is more intricate, for policymaking as governing often requires something tangible and material. Governing abstractions may require certain ways of action, and one of the ways of this conduct in this case was to define and constitute performative agencies of ECS (NGO networks), which can help imagining the actuality of an abstract totality, ECS. That is, as those NGO networks have been made visible in Brussels and elsewhere in Europe, it was possible to think about a reality of an ECS, even though it might have been in its earlier stages of development. The EU has tried to achieve this intentionally, though central to the argument of this book is that the influences of non-intentional processes in shaping of a civil society discourse have of great significance. I covered the conceptual ground of this argument in Chapter 1 and two, thus here I would like to discuss some wider implications.

The White Paper as an intentional programmatic text involves invoking civil society to engage in governance (policymaking processes and service delivery). It also defines and constitutes European civil society and its subjects by opening a discursive field. Yet, this does not mean that civil society subjects are produced as by-products of this discourse.

> Discourse is not, for Foucault, a monolithic, anthropomorphized Subject that bludgeons its way through history leaving only hegemonic subjects in its wake; nor are Foucauldian subjects merely 'standardized products, of some discourse formation ... individual copies that are mechanically punched out.' On the contrary: although all subject-positions are 'subjected' to discourses that temporally and ontologically precede them, the inevitable multiplicity of those discourses ensures that subjectification invariably produces structurally incompatible (i.e., hegemonic and counter-hegemonic) subject-positions.
>
> (Heller 1996: 94)

What is the implication of this in our discussion? Emerged as a subject-position, an NGO, civil society activist, are both guided and encouraged by policies. These policies should not be considered pure political indoctrinations, because they are often informed by scientific discourses. In fact scientists can also engage in policy-making processes under governance settings. Even though policy-makers might align with a particular discourse on civil society, scientific discourses on civil society and civil society activists offer and defend different if not alternative visions.

For instance, other groups, such as environmentalists, human rights movements, and anti-globalisation and far-rights groups also lay claim over the definition of European civil society with alternative visions for Europe. This book suggests implications for NGOs involving in EU governance and governance settings because they are more or less constrained by the similar structures of governance procedures and constraints. This, however, has limited implications existing outside the governance settings and policy domain.

The EU's attempt to foster harmonisation in terms of organisational knowledge leading to isomorphism might be coercive and restrictive. NGO support policies of the EU are coercive, in the sense they require the NGOs to adapt managerial knowledges. These policies are also restrictive, because they draw an appropriate sphere of action, that of acting beyond ideologies, presenting technical information and organising in accordance with managerial principles. Though, still such political intervention cannot determine all possible actions of the actors due to several reasons:

a *If civil society is not initially and solely defined by the EU, then the ECS subjects cannot be by-products of the EU:* The notions of participation and civil society are not reduced to the EU, that is, the EU is not the intellectual centre which defines these notions. Civil society is a historical concept that can be even be traced back to Hobbes, and participation has been a central notion and practice of democracy since 1960s. What the EU does is to prioritise a particular notion of civil society, managerial and de-politicised. Then, if the EU is not the intellectual centre of the notions of civil society and participation and if these notions have been defined elsewhere and often in contested terms, and if the idea of incorporating civil society to governance has been indeed suggested and practiced in different contexts, then ECS subjects cannot be by-products of the EU's discourse.

b *If actors are free but informed by the discourse, then ECS subjects cannot be by-products:* Actors are not puppets of political power acting within a discursive field defined by the political programmes, when power and resistance are conceived of correlated (Rose *et al.* 2006). Although EU's intervention shapes the actions of the NGOs, they have free space for fulfilling the content of their work. In other words, political power restricts but not determines. Rather, it invokes NGOs to adopt managerial practices in their organisational structures, such as through funding requirements, while adapting to an environment that reinforces the homogenised regimen of NGO management and to an institutional environment of managerial governance.

c *ECS discourse constraints other subject positions:* It means that discourse constraints the participation of other civil society subjects by confining this domain to managerial and willing actors.
d *Language (EU texts) is not the unique aspect that explains the constitution of subject positions:* Although we have focused on texts, this does not mean that it is possible to achieve anything with the appropriate formulation of language. Rather, I examine the emergence and the evolution of the ECS against the background of a larger social processes and meaning structures, those of restructuring of the statehood, neoliberal capital accumulation, Third Way, third sector, and social inclusion. The EU-driven-discourse on ECS can have another *meaning* when it is elaborated from this larger frame:

- ECS discourse carries global meaning structures on practices, norms, values into Europe, such as 'participation', managerialism, Third Way and liberal conception of the state-society-market relationship;
- ECS discourse creates or reproduces new *meaning* structures in the context of Europe, such as European society, European citizenship, and active citizenship.

The EU has been promoting the discourse on civil society and participation/participatory democracy since the 1990s. Within the scope of this discourse, the Commission has related the organised civic actors to the context of EU integration and its institutional interests. For instance, in the late 1990s, the Commission related the civic actors to legitimising its regulatory role in social policy. In the early 2000s, the Commission linked the discourse on European civil society to administrative reform within EU institutions and the EU's legitimacy crises. With respect to the latter, in the late 2000s, the Commission focused on the ECS's role in bringing the EU back to its citizens, diagnosing the legitimacy crisis of EU governance in citizens' lack of knowledge on the EU.

The participation discourse has been particularly appealing to the Commission in the context of questioning a common European identity (or demos). The debate on the existence of a demos in Europe suggested two alternative views: (a) there is no European demos due to the absence of a common language and history (Cederman 2001) and (b) a European demos can be imagined (and invented), since rights and the law could provide a *thin* integrative base by detaching the ethno-cultural basis of identity from rights (Weiler 1999; Habermas 2003, 2001; Eriksen 2005). Participation discourse, in line with the latter view, is compatible with the project of constituting a rights-based society, a model which is fostered with the symbolic use of participation, i.e. the notion that 'you can feel a sense of belonging because you take part in decision-making', along with the notion of polity-building. Therefore, it can be argued that the Commission has created a discursive field through participation in order to intervene in new domains, including empowering NGOs and connecting with the European citizenry.

The Commission's civil society discourse has, thus, been criticised for embodying a symbolic function, as if the society were incorporated into the EU decision-making processes. Walters and Haahr (2005b: 79) question the Commission's attempts along these lines: 'The point is how many people really think that initiatives like internet forums, or even improved procedures or consultation in policy-making, are going to significantly enhance European democracy.' Walters and Haahr (ibid.) further suggest that the symbolic use of the discourse has preceded the very goal of realising political participation. Constructing the discourse without content though creates a peculiar situation in which the definition of participation remains obscure to the coordinator of one of the umbrella networks of civil society organisations, the Civil Society Contact Group, which is responsible for the promotion of the participation within civil society (L. Sedou, personal communication, May 2009).

The neo-Marxist critics of the participation discourse and NGOs argue that political authorities make use of NGOs in developing countries to garner public support for neoliberal policy reforms (Petras 1999, Leal 2007) or embed those reforms to society (Porter and Craig 2004). This might be another way of understanding the emergence of the NGO phenomenon after the Maastricht Treaty, because the EU has also tried to draw benefit from the NGOs' enhancing public support for the EU and associated their emergence with the Europe's economic and social governance. Participation discourse, in this respect, has been appealing to the EU in mobilising the NGOs under the scope of a normative symbolic framework and aiming for the *consent* of the governed. The participation discourse, however, has not merely played an instrumental role in putting the ambitions of the EU into practice, creating an illusion that public concerns are channelled through the NGOs. ECS discourse is not selling a project campaign in such way to conceal a hidden reality from the people by misleading them with symbolic participation. Invoking civil society symbolically is productive and real (Porter and Craig 2004; Jessop 2002b; Anheier 2004; Springer 2012; Larner 2000; Hall 2012).

In what follows I will elaborate some implications of the incorporation of NGOs into governance via political encouragement by drawing on the observations on the Platform.

Performing NGO participation in European governance

The contribution of NGOs in EU governance is found trivial by the earlier research (Obradovic 2005): it has not been possible to track the particular contributions, since the Commission has been providing general feedbacks. Besides, the Commission is not legally obliged to consider these inputs, and this situation has not changed in the Lisbon Treaty, even though it has introduced the norm of participatory democracy. Thus, the presence of the social actors has been within the confines of 'rights to be heard'. On this account, the ideas of an NGO might likely be circulating as *empty signifiers* in Brussels policy-making milieu, but these ideas may make of sense when they are considered in relation to the concerns like the governing of European governance, power/knowledge and studied as illustration of how a sponsored NGO perceives this process.

As the above has shown, the Platform has been defined and constituted by bureaucratic programming and its management structure and working strategies comply with the tenets of New Public Management and 'new managerialism', which are associated with neoliberal rationalities. It has been illustrated that the Platform's organisational structure, working methods, ways of communicating and ways of thinking have been shaped and guided by the EU's participation discourse – though, its meta-rationality (i.e. NPM and new managerialism) was not necessarily created by the EU. In turn, the structure and procedures through which the Platform has been incorporated into EU decision-making lead to several consequences.

First, the practice of the EU's participatory governance discourse contains several exclusionary elements, for the consultation settings exert a pressure on interested groups to be capable of following the complex requirements. Bouwen (2004) argues that this has not only shaped the social actors, but also the business groups. He also argues that the Commission's role is overlooked with this regard. On the other, the Commission's interest intermediation policy categorise NGOs as interest groups, i.e. like any other group (e.g. corporate and business groups) that endeavours to influence EU politics.

Second, to hear it from the documents of the Platform, the NGO community is well-interconnected between different sectors as well as different levels (e.g. the national and European levels). On paper, this looks like a well-functioning state/society relationship, in which the different levels of the civil society communicate each other, so that any discourse that emerges within these deliberations are linked to the political public spheres. Nevertheless, the inquiry into the networking system of European NGOs demonstrates that this networking mechanism does not function perfectly. The rationale behind the network system rests on the idea of a linear interconnection that runs from the local NGOs to umbrella national networks, from umbrella national networks to European umbrella networks, and European umbrella networks to second-level umbrella networks. Nevertheless, national organisations have but a minor impact on the work of the Social Platform, while the right to participate in decision-making processes (management committees, steering committees, and working groups) is assigned to European-level NGO networks. In addition, the Platform defines itself as a European lobbying organisation whose objective is to provide advocacy to EU institutions.

Third, in fact, the very idea of a European NGO network excludes some voices from the notion of European civil society projected in the Commission's civil society discourse. Even though the Platform claims to channel *the* voice of the European civil society, it restricts the privilege of interacting with political institutions to only those organisations that are recognised and accredited by the EU institutions. The Platform defends this arrangement on the grounds that the Commission should implement an accreditation system in order to incorporate the representatives of the NGO sector into EU decision-making structures. It can be argued that it supports this idea to consolidate its position. However, this could also lead to a competition for power among civil society actors in order to be formally recognised by the EU institutions. Moreover, the Platform reinforces the Commission's conception of European civil society, which draws the legitimate boundaries of civil society according to those actors that are capable and enthusiastic about engaging in governance choreography (i.e. Europe talks to Europe). Having defined itself as a peaceful and constructive representative of civil society, it leaves out groups which challenge the ethos of European integration – anti-capitalists, anti-globalisation/alternative globalisation groups, anarchists, Eurosceptics, etc. – from the very definition of civil society. One can argue that political power would not be willing, surely, to establish dialogue with anti-systemic movements through formal structures. Neither would some social groups prefer lobbying and advocacy work as a strategy of defending their claims (Young 2001). Thus, the argument supported here is that the inclusion of 'other' and 'many' voices (and groups), including the most contentious, would not necessarily make the consultations more democratic. Rather, the implication of the Commission's discourse is that it fosters a *meaning* of civil society, which is restricted to actors that are docile and conform to the system. Our survey has shown how docile actors are managed and trained, thus being constituted by political rationalities.

Fourth, an NGO is entitled the status of 'stakeholder' in EU governance, however this notion is 'necessarily constrained and limited in terms of who can, is, or will be allowed to participate' (Swyngedouw 2005: 2000). Stakeholder status determines the participants in governance; however, 'in most cases, entitlements are conferred upon participants by those who already hold a certain power or status. Of course, the degree to which mobilisations of this kind are successful depends, *inter alia*, on the degree of force and/or power such groups or individuals can garner and on the willingness of the existing participants to agree to include them' (ibid.). This statement accurately reflects the Platform. The Platform mainly recruits people who hold a degree in European studies or have experience in European-level NGO management. In this sense, the Platform can be defined as a European elitist organisation. The people it recruits are those who prove willing to participate in the new governance setup, including the consultations with the Commission, the AGORA meetings with the European Parliament, Liaison group of the European Economic and Social Committee. They are also willing to work for the deepening of European integration. The Platform, after all, is an organisation whose interest and energy is directed towards the EU institutions and the idea of Europe. Furthermore, it works to Europeanise the interests of national NGOs, by which I mean it directs its energy and activities towards European institutions and the tools of European governance (e.g. the Open Method of Coordination). Thus, the Platform fits well into a functionalist conception of a Europeanised and Europeanising institution (Streeck and Schmitter 1991); its origins can be found in Monnet's thoughts, which has been rejuvenated and put into language with 'European Economic and Social Space' by Delors, put into practice by Santer, and developed by Prodi and Barroso Commissions. The aspects and several implications of Europeanisation can be outlined as follows.

First of all, the Platform was constituted deliberately by the Commission in order to act as an interlocutor of the Commission against the EU NGOs, particularly which work in social sector. Since its establishment, the Platform has been helping the Commission organise *European Social Policy Forums*,[1] the practice of which was later was called civil dialogue. Second, to the extent that the Platform has internalised the Commission's civil society and participation discourse, it has moved from the traditional tenets of civic action (i.e. voluntarism); and has become an enterprise-like organisation governed through a managerial mentality. Third, Platform has been considered a channel of European citizenry through linking public concerns into the EU level, thus suggesting a solution for the democratic deficit of the EU, which is perceived to be caused by the gap between the EU and its citizens. Nonetheless, this book argues that the Platform's (and some other NGOs' alike) involvement into the Commission's consultation regime is not a democratising act per se. In practice, the Platform (and other EU NGOs alike) can hardly represent European civil society as such, considering the Commission's opaque sponsorship, which is considered as the principal obstacle against the autonomy of civil society; its disconnection with the grassroots; and its resemblance like an exclusive club for the EU oriented NGOs – thus categorically excluding many voices of civil society, including anti-systemic groups.

Given that the Platform's influence on the Commission's consultations is rather trivial; thus, this book's proposal to concentrate on the NGO phenomenon in relation to a governmentality and power/knowledge relation might suggest an alternative analytical tools to understand governance and its subjects. The Platform may rather be conceived as an agent of government, which endeavours to tailor a harmonised organisational model for the social NGO community (both at EU and national level) along with a shared understanding of the notions of civil society and participation in such way complying with the tenets of 'new managerialism' and New Public Management. The critique of this book is that it sheds light on a contemporary process transmogrifying some civic activists into managers; the conception of civil society into a stakeholder of governance; and participation into bureaucratically controlled de-politicised action for mere efficient problem solving.

This observation implies that the Platform's organisational structure, working methods, communication methods and even ways of thinking and doing things have been, to a certain extent, shaped by the deliberate instruments of the Commission, such as via the requirements for the Platform report its achievements, the pressure on proving its representativeness, and improving its accountability and transparency. The Platform's organisational structure and management techniques largely complies with the tenets of new managerialism and NPM, which refers to all organisational changes happened after 1980s with regard to the dominance of market mentality and economic rationalities in public administration. This argument can be clarified as follows: the Platform follows a results-based, management-oriented working method, and thus aims to achieve certain objectives, which are calculable and auditable in a given period of time. These practices, in turn, have likely repercussions on what is being voiced; since, such management frame prioritises *know how rather know what*. Practiced in this way, 'participation' is conceptualised as an effective and efficient problem-solving activity, and is thus prone to de-politicisation by treating the objects of participation and the very notion of participation in itself as *things* to be achieved.

From a larger perspective, the emergence of an NGO phenomenon is related to (good) governance discourse, which was created by World Bank and United Nations in the context of economic development. It prescribes a particular role for the NGOs in accountable and legitimate governance as well as mobilising the grassroots (i.e. a catalyst of a democratic society). Rationalities and technologies behind the constitution of the Platform are not, therefore, reduced to the EU. The EU itself is exposed to the same process defining the ideas and practices of organisation, considering the Commission has conducted an administration reform during 1999–2004, one that can be associated with NPM (Kassim 2008). The EU, hence, is not necessarily seen as the intellectual centre that creates the techniques of NGO management, but an actor playing a role in carrying it into the European context.

Governmentality and NGO phenomenon

Against this backdrop, the book has, first, elaborated conceptual grounds of discussing governmentality in the context of incorporation of NGOs into decision-making structures. Second, it has investigated the global dynamics in order to refute the *sui generis* nature of the EU. Third, it has examined the ways in which the European civil society (ECS) discourse has evolved and transformed within the EU institutional milieu. Fourth, it has analysed the Social Platform, one of the more prominent actors in the EU NGO community, to observe how it has received and perceived the participation and civil society discourses.

This survey departs from the current debate that examines how NGOs are conducive to democratisation of EU governance. It has revealed: how the EU might *carry* the contemporary discourse on participation and (good) governance and managerialism; and *exert* the former with respect to a project of strengthening its institutional power as well as creating certain types of subjects who are willing and able to take part in its assignments, including to join to its consultation regime as a legitimating factor and helping in creating a symbolic link between the EU and its citizens.

Foucault's emphasis on governmentality in this sense provides an analytical tool for examining the relationality between the Commission's project of empowering supranational intermediaries of European civil society, new modes of governance (i.e. Open Method of Coordination), the Commission's administrative reform – which was completed during 1999–2004; and the management methods of the Platform. In this case relationality concerns common *episteme* (or set of principles and frameworks), *telos, techne* and *identities* of European governance. Foucault's concepts provides a frame for the context in which the discourse of the involvement of the civil society evolved; which technologies and strategies this discourse entailed; what this discourse has aimed to achieve; which strategies it has employed, and how the objects of this discourse have perceived and received this process. Our survey has examined the implications of political rationalities on the constitution of the self, organisations and state-society relations.

I have argued that the participation discourse, among others, is a constitutive element of the art of government and political power. As mentioned, the EU has attempted to develop a discourse on participation in order to gain public support – just as the notion has been used in developing countries. However, the EU also adopts the knowledge of managing this discourse, e.g. the logical framework and results-based management (which have been devised by the World Bank) as techniques of organisational structuring. What does this suggest and why is this has significance? From Foucault, we learned how state-formation is related to self-formation (Jessop 2011, 2007). The implication of this argument in this present debate is that re-structuring of the political institutions and their management is not external to organisation of non-political institutional actors and behaviours of the individuals constituting those institutions.

On this account, the ECS discourse might be considered as an effect of an larger dynamics, though which has constitutive effects on formation of subjects: the emergence of the NGO phenomenon and its activities are constituted, shaped and guided in several aspects.

First, the structure through which an NGO has been involved in EU politics may well be thought of in relation to the moral and ethical aspects of governmentality (Rose 1996). This statement implies that partnership arrangements with the political institutions are the good and appropriate way of mobilising civil society (as opposed to e.g. protests). The Platform, for instance, defines itself as a peaceful and constructive organisation that works for the European common good. Although it strives to secure legal guarantees for its interactions, in the meantime, the Platform seems not to abandon protest from its repertoire of action entirely. For instance, on one unique occasion, in 2010, the Platform was involved in street protests against the financial austerity programmes. Further, in its communication tools, particularly those that address its members, the Platform also uses visual illustrations of protest. While the Platform still defines itself as a Europeanised lobbying organisation, it can be argued that protest refers to the Platform's alter-ego, keeping it connected with social movement discourse and thus distancing itself from being a mere lobbying association. Nonetheless, in practice, the Platform works like a Europeanised lobbying organisation and an exclusive EU-oriented NGO club, while it endeavours to motivate local NGOs to seek legal guarantees to be recognised as formal partners of within the frame of participatory governance.

Second, an NGO that engages in European governance by receiving European grants is subject to technologies of performance and managerialism. For the ethos of neoliberal governmental rationalities is regarded as goal-orientation and outcome achievement (Dean 1999), this ethos projects a *performance machine*-like subject, including the states, organisations and the individual. We see solidification of this in the example of the Platform: that is, it has to perform a set of goals, which are planned, carefully calculated, and inscribed into reports. Its funding by the Commission is contingent on the accomplishment of certain pre-planned objectives, and its overall activities, reports, and tools of communication are all related to its technologies of performance, and these goals are represented in a special way, i.e. through the techniques of professional PR. Moreover, the Platform's bureaucratic decision-making structures, professional working methods and techniques of communication stem from managerialism. Given that managerialism implies an understanding that anything can be managed with a certain set of rules independent from what is being managed (Burnham 1942; Parker 2002), we observe the managerial mentality of the Platform in terms of its negotiations, communication and organisational techniques. The Platform has adopted expert skills, new management structures, new financing mechanisms, and a results-based working strategy to be able to connect with public authorities. To negotiate with the public authorities and compete with other interest groups, the Platform was also required to learn negotiation techniques and communication skills.

Furthermore, to prove its legitimacy to EU institutions, for instance, an NGO is required to adopt a formal statute and a transparent internal governance structure (Com 2000, 11 final). This reinforces similar organisational structures among the NGO community, and we see an illustration in that of the Platform: such as one coordinator, one communication officer, and several policy officers. The Platform convenes *general assemblies*, in which all members gather twice a year; *steering committees*, which take the important decisions; *working groups* that produce the institutional outputs; and a *management committee* to review overall organisational performance. In addition, the Platform inscribes yearly *activity reports* to the Commission, and disseminates and exploits their achievements through newspapers, webpages, conferences, toolkits, and position papers. These activities to a great extent reflect the Commission's activity-based management (i.e. in use since 1999) and institutional structure: for example, the Platform models the subsidiarity principle as a strategy for dividing responsibilities between its members and its secretariat (Alhadeff and Wilson 2002). That the EU applies a coherent attitude toward the other participants of European governance including the NGO community, which is enshrined into the white papers, green papers and funding programmes, there is good reason to expect similar organisational patterns and acts in them too.

For instance, the coordinator of the Civil Society Contact Group (L. Sedou, personal communication, May 2009) explains the tension between professionalism and the traditional ethos of civil society:

> There is a main tension within the NGOs in the sense that we [the NGO community] are required to be professionalised, whereas on the other hand, we are required to be a civil society organisation – a citizen organisation. How do we balance these two sometimes contradictory situations?

Some commentators have expressed the negative consequences of managerialism in civil society in terms governmentalisation of civil society (Morrison 2000; and MacKinnon 2007) and the replacement of the volunteer spirit with a management mentality (Skocpol 2003). The critique of the dominance of managerialism and bureaucracy within civil society further suggests that managerialism and bureaucracy might likely foster *exclusion, de-politicisation* and *colonisation.* That is, fierce competition to obtain EU funding, to become a stakeholder, and to fit into the EU institutional environment may result in an institutional Darwinism, in that the fittest among the institutions survive. Being fit, in this case, concerns the ability to perform the requirements of the governance system (i.e. running an organisation, inscribing reports, negotiating with other stakeholders). Thus, not surprisingly, the organisations that are willing to play the game according to the rules would likely to remain within the institutional milieu.

To continue with the influences of political rationalities on an NGO, the third one suggest to detect the underlying mechanisms through which power relations are exerted, authority is built and political obedience is achieved. Concerning the relationship between and NGO and the Commission, disciplining aspects of power relations originate primarily from funding. Most of the NGOs are funded by the Commission on the basis of a contract. The contractual relationship between the Commission and an NGO can be considered one of the mechanisms through which a participant of European governance is disciplined and made and both subject and object of governing. The Commission finances the supranational intermediaries of European civil society, but in order to access and sustain funding, an NGO has to adopt certain procedural requirements, including an administrative structure and internal governance mechanism. In addition to these, an NGO has to work in a professional way due to the requirements of contractual obligation and the EU decision-making design. Contractual requisites of the Commission and the requirements of the EU grant suggest the actors to set yearly objectives, prepare annual reports to document the performances. Thus, the most important factor undermining the independence of an NGO is the requirement for the Commission funding and because of the mentioned reasons, public finding pose a threat to autonomy of an NGO autonomy and independence.

Dependence on funding could also undermine the raison d'être of an organisation in question. For instance, some of the organisations that represent the needs of specific population segments (i.e. the excluded and marginalised) could start concentrating on transversal issues – or on those issues which are drawn up by the funding bodies – to obtain funding (Fazi and Smith 2006). The Platform may conform well to this process, as it endeavours to create a 'common' voice from a coalition of different sectors and ideological positions, including religious and leftist groups, notwithstanding leftists groups and the representative network of women's groups, the European Women's Lobby, seems to dominate the administrative structure and the final decisions (see also Cullen 2005).

Fourth, European governance entails postmodern patterns of surveillance, such as evaluation and auditing. Central to this argument is that the very system of reporting and evaluation might be conceived of a mechanism of surveillance.

According to this interpretation, reporting is not merely documenting a set of outcomes, as the structuring of reporting may shape actions by creating a certain cognitive framework to relate to the social phenomenon, i.e. in inscribing the methods of reaching objectives and the representation of end results. For instance, the communication tools of European governance privilege flow charts, bullet points and short summaries in its reports and position papers. In itself, this is not an interesting finding; nonetheless, these methods of visualisation make the governance governable, and they are endogenous to the managerial practices and a results-based working strategy.

Fifth, an NGO might not necessity bring authentic or alternative views into governance, but might refer to or be informed by already view, perspectives or ideologies. For example, the Platform's reactions to EU social policy reforms, on the one hand, recognise a new paradigm change due to a transformation entailed by economic restructuring; however, on the other, these reactions lead to several points of criticism. The Platform principally supports the Europeanisation of social policies, advocating the social inclusion discourse and the empowerment of the individual through techniques of lifelong learning and training. Suggested in this way, the Platform's suggestions can be seen pertinent with the tenets of Third Way, combining the social democratic spirit of state regulation with communitarian ideas of solidarity as well as policies of activation – which makes the human capacities amenable to political intervention and economic logic. One of the most pressing proposals of the Platform, in this respect, is the introduction of a minimum income within the EU. The Platform also supports policies of skill developing in order to adapt to changing economic conditions; this may well be regarded pertaining to the conduct of conduct via the political programme of forming a new subjectivity of an active citizenship who is empowered, but left with the responsibility of bearing the all risks.

The Platform's position on the EU social policies has been one of the focuses of this work. However, this inquiry of the relationship between the Platform and European social policy *qua* social policy should move beyond the Platform's mere thoughts and also consider the context of its emergence. This concerns the relative enhancement of the EU competencies with respect to social policies at Maastricht Treaty (1992), acceptance of the employment as a common European problem with the Amsterdam (1997), the launch of European Employment Strategy (1997) and the introduction of the Lisbon strategy (2000). The Platform's establishment, in this context, has been explained with the Commission's aspirations of strengthening its institutional legitimacy via mobilising collective action with an explicit (and implicit) connotation in that it represents the common European interests with respect to regulation of European social policy (e.g. Cram 2006). Yet, the Commission has tried to justify its sponsorship with its reliance on the external expertise for the task of proposal preparations, as recognised in EU treaties; it implies the Platform's position papers, which are elaborated above, would function to supply *epistemic* assistance.

Furthermore, the particular focus on the Social Platform suggests that the Social NGOs have a tendency in agreeing on referring to Third Way interpretation of social and economic policies. From a post-structural perspective this finding suggests that the Platform has been informed by an existing discursive framework (Third Way), and has not advanced possible alternative *meanings*.

The sixth aspect concerns the influences of an NGO network on other NGOs. The previous aspects focus on a Brussels-based NGO as its object of inquiry: in the example of the Platform, they suggest how an NGO is built as a form of subject, in fact a prototype subject which is compatible with the tenets of the new modes of governance. The present aspect, however, suggests studying how a network NGO might transfer the knowledge of its self-constitution to its members and the NGO community. In other words, this implies, as an agent of government, an NGO network might be considered both *constituted* and *constituting*. The main technology through which an NGO network might shape its members and the local NGO community is its capacity building activities – training, seminars, conferences, and tools of communication. As the new forms of governance entails a project of integrating enterprising subjects as a stakeholder in the governance of Europe, an NGO network in Brussels such as the Platform may be seen as a nuclei and carrier of this project.

If the aforementioned argument is true, an NGO network, then, acts as the subjects of government, taking a role in conducting the NGO community. For instance, the Platform tries to translate *the knowledge, tools of representation, techniques of governance*, and *identity* of the new modes of governance to national NGOs and other NGO networks. The conclusion to be drawn is through the objective of *strengthening the sector* (which is the one of three objectives of the Platform) and techniques of capacity building (e.g. benchmarking and sharing experiences), the Platform engages in an effort in fostering a specific type of civil society. In other words, the Platform tries to create Platform-like entities within civil society, as well as playing a role in normalisation of the legitimacy of EU in given policy areas. For example, the Platform arranges conferences about the OMC, effective lobbying strategies to the EU institutions and participation, which it implicitly (or explicitly) help justifying the EU rule and government.

The Platform also attempts to relate to the national organisations and to transform the interests of the constituents within the network. In contrast to a bottom-up organisational structure, however, the Brussels office plays a dominant role. In other words, while the Brussels headquarters – also called as the secretariat – to a great degree acts autonomously, it reinforces professional and managerial knowledge among the NGO community. This networking relationship, then, can result in colonisation of civil society, as the Platform carries the political rationalities to its members and the local NGOs. For instance, the Platform has been engaged in training the NGOs by translating the knowledge of how to run an organisation and how to communicate with the political authorities.

With respect to this reading, the activities of an NGO might correspond to a two-track model of colonisation: colonisation of the colonised.

In the first tier of this model, an NGO is colonised by the political and/or hegemonic discourse. The second tier concerns *colonisation through its own actions*. To illustrate this with the Platform, it disperses the idea that NGOs should orient their actions towards the EU institutions, and that they should include a 'European dimension' in their works. Put another way, the Platform imposes a *problematic* on the local NGOs: that is, the EU creates a discursive field in which the practice of its power is rationalised, and in which the EU is rendered knowable, such as through its 'connecting with the citizens' discourse. The Platform, then, transfers this discourse to its members. A Gramscian interpretation would argue that the Platform carries the hegemonic discourse on EU governance, as well as the knowledge necessary for restructuring the capital accumulation. Furthermore, it would also suggest that incorporating the NGOs in the new governance mechanisms is an attempt to integrate them into the historical bloc, where they are defined as the constituents of the new establishment. The Platform, then, in a Gramscian reading, helps maintain political integrity and stability vis-à-vis any popular discontent.

From a Foucauldian perspective, the Platform *guides the conduct of its members* through training in several areas, such as how to lobby EU institutions and national governments and how to organise an efficient NGO. The Platform also organises conferences and seminars for these purposes, and these activities require an alternative interpretation than the one that portrays them as spaces of public sphere, forums for critical discussion (Bohman 2004). That is, it is not possible to expect a critical atmosphere in those training conferences and seminars, for the Platform *circulates* the knowledge of EU governance (such as the Open Method of Coordination), imposes a problematic on the NGOs (that of directing their interests towards EU institutions), and shapes their behaviour (through training on NGO management and communication skills). In other words, the Platform shapes the conduct of conduct, normalising a certain form of governance and organisational knowledge. For instance, one of the objectives of Platform's attempts at training is the portrayal of professional lobbying as the technique NGOs should use in their relations with EU governance. Yet, we have already suggested that lobbying potentially removes the ethos of protest and voluntarism from an NGO's repertoire of action by defining an NGO as the partner and stakeholder within policy-making processes.

As a consequence of all of those aspects, this book, therefore, differs from approaches that define EU governance as a zero-sum game in which the power of the state is distributed between supranational, transnational, regional, and local actors. Our study reveals that the EU's civil society discourse has constitutive and productive features, which are not adequately uncovered by other studies on European civil society, such as normative, social movements and governance approaches. In other words, the Commission's understanding of European governance does not rest on an understanding of engaging different and multiple actors in effective and efficient problem-solving mechanisms in terms of what they are. Rather, it aims partly deliberately and to a certain extent unintentionally creating new actors and shaping the behaviours of already existing ones in order to adapt to the requirements of new forms of governance. The Commission with this regard has a legacy of developing projects and mentalities that aim to shape the European social and political environment; yet, sometimes by pushing its legal limits. Partially, some of these projects proved to be successful in time, particularly those originated during Hallstein and Delors Commissions.

The participation discourse in this respect can be considered as one of the projects through which the Commission endeavours to further the European integration by taking action on behalf of the EU, and arguably Europe at large. In turn, it aims at legitimising its actions, while acquiring the consent of the citizens. NGO phenomenon, as we see in the example of the Social Platform, then, has been made up by the forms of knowledge, morality and technologies that are rendered by the EU. In the example of the Platform, we also see that an NGO might be engaged in carrying the knowledge, morality and technologies to local NGOs in order to disperse a certain type organisational structure and civic activism.

Consequently, the participation discourse, on the one hand opens a discursive field for the EU's actions; on the other, it help to exercise a symbolic power as if the interests of the citizens are integrated into EU decision-making processes, thus mitigating the EU's legitimacy crises. The discourse further fosters promoting ethos of managerialism and performance-machine like subjects within the organised actors of civil society. Nonetheless, it should also be stated that this should be thought of as an open-ended process: that is, the analysis that has been carried out here gives a temporal picture. The nature of the relationship between the NGO community and European governance might to transform. For instance, the Commission's relationship with the social actors have been started within the framework of consultations and then evolved into participation. It is a possibility that the NGOs might become legally recognised actors in the very near future. The future configurations about the EU polity on the other hand might either favour or marginalise the NGOs. It is even a possibility the Commission and even the EU might collapse. With regards to the temporality of the process, the survey advanced in this book can be seen as an attempt of describing how the social actors transform into the managers and civil society institutions into corporate-like governed associations. Although this has currently has an implication on some sections of the civic sector, this might likely spread over a larger space. This process can lead to what Burnham conceptualised in 1942 as managerial revolution, which implies the rule of society by managers (or group of experts), as the new ruling class. Burnham developed this concept by observing the technocratic rule in Soviet Union and the Nazi regime in Germany. Different than the totalitarian implications of the concept, managerialism in the contemporary circumstances can lead to transformation of democracies into corporate-like governance, wherein all of the organised activity, including political settings and organised civil society, is administered like firms and according to principles of neoliberalism. Instead of this pessimistic scenario, it might however be more appropriate to end this work with optimism, underling the inherent contestations, resistances, and failures of any governmentality. This multi-directionality and reversibility of the social processes nourish anticipations for optimism.

Note

1 This should not to be mixed with the European Social Forum (ESF), a voluntary network with the purpose of opposing neoliberalism and a world dominated by capital and any form of imperialism. Yet, in order to discuss an alternative *modus operandi* for collective action, further research might compare the Platform (and the Commission supported NGOs alike) with the ESF. This discussion may include the promise of protest – the traditional method of contention – in raising the public awareness, fostering public deliberation and/or resistance to contemporary rationalities and practices, which are mostly regarded as the source of ever growing inequalities between different classes and regions. The potential of the Platform can be considered scant, if not epiphenomenal, with this regard.

References

Alhadeff, G. and Wilson, S. (2002) 'European Civil Society Coming of Age'. Online. www.globalpolicy.org/component/content/article/177/31558.html (accessed 15 May 2009).

Allen, B. (1998) 'Foucault and Modern Political Philosophy', In Moss, J. (ed.) *The Latter Foucault: Politics and Philosophy*, London; California; Delphi: Sage.

ALTER-EU and EU Civil Society Contact Group (2008) How to make a transparent registration in the European Commission Register of Interest Representatives.

Anderson, P. (2000) 'Renewals', *New Left Review*, 11(1): 5–24.

Anheier, H. (2004) 'Third Sector–Third Way: Comparative Perspectives and Policy Reflections', in Lewis, J. and Surrender, R. (eds), *Welfare State Change Towards a Third Way?*, Oxford: Oxford University Press.

Apeldoorn, van B. (2002) *Transnational Capitalism and the Struggle Over European Integration*, London and New York: Routledge.

Armstrong, K.A. (2002) 'Rediscovering Civil Society: The European Union and the White Paper on Governance', *European Law Journal*, 8(1): 102–32.

Australian Agency for International Development (AusAID) (2005) 'AusGuideline for Logical Framework Approach', Canberra: Australian Agency for International Development.

Avelino, F. and Rotmans, J. (2009) 'Power in transition: an interdisciplinary framework to study power in relation to structural change', *European Journal of Social Theory*, 12(4): 543–69.

Balme, R. and Chabanet, D. (2008) *European Governance and Democracy: Power and protest in the EU*, Rowman & Littlefield.

Barber, Benjamin R. (1984) *Strong Democracy: Participatory Politics for a New Age*, University of California Press: Berkeley.

Barry, A., Osborne, T. and Rose, N.S. (eds) (1996) *Foucault and Political reason: Liberalism, Neo-liberalism, and Rationalities of Government*, London: University of Chicago Press.

Bebbington, A. (2004) 'Theorizing participation and institutional change: ethnography and political economy', in S. Hickey and G. Mohan (eds) *Participation–From Tyranny to Transformation?: Exploring New Approaches to Participation in Development*, 278–84: London, New York: Zed Books.

Beger, N. (2004) 'Participatory Democracy, Organized Civil Society and the "New" Dialogue', *The Federal Trust Constitutional Online Papers* (09/04).

Begg, I. and Berghman, J. (2002) 'Introduction: EU social (exclusion) policy revisited?', *Journal of European Social Policy*, 12(3): 179–94.

Benhabib, S (1996) 'Towards a Deliberative Model of Democratic Legitimacy', in Seyla Benhabib (ed.), *Contesting the Boundaries of the Political*, Princeton, N.J: Princeton University Press.
Bevir, M. (2010) *Democratic Governance*, New Jersey: Princeton University Press.
—— (1999) 'Foucault, power, institutions', *Political Studies*, 47(2): 345–59.
Billig, M. (1995) *Banal Nationalism*, London, California, New Delhi: Sage.
Bohman, J. (2005) 'Reflexive Constitution Making and Transnational Governance', in E.O. Eriksen *et al.*, *Making the European Polity: Reflexive Integration in the EU*, London and New York: Routledge.
—— (2004), 'Constitution Making and Democratic Innovation: the European Union and Transnational Governance', *European Journal of Political Theory*, 3(3): 313–3337.
Bouwen, P. (2009) 'European Commission' in D. Coen and J.J. Richardson (eds) *Lobbying the European Union*, Oxford: University of Oxford Press.
—— (2004) 'Exchanging access goods or access: a comparative study of business lobbying in the European Union Institutions', *European Journal of Political Research*, 43(3): 337–69.
Burchell, G. (1991) 'Peculiar interests: civil society and governing "the system of natural liberty"', in G. Burchell, C. Gordon and P. Miller (eds), *The Foucault effect: Studies in governmentality*, Chicago University of Chicago Press.
Burnham, J. (1942) *The Managerial Revolution*, London: Putnam.
Butler, J. (1988) 'Performative acts and gender constitution: An essay in phenomenology and feminist theory', *Theatre journal*, 40(4): 519–31.
Carmel, E. (2003) 'What is European and social about European social policy? Some remarks on the Open Method of Co-ordination?', Paper presented to ESPAnet conference, Copenhagen, 14–17 November.
Cederman, L.E. (2001) 'Nationalism and Bounded Integration: What would it Take to Construct a European Demos', *European Journal of International Relations*, 7(2): 139–74.
Chambers, R. and Petit, J. (2004), 'Shifting Power to Make a Difference' in L. Groves and R. Hinton (eds) *Inclusive Aid: Changing power and relationships in international development*. Earthcan, London.
Chari, A. (2010) 'Toward a political critique of reification: Lukács, Honneth and the aims of critical theory'. *Philosophy & Social Criticism*, 36(5): 587–606.
Civil Society Contact Group (2008) 'A value-added and rights-based budget', Brussels: CSCG.
—— (2006), Making Your Voice Heard in the EU: A Guide for NGOs, Brussels: CSCG.
Clarke, J. (2005) 'New Labour's citizens: activated, empowered, responsibilized, abandoned?', *Critical Social Policy*, 25(4): 447–63.
Cohen, J. and Arato, A. (1992) *Civil Society and Political Theory*, Massachusetts: MIT Press.
Cohen, J. and Rogers, J. (1995) *Associations Democracy*, London: Verso.
Cohen, J. and Sabel, C. (1997) 'Directly-deliberative polyarchy', *European Law Journal*, (3): 313–42.
Considine, M and Painter, M. (1997) *Managerialism: The Great Debate*, Victoria Melbourne University Press.
Cooke, B. and Kothari, U. (2001) *Participation, The New Tyranny?*, London: Zed Books.
Cox, R. (1999) 'Civil society at the turn of the millennium: prospects for an alternative world order', *Review of International Studies*, (25): 3–28.
Cram, L. (2006a) 'Civil society, participatory democracy and the governance of the

Union: the institutionalisation of a fiction', paper for discussion at Osnabruck Workshop on European Governance, 2–4 November 2006.

—— (2006b) 'Inventing the people: civil society participation and the enhabitation of the EU' in S. Smismans (ed.) *Civil society and legitimate European governance*, Massachusetts: Edward Elgar Publishing.

Cruikshank, B. (1999) *The Will to Empower: Democratic Citizens and Other Subjects*, Ithaca, New York: Cornell University Press.

Cullen, P. (2010) 'The Platform of European Social NGOs: ideology, division and coalition', *The Journal Political Ideologies*, 15(3): 317–31.

—— (2005), 'Cooperation and conflict within the Platform of European Social NGOs', in J. Bandy and J. Smith (eds) *Coalition Across Borders: Transnational Protest and Neoliberal Order*, Oxford: Rowman & Littlefield Publishers.

Curtin, D. M. (1999) 'Transparency and political participation in EU governance: A role for civil society?', *Journal for Cultural Research*, vol. 3, no. 4, pp. 445–71.

Daly, M. (2006) 'EU Social Policy after Lisbon', *Journal of Common Market Studies*, 44(3): 461–81.

De Schutter, O. (2002), 'Europe in Search of its Civil Society', *European Law Journal*, 8(2): 198–217.

Dean, H. (2006) 'Activation policies and the changing ethical foundations of welfare', paper presented at the ASPEN/ETUI conference: Activation policies in the EU, 20–21 October 2006, Brussels. Online. http://eprints.lse.ac.uk/3784/ (accessed 15 April 2010).

Dean, M. (2010) *Governmentality: Power and Rule in Modern Society*, London, California, New Delphi: Sage.

—— (2002) 'Liberal government and authoritarianism', *Economy and society*, 31(1): 37–61.

—— (1999) *Governmentality: Power and Rule in Modern Society*, London, California, New Delhi: Sage.

—— (1994) *Critical and Effective Histories*, London: Routledge.

Delanty, G. (2005) 'The Quest for European Identity', in E.O. Eriksen (ed.) *Making the European Polity: Reflexive Integration in the EU*, New York: Routledge.

Deleuze, G. (1988) *Foucault*, trans. S. Hand, Minneapolis: University of Minnesota Press.

Della Porta, D. (2007) 'The Europeanization of Protest: a typology and empirical evidence', in B. Kohler-Koch and B. Rittberger (eds) *Debating the Democratic Legitimacy of the European Union*, Plymouth: Rowman & Littlefield Publishers.

Della Porta, D. and Caiani, M. (2009) *Social Movements and Europeanization*, Oxford: Oxford University Press.

Della Porta, D. and Diani, M. (1999) *Social Movements: An Introduction*, Malden, Oxford and Carlton: Blackwell Publishing.

Demirovic, A. (2003) 'NGOs, the State, and Civil Society: The Transformation of Hegemony', *Rethinking Marxism*, 15(2): 213–35.

Detel, W. (2005) *Foucault and Classical Antiquity: Power, Ethics and Knowledge*, Cambridge: Cambridge University Press.

Dryzek, J.S. (1999) 'Transnational democracy', *The Journal of Political Philosophy*, 7(1): 30–51.

Eberlein, K. and Kerwer, D. (2004), 'New governance in the European governance: A theoretical perspective', *Journal of Common Market Studies*, 42(1): 121–42.

Economist, The (2004), 'A rigged Dialogue with society', print edition 23 October.

Eising, R. and Kohler-Koch, B. (1999) 'Introduction Network Governance in the

European Union', in R. Eising and B. Kohler-Koch (eds) *The Transformation of Governance in European Union*, London: Routledge.

Eriksen, E.O. (ed.) (2005) *Making the European Polity: Reflexive Integration in the EU*, New York: Routledge.

Eriksen, E.O. (2005) 'An emerging European public sphere', *European Journal of Social Theory*, 8(3): 341–63.

—— (2001) 'Democratic or Technocratic Governance' in C. Joerges, Y. Mény and J.H.H. Weiler (eds) *Mountain or Molehill? A Critical Appraisal of the Commission White Paper on Governance*, Jean Monnet Working Papers 6/10, New York: NYU School of Law.

European Commission (2008) 'Debate Europe – building on the experience of Plan D for Democracy, Dialogue and Debate', COM (2008) 158/4, Brussels: European Commission.

—— (2008) 'Communication from the Commission: European Transparency Initiative: A Framework for Relations with interest representatives (Register and Code of Conduct)', COM (2008) 323 final, Brussels: European Commission.

—— (2008) 'European Transparency Initiative: A framework for Relations with Interest Representatives (Register and Code of Conduct)', COM(2008) 323 final, Brussels: European Commission.

—— (2007) 'Communication from the Commission to the European Parliament, the Council, European Economic and Social Committee and Committee of the Regions: Communicating Europe in Partnership', COM (2007) 569 final, Brussels: European Commission.

—— (2007) 'Commission Working Document: Proposal for an Inter-Institutional Agreement on Communicating Europe in Partnership', COM (2007) 568 final, Brussels: European Commission.

—— (2007) 'Follow up to the Green Paper 'European Transparency Initiative', COM (2007) 127 final, Brussels: European Commission.

—— (2006) White Paper on a European Communication Policy, COM (2006) 35 final, Brussels: European Commission.

—— (2006) 'Key Competences for Life Long Learning: European Reference Framework', Brussels: European Commission.

—— (2006) 'Green Paper – European Transparency Initiative', Com (2006) 194 final, Brussels: European Commission.

—— (2005) 'Strategic Objectives 2005–2009', COM (2005) 12 final, Brussels: European Commission.

—— (2005) 'Plan D for Democracy, Dialogue and Debate', COM (2005) 494 final, Brussels: European Commission.

—— (2004) 'Project Cycle Management Guidelines, Europe Aid Cooperation Office', Brussels: European Commission.

—— (2002) 'Towards a Reinforced Culture of Consultation and Dialogue – General Principles and Minimum Standards for Consultation of Interested Parties by the Commission, COM (2002) 704 final, Brussels: European Commission.

—— (2001) 'A White Paper on European Governance', COM (428 final), Brussels: European Commission.

—— (2000) 'Prodi-Kinnock: The Commission and Non-Governmental Organisations: Building a Stronger Partnership', COM (2000) 11 final, Brussels: European Commission.

—— (2000) 'European employment and social policy: a policy for people', DG Education and Culture, Brussels: European Commission.

References

—— (1997) 'Promoting The Role of Voluntary Organisations and Foundations in Europe', COM (97) 241 final, Brussels: European Commission.
—— (1993) 'Green Paper on Social Policy', COM (93) 55, Brussels: European Commission.
—— (1992) 'An open and structured dialogue between the Commission and special interest groups', COM (1992), Brussels: European Commission.
European Council (2006) 'Review of the EU Sustainable Development Strategy (EU SDS) – Renewed Strategy', 10917/06, 26 June 2006, Brussels: European Council.
European Economic and Social Committee (2009) 'The EESC: a bridge between Europe and organised civil society', Brussels: EESC.
—— (2006a) 'Opinion on the Green Paper – European Transparency Initiative', CESE 1373/2006, SC/028, Brussels: EESC.
—— (2006b) 'Opinion on the representativeness of European civil society organisations in civil dialogue', CESE 240/2006, SC/023Brussels: EESC.
—— (2002) 'Opinion on 'European Governance – a White Paper', CES 357/2002, Brussels: EESC.
—— (1999) 'Opinion on 'The role and contribution of civil society organisations in the building of Europe' – Ref.: CES 851/99, Brussels: EESC.
European Parliament (2008)' On the perspectives for developing civil dialogue under the Treaty of Lisbon', Genowefa Grabowska, Brussels: European Parliament.
Fazi, E. and Smith, J. (2006) 'Civil Dialogue: Making it better', commissioned report for Civil Society Contact Group, Brussels: CSCG.
Ferrera, M., Matsaganis, M. and Sacchi, S. (2002) 'Open coordination against poverty: the new EU "social inclusion process"', *Journal of European Social Policy*, 12(3): 227–39.
Finke, B. (2007) 'Civil society participation in EU Governance', *Living Rev. Eur.* 2(2): 1–29.
Fisher, W.F. (1997) 'Doing good? The politics and antipolitics of NGO practices', *Annual Review of Anthropology*, 439–64.
Fossum, J.E. and Trenz, H.J. (2006) 'The EU's fledgling society: from deafening silence to critical voice in European constitution making', *Journal of Civil Society*, 2(1): 57–78.
Fossum, J.E. and Menendez, A. (2005) 'The Constitution's Gift? A Deliberative Democratic Analysis of Constitution Making in the European Union', *European Law Journal*, 11(4): 380–410.
Foucault, M. (2009) *Security, territory, Population: lectures at the College de France 1977–1978*, M. Senellart (ed.), trans. G, Burchell, Hampshire and NY: Palgrave Macmillan.
—— (1991) 'Governmentality' in G. Burchell, C. Gorden and P. Miller (eds) *The Foucault effect: the studies in governmentality*, Chicago: The University of Chicago Press.
—— (1984) 'What is Enlightenment?' ('Qu'est-ce que les Lumières?'), in P. Rabinow (ed.) *The Foucault Reader*, New York: Pantheon Books.
—— (1982) 'The subject and power', *Critical Inquiry*, 8(4): 777: 95.
—— (1977) *Discipline and Punish: The Birth of the Prison*, London: Allen Lane, Penguin.
—— (1976) *The Will to Knowledge: The History of Sexuality: 1*, London: Allen Lane, Penguin.
Fyfe, N.R. (2005) 'Making space for "neo-communitarianism"? The third sector, state and civil society in the UK'. *Antipode*, 37(3): 536–57.

Føllesdal, A. (2003) 'The political theory of the White Paper on Governance: hidden and fascinating', *European Public Law*, 9(1): 73–86.
Gaventa, J. (2004) 'Towards participatory governance: assessing the transformative possibilities' in S. Hickey and G. Mohan (eds) *Participation: From tyranny to transformation: Exploring new approaches to participation in development*, London: Zed Books.
Geyer, R. (2001) 'Can European Union (EU) Social NGOs co-operate to promote EU social policy', *International Social Policy*, 30(3): 477–93.
Gillingham, J. (2003) *European Integration, 1950–2003: Super-state or New Market Economy*, Cambridge: Cambridge University Press.
Greenwood, J. (2007a) *Interest Representation in the European Union*, New York: Palgrave Macmillan.
—— (2007b) 'Review Article: Organized Civil Society and Democratic Legitimacy in the European Union', *British Journal of Political Science*, 37: 333–57.
Grimm, D. (1995) 'Does Europe Need a Constitution?', *European Law Journal*, 1(3): 282–302.
Haahr, H.H. (2005) 'Governmentality and the Problem of Democracy in European Integration', Center for Democratic Network Governance, Working Paper Series No. 1.
—— (2004) 'Open Method of coordination as advanced liberal government', *Journal of European Public Policy*, 11(2): 209–30.
Haas, E.B. (1958) *The Uniting of Europe: Political, Social and Economic Forces, 1950–1957*, Stanford: Stanford University Press.
Habermas, J. (2003) 'Toward a cosmopolitan Europe', *Journal of Democracy*, 14(4): 86–100.
—— (2001a) 'Why Europe Needs a Constitution?', *New Left Review*, 11: 5–26.
—— (2001b) *The Postnational Constellation. Political Essays*, Cambridge: Polity.
—— (1996) *Between Facts and Norms. Contributions to a Discourse Theory of Law*, Cambridge, Massachusetts: MIT.
Hall, S. (2011) 'The neo-liberal revolution', *Cultural studies*, 25(6): 705–28.
Hall, S. (ed.) (1997) *Representation: Cultural representations and Signifying Practices*, London, California, and New Delphi: Sage.
Hall, S. (1988) 'The Toad in the Garden: Thatcherism among the Theorists', in C. Nelson and L. Grossberg, (eds), *Marxism and the Interpretation of Culture*, London: Macmillan Education.
Harvey, D. (2005). *A brief history of neoliberalism*, Oxford: Oxford University Press.
Held, D. (2004) *Global Covenant: The Social Democratic Alternative to the Washington Consensus*, Cambridge: Polity Press.
Heller, K.J. (1996) 'Power, subjectification and resistance in Foucault', *SubStance*, 25(1): 78–110.
Heritier, A. (1999) 'Elements of Democratic Legitimation in Europe: An Alternative Perspective', *Journal of European Public Policy*, 6(2): 269–82.
Hickey, S. and Mohan, G. (eds) (2004) *Participation–from Tyranny to Transformation?: Exploring New Approaches to Participation in Development*, London: Zed Books.
Hooghe, L. and Marks, G. (2001) *Multi-Level Governance and European Integration*, Lanham, MD: Rowman & Littlefield.
Horeth, M. (1999), 'No Way Out of the Beast? The Unsolved legitimacy problem of European Governance', *Journal of European Public Policy*, 6(2): 249–68
Huller, T. (2010) 'Playground or Democratization: New Participatory Procedures at the European Commission', *Swiss Political Science Review*, 16(1): 77–107.

References

Imig, D. and Tarrow, S. (eds) (2001) *Contentious Europeans: Protest and Politics in an Emerging Polity*, Lanham, MD: Rowman & Littlefield.

Jachtenfuchs, M. (2001) 'The Governance Approach to European Integration', *Journal of Common Market Studies*, 39(2): 245–64.

Jaeger, H.M. (2007) 'Global civil society and the political depoliticization of global governance', *International Political Sociology*, 1(3): 257–77.

Jeffery, C. (2002) 'Social and regional Interests: ESC and the Committee of the Regions' in J. Peterson and M. Schackleto (eds) *The Institutions of the European Union*, Oxford: Oxford University Press.

Jensen, M.N. (2006) 'Concepts and conceptions of civil society', *Journal of Civil Society*, 2(1): 39–56.

Jessop, B. (2011) 'Constituting another Foucault effect: Foucault on states and statecraft', in U. Bröckling, S. Krassmann and T. Lemke (eds) *Current issues and future challenges*, Ney York: Routledge.

—— (2007) *State Power: A Strategic-Relational Approach*, Cambridge: Polity.

—— (2006) 'State-and Regulation-theoretical Perspectives on the European Union and the Failure of the Lisbon Agenda', *Competition & Change*, 10(2): 141–61.

—— (2004) 'The European Union and recent transformations in statehood' in S.P. Riekmann, M. Mokre and R. Latzer (eds) *The state of Europe: transformations of statehood from a European perspective*, Frankfurt, Main: Campus Verlag.

—— (2002a) *The Future of the Capitalist State*, Cambridge: Polity.

—— (2002b) 'Liberalism, neoliberalism, and urban governance: A state–theoretical perspective', *Antipode*, 34(3): 452–72.

Joerges, C., Meny, Y. and Weiler, J.H.H. (eds) (2001) *Mountain or Molehill? A Critical Appraisal of the Commission White Paper on Governance*, Jean Monnet Working Papers 6/10, New York: NYU School of Law.

Joerges, C. and Neyer, J. (1997) 'Transforming Strategic Interaction into Deliberative Problem-Solving. European Comitology in the Food Stuffs Sector', *Journal of European Public Policy*, 4(4): 609–25.

Kaldor, M. (2005) 'The idea of global civil society', in G. Baker, and D. Chandler (eds) *Global Civil Society: Contested Futures*, New York: Routledge.

Kassim, H. (2008) 'Mission impossible, but mission accomplished: the Kinnock reforms and the European Commission', *Journal of European Public Policy*, 15(5): 648–68.

Keck, M. and Sikkink, K. (1998) *Activists beyond borders*, Ithaca: Cornell University Press.

Kendall, J. and Anheier, H.K. (1999) 'The third sector and the European Union Policy Process: an initial evaluation', *Journal of European Public Policy*, 6(2): 283–307.

Kohler-Koch, B. (2010) 'Civil society and EU democracy: "Astroturf" representation?', *Journal of European Public Policy*, 17(1): 100–16.

—— (2009). 'The three worlds of European civil society – What role for civil society for what kind of Europe?', *Policy and Society*, 28: 47–57.

Kohler-Koch, B. and Finke, B. (2007) 'The Institutional Shaping of EU-Society Relations: A Contribution to Democracy via Participation?', *Journal of Civil of Civil Society*, 3(3): 205–21.

Kohler-Koch, B. and Rittberger, B. (2006) 'Review Article: the 'governance turn' in EU studies', *Journal of Common Market Studies*, 44(1): 27–49.

Kooiman, J. (1993) *Modern Governance, New Government-Society Interactions*, London, London, California, and New Delhi Sage.

Kröger, S., and Friedrich, D. (2013) 'Democratic representation in the EU: two kinds of subjectivity', *Journal of European Public Policy*, 20(2): 171–89.

Kumar, K. (2007) 'Global civil society', *European Journal of Sociology*, 48: 413–34.
Leal, P.A. (2007) 'Participation: the ascendancy of a buzzword in the neo-liberal era', *Development in Practice*, 17(4–5): 539–48.
Larner, W. (2000) 'Neo-liberalism: policy, ideology, governmentality', *Studies in Political Economy*, 63: 5–24.
Lemke, T. (2007) 'An Indigestible meal? Foucault, Governmentality and State Theory', *Diskintion*, 15: 43–64.
—— (2002) 'Foucault, Governmentality, and the Critique', *Rethinking Marxism*, Vol. 14, No. 3, 49–63.
—— (2001) 'The Birth of Bio-politics: Michel Foucault's lecture at the College de France on neoliberal governmentality', *Economy and Society*, 30(2): 190–207.
Linklater, A. (2007) 'Public spheres and civilizing process', *Theory, Culture and Society*, 24(4): 31–8.
—— (2005) 'A European Civilizing Process?', in C. Hill and M. Smith (eds) *International Relations and the European Union*, Oxford: Oxford University Press.
Lord, C. and Beetham, D. (2001) 'Legitimizing the EU: Is there a "Post-parliamentary Basis" for its Legitimation?', *Journal of Common Market Studies*, 39(3): 443–62
MacKinnon, D. (2000) 'Managerialism, governmentality and the state: a neo-Foucauldian approach to local economic governance', *Political Geography*, 19(3): 293–314.
Magnette, P. (2003) 'European governance and civic participation: beyond elitist *Citizenship*', *Political Studies*, 5(1): 144–60.
—— (2001) 'European Governance and Civic Participation: Can the European Union be politicised' in C. Joerges, Y. Meny and J.H.H. Weiler (eds) *Mountain or Molehill? A Critical Appraisal of the Commission White Paper on Governance*, Jean Monnet Working Papers 6/10, New York: NYU School of Law.
Mahoney, C. (2004) 'The power of institutions: state and interest group activity in the European Union', *European Union Politics*, 5(4): 441–66.
Majone, G. (1996) *Regulating Europe*, London, New York: Routledge.
McKee, K. (2009) 'Post-Foucauldian governmentality: What does it offer critical social policy analysis?', *Critical Social Policy*, 29(3): 465–86.
Mercer, C. (2002) 'NGOs, civil society and democratization in the developing world: a critical review of the literature', *Progress in Development Studies*, 2(1): 5–22.
Merlingen, M. (2006) 'Foucault and World Politics: Promise and Challenges of Extending Governmentality Theory to the European and Beyond', *Journal of International Studies*, 35(1): 181–96.
—— (2003) 'Governmentality towards a Foucauldian framework for the study of IGOs', *Cooperation and Conflict*, 38(4): 361–84.
Miller, P. (1992) 'Accounting and objectivity: the invention of calculating selves and calculable spaces', *Annals of scholarship*, 9(1/2): 61–86.
Minogue, M., Polidano, C. and Hulme, D (eds) (1998) *Beyond the New Public Management*, Cheltenham: Edward Elgar.
Mitchell. K. (2006) 'Neo-liberal governmentality in the European Union: Education, training and technologies of citizenship', *Environment and Planning D: Society and Space*, 24(3): 389–407.
Moravsick, A. (1995) 'Liberal intergovernmentalism and Integration. A Rejoinder', Journal of Common Market Studies, Vol. 4, No. 4, pp. 611–28.
—— (1993) 'Preferences and Power and European Community', *Journal of Common Market Studies*, 31(4): 473–524.

Morrison, J (2000) 'The government-voluntary sector compacts: Governance, governmentality and civil society', *Journal of Law and Society*, 27(1): 98–132.

Mosher, J.S. and Trubek, D.M. (2003) 'Alternative Approaches to Governance in the EU: EU Social Policy and the European Employment Strategy', *JCMS: Journal of Common Market Studies*, 41(1): 63–88.

Moss, J. (ed.) (1998) *The Latter Foucault: Politics and Philosophy*, London, California, and Delphi: Sage.

Mouffe, C. (2005) *On the Political*, London and New York: Routledge.

Nanz, P. (2007), Multiple Voices: An Interdiscursive Concept of the European Public Sphere, CIDEL Report.

Nugent, N. (2010) *Government and Politics of the European Union*, New York: Palgrave Macmillan.

Obradovic, D. (2005) 'Civil and Social Dialogue in European Governance', NEWGOV Project Report, ref: no: 24/D01, Amsterdam.

OECD (2002), Glossary of key terms in evaluation and results-based management. Online. www.oecd.org/dac/evaluation (accessed 13 May 2010).

O'Malley, P., Weir, L. and Shearing, C. (1997) 'Governmentality, criticism, politics', *Economy and Society*, 26(4): 501–17.

Papadolous, Y. (2002) 'Is governance a form Deliberative Democracy,' Joint Sessions of Workshops Turin, 22–27 March, The Politics of Metropolitan Governance.

Parker, M. (2002) *Against Management*, Cambridge: Polity.

Parker, O. (2012) *Cosmopolitan Government in Europe: Citizens and Entrepreneurs in Post-national Politics*, New York, London: Routledge.

Pateman, C. (1970) *Participation and democratic theory*, Cambridge: Cambridge University Press.

Patton, P. (1998) 'Foucault's Subject of Power', in J. Moss (ed.) *The Later Foucault. Politics and Philosophy*, London, Thousand Oaks, and New Delhi: Sage.

Peck, J. and Tickell, A. (2002) 'Neoliberalizing space', *Antipode*, 34(3): 380–404.

Petras, J. (1999) 'NGOs: In the service of imperialism', *Journal of Contemporary Asia*, 29(4): 429–40.

Phillips, L. and Ilcan, S. (2004) 'Capacity-building: The neo-liberal governance of development', *Canadian Journal of Development Studies*, 25(3): 393–409.

Pierre, J. (2000) (ed.) *Debating Governance*, Oxford: Oxford University Press.

Polanyi, K. (1944) *The great transformation: Economic and political origins of our time*, New York: Rinehart.

Porter, D. and Craig, D. (2004) 'The third way and the third world: poverty reduction and social inclusion in the rise of "inclusive" liberalism', *Review of International Political Economy*, 11(2): 387–423.

Power, M. (2011) 'Foucault and sociology', *Annual Review of Sociology*, 37: 35–56.

Putnam, R.D. (1995) 'Bowling alone: America's declining social capital', *Journal of Democracy*, 6(1): 65–78.

Rhodes, R. (1996) 'The new governance: governance without government', *Political Studies*, 44(4): 652–67.

Roberts, S.M., Jones III, J.P. and Fröhling, O. (2005) 'NGOs and the globalization of managerialism: A research framework', *World Development*, 33(11): 1845–64.

Rose, N. (1996) Governing advanced liberal democracies. In A. Barry *et al.*, Foucault and political reason: liberalism, neo-liberalism and rationalities of government, pp. 37–64, London: UCL Press.

—— (1992) 'Governing the enterprising self', in P. Heelas and P. Morris (eds) *The values of the enterprise culture: The moral debate*, New York: Routledge.
Rose, N. and Miller, P. (1992) 'Political Power Beyond the State: Problematics of Government', *British Journal of Sociology*, 43(2): 172–205.
—— (2008) *Governing the Present: administering economic, social and personal life*, Cambridge: Polity.
Rose, N., O'Malley, P. and Valverde, M. (2006) 'Governmentality', *Annual Review of Law Society and Science*, 2: 83–104.
Rosenau, J.N. (1998) 'Governance and democracy in a globalizing world', in D. Archibugi, D. Held and M. Köhler (eds) *Reimagining Political Community*, Cambridge: Polity Press.
Ruzza, C. (2004) *Europe and civil society: movement coalitions and European governance*, Manchester: Manchester University Press.
Ruzza, C. and Salla, V.D. (eds) (2007) *Governance and Civil Society in the European Union, volume 2*, Manchester University Press.
Sabel, C.F. and Zeitlin, J. (eds). (2010) *Experimentalist governance in the European Union: towards a new architecture*, Oxford: Oxford University Press.
Sánchez-Salgado, R. (2007) 'Giving a European Dimension to Civil Society Organizations.' Journal of Civil Society, 3(3): 253–69.
Sauregger, S. (2006) 'The professionalization of interest representation: a legitimacy problem for civil society in the EU?', in S. Smismans (ed.) *Civil Society and Legitimate European Governance*, Cheltenham: Northampton; Edward Elgar.
Savio, A. and Palola, E. (2004) 'Post-Lisbon social policy – inventing the social in the confines of the European Union', paper presented to second ESPAnet Annual Conference European Social Policy: Meeting the Needs of Europe, Oxford, 9–11 September.
Scharpf, F. (1997) 'Economic integration, democracy and the welfare state', *Journal of European Public Policy*, 4(1): 18–36.
Schlesinger, P. (2007) 'A Cosmopolitan Temptation', *European Journal of Communication*, 22(4): 413–26.
Schmitter, P. (2003a) 'Neo-neo-functionalism', in A. Wiener and T. Diez (eds) *European Integration Theory*, Oxford: Oxford University Press.
—— (2003b), 'Democracy in Europe and Europe's Democratization', *Journal of Democracy*, 14(4): 71–84.
Scholte, J.A. (2002) 'Civil society and democracy in global governance', *Global Governance*, 8(3): 281–304.
Sending, O.J. and Neumann, I.B. (2006) 'Governance to Governmentality: Analyzing NGOs, States, and Power', *International Studies Quarterly*, 50: 651–72.
Shore, C. (2009) 'European governance or governmentality?: Reflections on the EU's system of government', *Constitutionalism Web-Papers ConWEB* No: 3.
—— (2006) 'Government without statehood? Anthropological Perspectives on Governance and Sovereignty in the European Union?', *European Law Journal*, 12(6): 709–24.
Simons, J. (1995) *Foucault and the Political*, London, New York: Routledge.
Skocpol, T. (2003) *Diminishing democracy*, Norman: University of Oklahoma Press.
Smismans, S. (2007), 'European civil society: shaped by discourses and institutional interests', *European Law Journal*, 9(4): 473–95.
Smismans, S. (ed.) (2006) *Civil Society and Legitimate European Governance* Cheltenham, Northampton: Edward Elgar.

Social Platform (2009) 'Social Platform's Response to the Green paper on Equality and non-discrimination in an enlarged Union', Brussels: The Platform of European Social NGOs.
—— (2008) 'Evaluation letter to the EP President for the AGORA 2007–2008', Brussels: The Platform of European Social NGOs.
—— (2008) 'Social Platform reference paper: Shaping an effective civil dialogue at national and European level – "policies for people with people"', Brussels: The Platform of European Social NGOs.
—— (2007) 'The EU budget: more than money – solidarity and democracy for a social and sustainable future', Brussels: The Platform of European Social NGOs.
—— (2006) 'Communication: selling Europe or opening Europe? Response of the Platform of European Social NGOs to the White Paper on a European Communication Policy', Brussels: The Platform of European Social NGOs.
—— (2006) 'Strategic Action Plan', Brussels: The Platform of European Social NGOs.
—— (2006) 'Social Platform Internal rules, Brussels: The Platform of European Social NGOs.
—— (2006) 'Social Platform Membership', Brussels: The Platform of European Social NGOs.
—— (2005) 'Open consultation on the European Commission Future Programme on Active European Citizenship', Brussels: The Platform of European Social NGOs.
—— (2005) 'Contribution to Evaluation of the Open Method of Coordination (OMC)', Brussels: The Platform of European Social NGOs.
—— (2004) 'Making Work Pay' – Stigmatising the non-employed and endangering the European Social Model', Brussels: The Platform of European Social NGOs.
—— (2004) 'Contribution to Troika preceding the Informal Employment and Social Affairs Council', Brussels: The Platform of European Social NGOs.
—— (2002) 'Response to the White Paper on Governance', Brussels: The Platform of European Social NGOs, Brussels: The Platform of European Social NGOs.
—— (2001) 'Democracy, governance and European NGOs: Building a Stronger Structured Civil Dialogue', Brussels: The Platform of European Social NGOs.
—— (2000) 'Social Protection – Meeting the Challenges of the New Century', Brussels: The Platform of European Social NGOs.
—— (2000–2010) 'Working Reports', 2000–2010, Brussels: The Platform of European Social NGOs.
—— (2000–2010) 'Annual Reports', 2000–2010, Brussels: The Platform of European Social NGOs.
—— (1999) 'Developing civil dialogue in Europe to strengthen social exclusion: Lisbon Declaration', Brussels: The Platform of European Social NGOs.
—— (1998) 'Adopting to social changes', Brussels: The Platform of European Social NGOs.
—— (not dated) 'Social Platform Statutes', Brussels: The Platform of European Social NGOs.
Solidar (2009) 'Questionnaire, Capacity and legal status of CSOs in the Western Balkans', Brussels: Solidar.
Springer, S. (2012) 'Neoliberalism as discourse: between Foucauldian political economy and Marxian poststructuralism', *Critical Discourse Studies*, 9(2): 133–47.
Steffek, J., Kissling, C. and Nanz, P. (2007) *Civil Society Participation in European and Global Governance: A Cure for the Democratic Deficit*, Houndmills: Palgrave Macmillan.

Stenson, K. (2005). Sovereignty, biopolitics and the local government of crime in Britain. *Theoretical Criminology*, 9(3): 265–87.
Streeck, W. and Schmitter, P.C. (1991) 'From National Corporatism to Transnational Pluralism: Organized Interests in the Single European Market', *Politics and Society*, 19(2): 133–64.
Sum, N.L. (2009) 'The production of hegemonic policy discourses: "competitiveness" as a knowledge brand and its (re-)contextualizations', *Critical Policy Studies*, 3(2): 184–203.
Swyngedouw, E. (2005) 'Governance innovation and the citizen: the Janus face of governance-beyond-the-state', *Urban Studies*, 42(11): 1991–2006.
Tarasenko, A. (2010) 'Particularities of the European Policy Toward Social Nongovernmental Organisations', *Centre for German and European Studies (CGES) Working Papers*, No: 9.
Trenz, H.J., (2008) 'In search of the European public sphere', *RECON Working Papers*, No. 12.
Trenz, H.J. and Eder, K. (2004) 'The Democratizing dynamics of a European Public Sphere: Towards a Theory of Democratic Functionalism', *European Journal of Social Theory*, 7(1): 5–25.
Van de Steeg, M. (2002) 'Rethinking the conditions for a public sphere in the European Union', *European Journal of Social Theory*, 5(4): 499–519.
Walters, W. (2012) *Governmentality: Critical Encounters*, Abingdon/New York: Routledge.
—— (2004) 'The Political Rationality of European Integration', in W. Larner and W. Walters (eds) *Global Governmentality*, London: Routledge.
Walters, W. and Haahr, J.H. (2005a) 'Governmentality and Political Studies', *European Political Science*, 4: 288–300.
—— (2005b) *Governing Europe: Discourse, Governmentality and European Integration*, London: Routledge.
Warleigh, A. (2001) 'Europeanizing civil society: NGOs as agents of political socialization', *Journal of Common Market Studies*, 39(4): 619–39.
Weiler, J.H.H. (1999) *The Constitution of Europe: 'Do the New Clothes Have an Emperor?*, Cambridge: Cambridge University Press.
Weiss, T. (2000) 'Governance, good governance and global governance: conceptual and actual challenges', *Third World Quarterly*, 21(5): 795–814.
World Bank (2000) *Logframe Handbook*, Washington: World Bank.
Wyplosz, C. (2010) 'The failure of the Lisbon Strategy'. Online. www.voxeu.org in (accessed 12 September 2011).
Yeatman, A. (1997) 'The reform of the Public Management', in M. Considine and M. Painter (eds) *Managerialism: The Great Debate*, Victoria: Melbourne University Press.
Young, I.M. (2001) 'Activist challenges to deliberative democracy', *Political Theory*, 29(5): 670–90.
Zimmel, A. and Freise, M. (2006) 'Brining Society Back in: civil society, social capital, and third sector'. Online. http://nez.unimuenster.de/download/CONNEX_22.feb.pdf (accessed 25 June 2009).
Žižek, Slovaj (1997) *The Plague of Fantasies*, London: Verso.

Index

Page numbers in *italics* denote tables.

accountability 57, 91, 99, 115, 141, 153, 159, 161
act4europe 121, 122
action: and knowledge 13, 39; and practice 13
action plans 31, 65, 128
Active Citizens for Europe 83
Active Citizenship 32, 33, 44, 58, 63, 69, 74, 75, 81, 83–5, 109, 136, 154–6, 161, 174, 183
Active Civil Society in Europe 83–4
Active European Remembrance 83, 84
advanced liberalism 104, 129, 168n16
agency 8, 29, 37, 58, 130
AGORA initiative 102, 108, 117, 119, 168n12, 177
Alhadeff, G. 138, 152, 181
ALTER-EU 90, 156, 157
Althusser, L. 27
Amato, G. 121
Amnesty International 114
Amsterdam Treaty (1997) 61, 62, 65, 66, 89–90, 136, 183
Anderson, P. 54
Anheier, H. 16n1, 19, 46, 54–5, 58, 175
Apeldoorn, van B. 2
Arato, A. 20, 106
Armstrong, K.A. 2, 14, 17, 20, 64, 95, 102, 156
asceticism of government 34–5, 127
associational democracy 130
associational revolution 15, 45
auditing 42, 149–50, 182
Australian Agency for Development (AusAID) 142
autonomy/autonomisation 24, 27, 28, 29, 39, 41, 42, 51, 178, 182

Balme, R. 101
banal Europeanism 113
Barber, B.R. 84, 150
Barroso Commission 177
Barry, A. 23, 25, 27, 104, 127
base-superstucture model 25

Bebbington, A. 58
Beetham, D. 16n1
Beger, N. 110n24, 158
Begg, I. 126, 127
benchmarking 31, 37, 38, 128, 142, 150
Benhabib, S. 18
Berghman, J. 126, 127
best practice 31, 38; exchange of 150–1, 163
Bevir, M. 24, 27, 29, 38
Billig, M. 113
Blair, T. 63
Bohman, J. 2, 7, 112, 185
Bouwen, P. 20, 176
budget process 132–3
Burchell, G. 29
Bureau Européen des Unions Consommateurs (BEUC) 114
bureaucracy/bureaucratisation 5, 137, 182
Burnham, G. 37, 38, 181, 186
business 2, 89, 106, 107
Butler, J. 9–10

Caiani, M. 6, 14, 17
capacity-building 42, 49, 58, 109, 163, 164, 184; Social Platform 38, 113, *145*, *146*, 160
capital accumulation 45, 46, 47, 174, 185
capitalism 15, 24
Carmel, E. 126
Catholic Church 22
Cederman, L.E. 85, 174
Central and Eastern Europe 124; and civil society discourse 86, 88; democracy 72
Chabanet, D. 101
Chambers, R. 148
Charhon, P. 117, 138
Chari, A. 139
Charter of Fundamental Rights 121, 134
Chicago School 128, 129
children's activities 77–8
Chirac, J. 63
Christianity 34

citizens: bridging the gap with 74–88, 124–5; use of as a concept 76
Citizens' Assembly project 121, 122, 123
citizen's associations 129–30, 159
Citizens for Europe 81
citizenship 54; European 60, 61, 66, 69; *see also* Active Citizenship
civil dialogue 158, 178; and European Commission 64, 67, 78–9, 88–95, 97, 98, *103*, 105, 106, 107, 163; and European Economic and Social Committee (EESC) 97–8, 100, *103*, 109; and Social Platform 12, 123, 125, *145*, *146*, 148, 157, 159–62, 163–4
Civil Dialogue conference (2008) 12, 157, 163–4
Civil Society Contact Group (CSCG) 12, 16n4, 113, 114, 121–2, 132, 133, 139, 156, 157, 164, 175, 181
Civil Society Development in Southeast Europe conference (2008) 88
civil society organisations (CSOs) concept 14, 67, 105, 159
Clarke, J. 13, 25
co-decision procedure 61
codes of conduct 35, 172; interest groups 90–1, 93, 101, 110n30
Cohen, J. 6, 7, 20, 57, 106, 130
coherence 91, 153
colonisation 184–5
Committee of the Regions (CoR) 13, 89, 94, 95, 101, 108
Common Agricultural Policy (CAP) 60
Common Foreign and Security Policy (CFSP) 63
Common Security and Defence Policy (CSDP) 61
Communicating Europe in Partnership 75
communication: Social Platform tools 138–40; technologies of 74–88
Communication Policy 12, 15, 67, 69, 74, 78–82, 85, 86, 105, 154–6
communicative rationality 20, 21
Community Action Programme to Promote Active European Citizenship 117
CONCORD alliance 114
conduct 22, 148; of conduct 22, 31, 56, 113, 148, 172; *see also* codes of conduct
CONNECCS (Consultation, the European Commission and Civil Society) 91
consensual aspects of politics 4
consent 57, 76, 104, 175
Considine, M. 37
Constitution for Europe 16n1, 18, 60, 121; constitutional treaty 62–3, 66, 122, 172
consultancy firms 2, 106
consultation 20, 64–5, 67, 76, 88–95, 97, 98, 106, 162, 165; internet 77, 155, 156, 158
contracting out 38
contractual relations 37, 39, 182
Convention on the Constitution of Europe 95

Convention on the Future of Europe 62, 121–3
Convention method 18
Cooke, B. 50, 58
corporate governance 19
corporate management mentalities 5
corporate sector 107; representation 100
Council of Ministers 61
counter-hegemony 20, 21
counter-ideology 50
Country Assistance Strategies (CAS) 58
Cox, R. 49, 50
Craig, D. 47–8, 49, 51, 52, 55, 58, 175
Cram, L. 65, 66, 113, 114, 123, 125, 136, 183
critical public management 25
critical social policy 25
critical theory 4, 17
Cruikshank, B. 104, 127
Cullen, P. 14, 17, 18, 114, 115, 136, 138, 152, 165, 182
cultural differences 69, 163
culture, European 84, 85
Curtin, D. M. 16n1, 17, 18, 95
Cyprus 124
Czech Republic 124

Daly, M. 34, 126–7
De Schutter, O. 2, 6, 17, 18, 20, 112, 121
Dean, H. 13, 25
Dean, M. 4, 22, 23, 24, 25–6, 27, 28, 29, 34, 35, 37, 39–40, 51, 52–3, 127, 133, 141, 180
Debate Europe 67, 77–8, 85, 86, 155
Delanty, G. 84
Deleuze, G. 52
deliberative democracy 56–7, 161
Della Porta, D. 6, 14, 17, 18, 86, 106
Delors, J. 52, 60–1, 64, 119, 177, 186
Demirovic, A. 49
democracy 10, 14, 18, 21, 33, 69, 96, 112; associational 130; Central and Eastern Europe 72; deliberative 56–7, 161; developing countries 72; and governance 20; and interest regulation 95; liberal 3, 49; normative 90, 95, 123; partnership 20, 72; problematisation of 31; radical 3; representative 6, 69, 72, 77, 101, 102, 123, 125, 161; stakeholder 20; *see also* participatory democracy
democratic deficit 56, 126, 153, 154, 178
democratic experimentalism 6
democratic legitimacy crisis *see* legitimacy crises
democratic renewal 124
democratisation 2, 6, 10, 20, 49, 50, 51, 52, 55, 56
demos, European 85, 174
Denmark, EU treaty referendums 62, 64
deontology 34, 35, 127
developing countries 72
development 5, 48, 49, 50, 53
Di Puppo, R. 138

Diani, M. 17, 106
direct deliberative polyarchy 6
Directorate-General for Employment, Social Affairs and Inclusion (DG EMPL) 12, 65, 114
disciplinary power 7
discipline 7, 21
discourse 4–5, 8, 10–11, 172
discourse analysis 5
discursive representation 57
domination 22
donor institutions 58
double movement argument 48, 49, 54
Dryzek, J.S. 57

Eastern Europe *see* Central and Eastern Europe
Eberlein, K. 6, 120, 126
economic crises 48
economic integration 48, 61
economic liberalisation 48, 61
economism 36
Eder, K. 16n1
education 35–6, 81, 131, 135–6
effectiveness 19, 37, 91, 153
efficiency 19, 37, 38
Eising, R. 17
elections, European Parliament 79, 80
elitism 2
employability 34, 66, 127, 129, 131, 134, 135
employability insurance 131
employers 105, 106, 107; and EESC 96; and Social Dialogue 61, 64
employment 34, 61, 64, 66, 68, 127, 128, 129, 131, 134
empowerment 23–4, 34, 58, 112, 129–30, 134, 136, 160, 163–4
'empty chair' crisis 60
ENGAGE 141
enlargement of EU 62, 72, 73, 86, 88, 119, 124
entitlement 54
entrepreneurship 35, 36, 66
equality 127, 131, 160
Erasmus programme 81
Eriksen, E.O. 6, 14, 16n1, 17, 56, 76, 85, 90, 174
ethical liberalism 135–6
ethical self-government 34–5
ethics 10, 23, 25, 29, 30, 32, 75, 77, 79, 126, 127, 152, 180; of the self 34, 44
EU at a Glance website 89
Eurapathy 154
Europe for Citizens 12, 15, 63, 67, 74, 75, 83–4, 84–5, 85, 86, 105, 158
Europe is our Future declaration 121
European Anti Poverty Network (EAPN) 114
European Atomic Energy Community (EURATOM) 60, 62
European Coal and Steel Community 31, 60, 64
European Commission 8, 15, 33, 35–6, 40, 57, 185–6; Active Citizenship Programme (ACP) 32, 33, 44, 58, 63, 69, 74, 75, 81, 83–5, 109, 136, 154–6; administrative reform of 61, 179; and civil dialogue 64, 67, 78–9, 88–95, 97, 98, *103*, 105, 106, 107, 163; and civil society discourse 66–88, 112, 119, 158, 174–5; Communication Policy 12, 15, 67, 69, 74, 78–82, 85, 86, 105, 154–6; Europe for Citizens programme 12, 15, 63, 67, 74, 75, 83–4, 84–5, 85, 86, 105, 158; evolution of relationship with social actors 64–6; interest intermediation policy 65, 66, 90–3, 101, 105, 106, 107, 108, 176; online consultation 77, 155, 156, 158; Plan D for Democracy (Debate Europe) 12, 15, 63, 67, 69, 74, 75, 76–8, 81, 85, 86, 105, 155, 158; project designer role 59–64; and Social Platform 117, 120, 125; *Your Voice in Europe* web portal 91; *Building a Stronger Relationship with NGOs* 72–3; *The Commission and Non-governmental Organizations* 67; *Green Paper on Social Policy* 114, 119, 125; *Promoting the Role of Voluntary Organisations and Foundations in Europe* 68–71; *White Paper on Communication* (WPC) 78–82; *White Paper on European Governance* (WPEG) 12, 16n5, 19, 31–2, 34–5, 42, 55, 64, 67, 73–5, 79, 89, 105, 119–20, 124, 152, 153–4, 172
European Council 62, 63, 82, 117, 121, 133
European Court of Justice (ECJ) 63, 140
European Disability Forum 114
European Economic Community (EEC) 31, 60
European Economic and Social Committee (EESC) 13, 64, 72, 89, 91, 94, 95–101, 102, 108, 115; and civil dialogue 97–8, 100, *103*, 109; on consultation 97, 98; Liaison Group 100–1, 177; on membership of NGOs 99–100; *Opinion on the White Paper on Governance* 99; on participation 97–8 (and pan-European identity 96–7); on representativeness of NGOs 98–9
European Employment Strategy (EES) 32, 55, 61, 66, 68, 127, 183
European Forum for Arts and Heritage (EFAH) 114
European identity 69, 74, 75, 83, 84–5, 86, 96–7, 107, 174
European integration 4, 6, 31, 45, 59–60, 72, 74, 85, 96, 123, 158, 177
European Network Against Racism (ENAR) 12, 113, 114, 116, 138
European Parliament 13, 16n1, 60, 69, 96–7, 101–2, 108, 109, 117; AGORA initiative 102, 108, 117, 119, 168n12, 177; and civil dialogue 101–2, *103*, 163; cooperation procedure 61; e-database for interest groups 93; and EESC 100;elections 79, 80; representativeness of 100; veto power 61
European public sphere 66, 67, 80–1, 86, 159–60, 172

Index 203

European Roundtable of Industrialists 120
European social and economic space 61, 64, 119, 171, 177
European Social Forum (ESF) 187n
European social funds 132
European Social Policy Forums 18, 67, 88, 114, 119, 122, 178
European Structural Funds 131
European Trade Union Confederation (ETUC) 61, 120
European Transparency Initiative (ETI) 90, 92, 93–4, 152, 156–7
European Union (EU) 15, 32, 57, 66, 69, 73, 76, 85, 124, 161, 174, 186; accession process 86, 88; budget 132–3; Charter of Fundamental Rights 121, 134; enlargement 62, 72, 73, 86, 88, 119, 124; legitimacy 16n1, 62, 67, 71–3, 75, 94, 96, 105; legitimacy crises 15, 32, 57, 66, 69, 73, 76, 85, 124, 161, 174, 186
European Women's Lobby (EWL) 114, 182
European Youth Forum (EYF) 114
Europeanisation 14, 112, 123, 126
Euroscepticism 154
eurosclerosis 60
exchange of practices 150–1, 164

Fazi, E. 89, 113, 117, 120, 182
Ferrara, M. 126
Finke, B. 14, 16n1, 17, 64, 65, 67, 75, 102, 124, 125, 136
Fisher, W.F. 3, 45, 49, 50
folding processes 52–3
Føllesdal, A. 153
Fordism 46
Fossum, J.E. 16n1, 18, 32
Foucault, M. 3–4, 21, 25, 36, 52, 56, 57, 112, 126, 129, 179–80; discourse 4, 10, 172; ethics of the self 34; governmentality 3, 8, 21–2, 23–4, 30, 39, 179; neoliberalism 128, 168n16; power relations 4, 7, 11, 14–15, 27–8, 29; regimes of truth 35
France: and 'empty chair' crisis 60; EU treaty referendums 62–3
Freise, M. 17, 19
Friedrich, D. 2
functional representation 57, 64, 98
funding 41–2, 69, 70, 109, 140, 163, 182; of Social Platform 117, 181
Future of Europe initiative 121–3, 157
The Future of Europe: The Citizen's Agenda conference (2007) 77
Fyfe, N.R. 58

Gabrowska report 117
Gaventa, J. 24, 58
genealogical approach 4
Geyer, R. 140
Giddens, A. 52, 54
Gillingham, J. 60, 61, 62
global governance 3, 5, 36, 45, 58

globalisation 73, 121
good governance 5, 6, 18–19, 24, 25, 33, 38, 41, 47, 53, 113, 164; UN promotion of 19, 65, 179; *White Paper on European Governance* principles of 153; World Bank promotion of 13, 19, 49, 58, 65, 153, 179
governance 4–5, 7, 13, 18–21, 33, 38, 52, 56, 104, 108, 119–25, 165, 175–9, 185; corporate 19; and democracy 20; global 3, 5, 36, 45, 58; meaning and use of the term 14, 19; multi-level 19; as new form of governmentality 29–44, 112; as a performative act 8–11; *see also* good governance
government 22, 29–31; art of 25–6, 27, 32, 39, 40, 57, 74, 104, 128, 129; episteme of 39–40, 40–1; technical aspects of 39, 40; techniques of 22
governmentality 3–15, 20, 21–9, 52, 56, 104, 113, 126–9, 141, 171, 178, 179–86; as form of power 22, 130; Foucault's concept of 3, 8, 21–2, 23–4, 30, 39, 179; governance as new form of 29–44, 112; neoliberal 25, 104, 128, 129, 160
Gramsci, A. 21, 25, 57
grassroots connection/activation 18, 19, 20, 96, 179
Green 8 114, 10 99, 100
Greenpeace 114
Greenwood, J. 2, 14, 16n1, 20, 95, 107, 114
Grimm, D. 16n1

Haahr, J.H. 4, 7, 24, 31, 38, 109, 113, 120, 128, 141, 175
Haas, E.B. 19
Habermas, J. 5, 6, 16n1, 18, 21, 56, 84, 85, 106, 139, 160, 174
Hall, S. 10, 11, 24, 25, 54, 175
Hallstein, W. 60
Hallstein Commission 60, 186
Harvey, D. 24
health care 131, 134
Held, D. 3
Heller, K.J. 7, 11, 172
Heritier, A. 16n1
Hickey, S. 51
history, European 84, 85
Hooghe, L. 19
Horeth, M. 16n1
Houses of Europe 78, 81
Hueller, T. 63, 104
human face analogy 47, 48, 49, 58, 82
Human Rights and Democracy Network 99, 100
Human Rights Development Network 114
Hungary 124

ideal civil society 2
identity 96–7, 104; European 69, 74, 75, 83, 84–5, 86, 96–7, 107, 174; national 96
ideology 161, 162

204 Index

Ilcan, S. 113
Imig, D. 14, 17, 18, 86, 106
income, minimum 134, 136, 183
individualisation 34, 35, 54, 129, 130, 134
information gap 82
Instrument for Pre-accession Assistance (IPA) 88
interest groups 14, 19–20, 67–8, 90, 106, 107; codes of conduct 90–1, 93, 101, 110n30; registration system 91–3, 95, 156–7, 158, 169n24
interest intermediation 17, 20, 65, 66, 90–3, 101–2, 105, 106, 107, 108, 176
interest politics 66, 67
interest representation 90, 94–5, 98, 100, 106
interest representativeness 94–5, 98, 99
internal market 61
International Monetary Fund (IMF) 48, 49
international organisations 31, 114
internet 82; access and skills 81; consultation 77, 155, 156, 158; interest group registration system 91–3, 95, 156–7, 158
Ireland: and constitutional treaty 62, 63; and Lisbon Treaty 63–4

Jachtenfuchs, M. 19, 74, 104, 123, 141
Jaeger, H.M. 16n2
jargon 89, 163
Jeffery, C. 96
Jensen, M.N. 106
Jessop, B. 4, 24, 31, 32, 35, 46, 47, 51, 58, 129, 133, 171, 175, 180
job creation 68, 132
Joerges, C. 90, 119
Juncker, J.-C. 63
Justice and Home Affairs (JHA) 61, 63

Kaldor, M. 3
Kant, I. 3, 29
Kassim, H. 33, 62, 119, 179
Keck, M. 165
Kendall, J. 16n1, 19
Kerwer, D. 6, 120, 126
Keynesian National Welfare State (KNWS) 46
Kinnock Report 119
knowledge 7, 21, 22, 26, 31, 186; and action 13, 39; and art of government 25, 27; *see also* power/knowledge relations
Kohler-Koch, B. 2, 14, 16n1, 17, 19, 20, 64, 65, 67, 74, 75, 102, 104, 123, 124, 125, 136, 169–70n28
Kooiman, J. 19, 52
Kothari, U. 50, 58
Kröger, S. 2
Kumar, K. 3

labour market 66, 68, 127, 134
Laeken Declaration (2001) 62
language 30, 32, 39, 174; barriers 69, 80, 163; common 85, 174; jargon 89, 163

Larner, W. 24, 25, 34, 126, 175
Latvia 124
Leal, P.A. 48–9, 50, 175
Legambiente 113
legitimacy 2, 57; EU 16n1, 62, 67, 71–3, 75, 94, 96, 105; input-oriented 18; NGOs 98, 100; outcome 141–2; output-oriented 18
legitimacy crises 15, 32, 57, 66, 69, 73, 76, 85, 124, 161, 174, 186
Lemke, T. 14, 22, 26, 27, 29, 39, 47, 56, 104, 127, 128–9
Liaison Committee of Development NGOs to the EU (CLONG) 114
liberal democracy 3, 49
liberal intergovernmentalism 86
liberal police 52–3
liberalisation: economic 48, 61; of markets 39, 48
liberalism 24; advanced 104, 129, 168n16; classical 128, 129, 168n16; ethical 135–6; *ordo* 128, 168m16
lifelong learning 34, 83, 127, 132, 133, 135–6
Linklater, A. 31, 160
Lisbon Strategy 55, 66, 127, 136, 183
Lisbon Treaty (2007) 33, 40, 61, 62, 66, 107, 112, 122, 125–6, 157–8, 175
lobbying 2, 18, 20, 21, 70, 90, 91, 93–4, 95, 101–2, 106, 107, 157, 169n24, 177, 185
logical framework analysis (LFA) 23, 142, *143*, 144, 148, 150, 172, 180
Lord, C. 16n1
Luxembourg 63
Luxembourg compromise (1966) 60
Luxembourg Summit (1997) 66

Maastricht Treaty (1992) 51, 61, 62, 64, 65, 119, 136, 175, 183
MacKinnon, D. 25, 182
Magnette, P. 2, 14, 16n1, 17, 20, 75, 102, 121, 156
Mahoney, C. 17
Majone, G. 104
managerial revolution 37, 186
managerialism 36, 37–8, 58, 137, 174, 179, 180, 181, 182, 186
markets, liberalisation of 39, 48
Marks, G. 19
Marxism 24, 27
McKee, K. 5, 13, 25, 46
media 80, 82, 106
membership: of organisations 99–100; Social Platform 116–17
Menendez, A. 16n1
Mercer, C. 3
Merlingen, M. 26, 109
Miller, P. 23, 25, 27, 30, 31, 46–7, 141
minimal state 19, 134–5
minimum income 134, 136, 183
Minogue, M. 52
Mitchell, K. 35–6, 135–6

Mohan, G. 51
Monnet, J. 31, 177
morals/morality 25–6, 29, 30, 31–2, 34, 35, 39, 41, 44, 69, 127, 151, 152, 158, 160, 161, 180, 186
Moravsick, A. 19, 56, 86
Morrison, J. 36, 37, 58, 182
Mosher, J.S. 66, 120, 126, 141, 151
Moss, J. 22, 29
Mouffe, C. 3
movement advocacy coalitions 14
multi-level governance 19
Multi-stakeholder Forum 120

Nanz, P. 16n1
national action plans 31, 128
national identity 96
Nazism 84, 186
negative rights 134
neo-corporatist policies 105, 106
neo-Gramscians 4
neo-Marxism 4, 49–50
neoliberal govermentality 14, 104, 128, 129, 160
neoliberal rationalisation 8, 14
neoliberalism 6, 8, 9, 14, 24, 38, 128–9, 137, 168n16, 175, 186; as governmentality 25; as an ideology 25; and participation policies 46–58; as a policy 24–5
Netherlands, EU treaty referendums 62–3
network communication 43–4, 176
Neumann, I.B. 4, 7, 16n2, 29, 36–7
new managerialism 5, 13, 38, 176, 178
New Public Management (NPM) 19, 24, 25, 33, 38, 58, 113, 137, 176, 178
Neyer, J. 90
Nice Treaty (2001) 62, 98
non-profit organisations 67, 68, 105
norm-building/reproduction 31, 42–4, 160
normative approach to civil society 17–18, 20, 104, 185
normative democracy 90, 95, 123
Nugent, N. 60, 61, 62, 63, 64

Obradovic, D. 17, 19, 42, 95, 125, 128, 175
O'Malley, P. 21, 27
online tools *see* internet
ontology 34, 43, 127
Open Method of Coordination (OMC) 31, 38, 61, 65, 66, 120, 125, 126, 128, 131, 134, 163, 164, 177, 179, 185
openness 19, 91, 101, 153
ordo liberalism 128, 168n16
out-put oriented legitimacy 18
outcome 142, *143*; legitimacy 141–2
outputs 142, *143*
Oxfam 114

Painter, M. 37
Palola, E. 126

Papadolous, Y. 76
Paris Treaty (1952) 64
Parker, M. 137, 181
Parker, O. 4
participation 1, 2, 3, 4, 19, 91, 95, 96, 148, 162, 171, 173, 174, 175; as buzzword 50; discourse on 5, 6, 10, 11, 12, 13, 14–15, 24, 48–9, 50, 51, 57–8, 59, 64, 69, 73–4, 85, 108, 112, 152–64, 179, 180, 186; EESC understanding of 96, 97–8; emancipatory dimension of 50–1; and European identity 96; as form of social control 50, 57; and neoliberalism 46–58; and political economy 45–58; popular 57; positive aspects of 58; techniques of 50
participatory democracy 15, 31, 40, 72, 74, 75, 77, 90, 105, 114, 148, 150–1, 174; and draft constitutional treaty 66, 122; and Lisbon Treaty 33, 40, 66, 89, 107, 157–8, 175; and Social Platform 152, 156, 157–64
particularisation 129–30
partnership 64, 162, 180; public-private 54
partnership democracy 20
Partnership for European Renewal 93
pastoral power 22
Pateman, C. 3
paternalism, postmodern 133–4
Patton, P. 29
Peck, J. 46
peer reviews/learning 128
pensions 131, 134
performance 34–5, 39, 148; measurement of 38; technologies of 37, 41, 141–2, 180–1
performance-machines 35, 41, 141, 148, 180–1, 186
performativity 8–11
Petit, J. 148
Petras, J. 49, 50, 175
Phillips, L. 113
Pierre, J. 153
Plan D for Democracy 12, 15, 63, 67, 69, 74, 75, 76–7, 78, 81, 85, 86, 105, 158; *see also* Debate Europe
Poland 63, 124
Polanyi, K. 47, 48
police, theory of 22, 52–3
policy framework analysis 126
political economy 8, 13–14, 15, 45
political parties 155
political programming 1, 7, 9, 21, 26–7, 30, 31–2, 33, 47
political rationalities 25–7, 32
political rights 79
political socialisation 75, 81, 124, 151
popular participation 57
Porter, D. 47–8, 49, 51, 52, 55, 58, 175
positive rights 134–5
post-Fordism 46
Post-national Schumpeterian Workfare State (PSWS) 46

post-structuralism 27, 30
postmodern paternalism 133–4
poverty 48, 50, 114, 115, 121, 132, 134, 138
Poverty Reducation Strategies 51, 58
Power, M. 47
power 7, 11, 21, 129; disciplinary 7; EU 11, 32, 56; govermentality as form of 22, 130; microphysics of 24; pastoral 22; postmodern interpretation of 30; state 6, 23–4, 26, 46–7
power relations 4, 7, 14–15, 26–7, 27–9, 41–2, 56, 112, 141, 182
power/knowledge relations 10, 41, 175, 178
power/subject relations 41, 127, 146, 148
practice, and action 13
problem-solving 19, 20, 75, 130, 141, 161, 178, 179, 185
Prodi, R. 119, 177
professionalism 36, 137, 181
project cycle management (PCM) 23, 172
project management 72
protest 123, 158, 185, 187n
public relations 75, 76
public sphere(s) 2, 7, 16n1, 17, 18, 21, 112; European 66, 67, 80–1, 86, 159–60, 172; local 80; national 80; regional 80
public–private partnerships 54
Putnam, R.D. 24, 52, 84, 85

qualitative criteria 100

radical democracy 3
rational-choice methodology 4
rationalisation 5–6; neoliberal 8, 14
rationalities, political 25–7
Red Card Campaign 140
redistribution 129, 132–3, 162
referendums, EU treaty 62–3
reflexive polity 6, 17
regimes of truth 35, 160
registration system, for interest groups 91–3, 95, 156–7, 158, 169n24
remembrance 83, 84
reporting 42, 149–50, 182–3
representation 56–7, 70; corporate 100; discursive 57; functional 57, 64, 98; interest 90, 94–5, 98, 100, 106; structure of 56
representative civil society 156
representative democracy 6, 69, 72, 77, 101, 102, 123, 125, 161
representativeness 115; of European Parliament 100; interest/NGO 94–5, 98, 99, 158, 159
responsibilisation 34, 39, 54, 129, 130–1
results-based management (RBM) 141–4, 148, 149, 180, 183
Reuter, C. 101, 117, 124–5, 138, 140, 159
Rhodes, R. 19, 20, 38
rights-based approach 133, 134–5, 174
risk management 54, 127
Rittberger, B. 19, 74, 75, 123
Roberts, S.M. 8

Rogers, J. 7, 57, 130
Rome, Treaties of (1957) 31, 60, 64
Rose, N. 4, 23, 25, 26, 27, 30, 31, 37, 41, 46–7, 127, 168n16, 171, 172, 173, 180
Rosenau, J.N. 3
Ruzza, C. 14, 152, 165

Sabel, C. 2, 6, 57
Salla, V.D. 14
Sánchez-Salgado, R. 114, 117
Santer Commission 61–2, 119, 177
Sauregger, S. 2
Savio, A. 126
Schlesinger, P. 16n1
Schmitter, P. 6, 7, 16n1, 19, 20, 112, 177
Scholte, J.A. 3
Schroeder, G. 63
Schuman, R. 31
scientism 38
Sedou, L. 117, 175, 181
self 41; ethics of the 34, 44; government of 22, 27, 29, 31, 34–5, 104
self-responsibility 34
Sending, O.J. 4, 7, 16n2, 29, 36–7
Shore, C. 7, 19, 30, 57, 75, 85, 108, 109
Sikkink, K. 165
Siklossy, G. 117
Simons, J. 27, 127
single currency 61
Single European Act (1986) 60–1, 62
skills upgrading/activation 34, 127, 135–6, 183
Skocpol, T. 182
Smismans, S. 16n1, 17, 18, 19, 20, 42, 66, 67, 71, 95, 96, 98, 100, 101, 102, 112, 123, 125
Smith, J. 89, 113, 117, 120, 182
social capital 10, 15, 24, 52, 135, 159, 171
Social Chapter 61
social constructivism 4
social control, participation as form of 50, 57
Social Dialogue 61, 64, 105, 106, 107
social exclusion 127, 132, 135
social inclusion 48, 51, 127, 128, 131, 134, 136, 160, 174, 183
social justice 127, 161
social movement discourse 6, 17, 18, 20, 86, 106, 152, 165, 180, 185
social organisations 66–7, 67–9; creation of a transnational space for 69–70; funding of 69, 70
Social Platform 11–14, 15, 18, 20, 21, 33, 39, 40, 44, 67, 88, 112–70, 171, 176–7, 178–9, 180, 181, 185, 186; act4europe campaign 121, 122; and Active Citizenship programme (ACP) 154–6, 183; administrative structure 137–8; advocacy work 138–9; aims and objectives 115–16, 144, *145*, *146*, *147*, 150, 176; capacity-building programmes 38, 113, *145*, 146, 160; Citizens' Assembly project 121, 122, 123; and civil dialogue 12, 123, 125, *145*,

146, 148, 157, 159–62, 163–4; and Communication Policy 154–6;
communication tools 138–40, 180; as techniques of subjectification 144–9
contacts with European institutions 117, *118*; and discourse on bridging the gap with citizens 124–5; and European Commission 117, 120, 125 (*White Paper on European Governance* 152, 153–4); funding 117, 181; Future of Europe initiative 121, 122; and lifelong learning 132, 133, 135–6; management of 137–52, 176, 178; membership 116–17; and NGO shaping and reshaping 150–2; organisational identity 140–1; and participation discourses 148, 149, 152–64, 178, 179; as performance-oriented subject 149–50, 181; Red Card Campaign 140; and social policy 34, 125–36, 183–4; subjectivisation of 153–4; and training strategies 38, 113, 124, 132, 134, 135–6, 184, 185; *Adapting to Social Changes* 129, 130–1, 134; *Making Work Pay* 131–2; *Reference Paper: Shaping Effective Civil Dialogue* 159–62; *Social Investment* 135; *Social Platform: Meeting the Challenges of the Century* 131
social policy 8, 13, 35–6, 51, 65–6, 148, 171; common 60; rights-based approach to 134–5; Social Platform and 34, 125–36, 183–4
social protection 129–30, 131–2, 133
Social Protocol 64
social responsibility 129, 130–1
socialisation, political 75, 81, 124, 151
Solidar 116, 138, 164
solidarity 129, 132, 136, 159, 161, 183
sovereignty 7
Spain, EU treaty referendums 62
Spring Day for Europe activities 77
Springer, S. 47, 175
stakeholder democracy 20
stakeholder status 56, 177
Stalinism 84
standardisation 31
state 4, 5, 6–7; govermentalisation of 24; minimal 19, 134–5; power of 6, 23–4, 26, 46–7
statehood 45, 46–7, 54, 174
statute requirement 99, 115, 181
Steffek, J. 16n1, 20
Stenson, K. 5, 46
Streeck, W. 177
structural adjustment programmes (SAPs) 48–9, 58
structure-centred approach 8
subject formations 8, 9, 21, 23, 32, 39, 44, 112
subject/power relations 41, 127, 146, 148
subjectification 39, 40, 41–2, 144–9, 172
subjectivation 40, 153–4
subjectivity 21, 23, 112, 126, 127; of EU institutions 11

subjects 27, 28–9, 41, 172
subsidiarity, principle of 65, 89, 130–1, 181
Sum, N.L. 4
supranationalism 17, 60, 130
surveillance 24, 42, 128, 149–50, 182–3
Swedish International Agency for Development (SIDA) 142
Swyngedouw, E. 18, 24, 30, 56, 57, 177

Tarasenko, A. 114
Tarrow, S. 14, 17, 18, 86, 106
teleology 34, 35, 127
third-sector 17, 47, 54, 55, 58, 66, 174
Third Way approach 15, 47, 51, 52, 53–6, 127, 136, 162, 171, 174, 183–4
three pillars method 61
Tickell, A. 46
Tocqueville, A. de 85
Together in Europe 83, 84
trade unions 61, 64, 89, 105, 106, 107
training 35, 36, 42, 58, 68, 163; Social Platform ideas on 113, 124, 132, 134, 135–6, 184, 185
translation of political programmes 26, 30
transnational coalitions 14, 165
transparency 19, 90, 92, 93–4, 98, 99, 141, 152, 156–7, 158–9, 181
Treaty on European Union (TEU) *see* Maastricht Treaty
Treaty on Functioning of the European Union (TFEU) 62
Trenz, H.J. 16n1, 18, 32
Trubek, D.M. 66, 120, 126, 141, 151
Turin Summit (1996) 64
Turkey 63

unemployment insurance 131
UNICE 61, 120
United Kingdom (UK) 63
United Nations 19, 65, 91, 112, 179
United States Agency for International Development (USAID) 8, 142
universal/particular relation 129–30

values, European 84, 85
Van de Steeg, M. 16n1
veto power: EU member states 60; European Parliament 61
visibility 39, 40
voluntary organisations 50, 54, 66, 68–9, 105; characteristics of *71*; creation of transnational space for 69–70; function of *71*; funding of 69, 70; role of 68–9, 70, *71*
voluntary work 68–9, 83

Walters, W. 4, 7, 21, 22, 24, 31, 64, 113, 175
Warleigh, A. 75, 102, 151
wealth, distribution of 132–3, 162
Weber, M. 5
Weiler, J.H.H. 85, 174
Weiss, T. 19, 65, 112, 153

welfare ethos 34, 36, 129
welfare policies 51
welfare services provision 19, 49
welfare state 46, 54; European 60
Wilson, S. 138, 181
workfare ethos 34, 46, 129, 131–2, 133, 134
World Bank 8, 45, 51, 57, 82, 142, 180; good governance discourse 13, 19, 49, 58, 65, 153, 179; and participation discourse 47, 48, 50, 108, 112; *Sub-Saharan Africa: From Crisis to Sustainability* 49

Wyplosz, C. 128

Yeatman, A. 38
Young, I.M. 123, 177
Your Voice in Europe–Žž 91
Youth in Action and Culture 81

Zeitlin, J. 2
Zimmel, A. 17, 19
Žižek, S. 162